A GEOGRAPHICAL ANALYSIS OF RURAL MARKETS AND RURBAN CENTRES

A GEOGRAPHICAL ANALYSIS OF RURAL MARKETS AND RURBAN CENTRES

Ashok Kumar Sinha
B.A. HONS, M.A., Ph.D., L.L.B.,
D.R.D. (IGNOU), P.G.D.E.E., READER,
Post Graduate Department of Geography,
MAGADH UNIVERSITY, BODH GAYA–824 234
(BIHAR), INDIA

Ess Ess Publications
4837/24, Ansari Road, Darya Ganj,
New Delhi-110 002
Phone : 3260807
Fax: 3274173
E–mail: essess@del3.vsnl.net.in

First Published 2000

ISBN : 81-7000-273-7

Price : Rs. 450/-

Published by :
Ess Ess Publications
4837/24, Ansari Road, Darya Ganj,
New Delhi - 110 002
Phone : 3260807
Fax: 3274173
E–mail: essess@del3.vsnl.net.in

Laser Typesetting :
CINOGRAPHICS
E-41, New Multan Nagar
New Delhi
Phone : 5583866

Printed at :
Printline, New Delhi

CONTENTS

List of Tables

Magadh Division

FOREWARD

"A Geographical Analysis of Rural Markets and Rurban Centres" has evolved out of Ph.D. Thesis submitted in Magadh University, Bodh Gaya by Mr. Ashok Kumar Sinha under my supervision. I had the pleasure to make minor modifications to attain uniformity in style and methods of treatment, when presented as Ph.D. Thesis it earned an appreciation and high commendation.

Dr. Ashok Kumar Sinha has projected profiles of natural and cultural landscapes to portray Country's Rural Markets and Rurban Centres. Several hundreds flock at a geo-economic segments for a fraction of a day to exchange their earnings and wants to function as a miniature hub of collection and distribution.

Dr. Sinha is one among few workers in this rare field. The spirit of his research contribution relates in areas and theme coverage the fundamental thrust on aspects of spatial organisation, the extent and intensity of inter-link and interalliance among elements of natural and cultural environs.

Dr. Ashok presents eight balanced chapters, numerous nice cartographical display, selected tables and a rich bibliography to analysis basis of theory and review of hierarchy of rural markets and rurban centres, spatiotemporal characteristics, functional and bahavioural characteristics of markets, analysis of rurban centres, micro-geography of sample markets, marketing and rural development.

Rural markets, in fact, function as levers of growth. They are still in its infancy and evolutionary phase. To portray rural markets in their multi-phases, it is essential to balance markets, traders, consumers goods movements and complexities.

Marketing is the biggest problem ever faced by advancing rural industrial sector. A creation of an effective marketing infrastructure is needed to produce products of rural industries. If agriculture function as the heart of economy, rural industries will act as its lungs to balance production of commodities and their sale on fair price in markets.

Dr. Ashok Kumar Sinha, in fact, has indentified the keystone of rural markets and rurban centres to erect the agricultural mansion with the help of evolving rural markets and developing rurban centres.

Dr. Sinha's work will pave the path of market-geography involving geographer's approach. Rural markets and rurban centres of Magadh Division have extensive spheres where complexities will be augmented to invite several researchers to make regional synthesis for further research work.

R.P. Singh,

M.A. (Alig) Ph.D. (London)

Retd. University Professor & Head,

P.G. Deptt. of Geography,

Magadh University Bodh Gaya

Ex - Vice-Chancellor,

Magadh University, Bodh Gaya

(BIHAR)

PREFACE

The idea of patronizing marketing geography as a special field of geographical studies was propounded to strengthen the study of market place exchange systems all over the world. Market place is a necessity of our time. It provides impetus for the development of activities of trade and commerce on one hand, and on the other, leaves its imprints on its land use pattern. The term 'market' is used to a public gathering of buyers and sellers of commodities meeting at an appointed or customary location at regular intervals ranging from daily to monthly. A market centre is focus of various human activities. Hence market centres also play a vital role in accelerating the process of regional development. Large rural settlements and small towns having certain facilities and services are called rurban centre.

Rural markets and rurban centre play an important role in a developed economy including India. In market places, not only the exchange of goods and services is performed but the exchange of ideas and information also takes place. These are the places of social contact. The study of periodic market places in terms of space and time relationship may help in assessing the role that the market centres can effectively play in rural development.

India is a country of six lakh villages and its real soul lives in her villages with 71% of its total population. The economy of India is a mixed type, but agriculture's share is more larger. Obviously most of the activities in most parts of the country are directly or indirectly outcome of agriculture. The society and economy of India largely operates through rural marketing systems. Rural market centre represent the cross profile of rural India.

Twentieth century economic development requires both functional and locational specilaizations. Rural markets and rurban centres work as catalyst for improvement of the rural environment through the backward and forward movement of technological advances and innovations.

Keeping in view, the vast rural population which contributes 71% of the total Indian population and about 90% of the state of Bihar and more than 91% of the Magadh Division is the primary consideration for selecting this research project to go into the details & depth of the various aspects, economy & problems of the Indian rural life and society and to forward a details useful suggestions for the rural development. In the present book entitled "A Geographical Analysis of Rural Market and Rurban Centres" physical, cultural landscapes of the Magadh Division of Bihar state & all aspects of market centres of the region have also been dealt in detail for their scientific and original interpretation.

I, however take the privilege to express my deep sense of gratitude to my reverend teacher and research supervisor Late Prof. (Dr.) R.P. Singh, M.A. Ph.D. (London) Retd. University Professor and Head of the Post Graduate Department of Geography, Magadh University, Bodh Gaya and Ex. Vice-Chancellor Magadh University. Bodh Gaya whose constant inspiration and excellent guidance has helped me in completing this research project successfully.

I am equally thankful to Dr. V.K. Shrivastava, University Professor and Head, Deptt. of Geography, DDU. University, Gorakhpur (U.P.) for his constructive suggestions, provision of books and journals and planning of chapters during discussions which have added new useful dimensions to my present research work. I must record my gratitutde to the teaching and non-teaching members of staff of the P.G. Deptt. of Geography, Magadh University, Bodh Gaya, Gaya College-Gaya, and S.M. S.G. College, Sherghati (Gaya) and other scholars & writers of my subject for their co-operation, goodwill, suggestions and wealth of study materials.

I am also indebted to scores of my students for the co-operation they offered me in compiling primary date during field work and survey.

Undoubtedly my biggest source of inspiration goes to my parents Late(Smt.) Jagdamba Devi and Shri Shiva Kumar Prasad, D.F.O. (Retd.), who always encouraged and blessed me to take up the job with due courage and self confidence.

I also offer my hearty thanks to my elder sister Smt. Kalindi Sharan of Mumbai and brother-in-law Shri J. Sharan, A.D. Enforcement, Jalandhar (Punjab), my elder brothers and bhahis Shri K.K. Prasad & Smt. Sushila Prasad, Plant Engineer, H.F.C. Barauni, Prof. (Dr.) R.K. Prasad & Smt. Neeta Prasad, University Professor and Head, Deptt. of Botany, S.M. S.G. College, Sherghati and Shri S.K. Prasad & Smt. Usha Prasad, Jt. Director General, Foreign Trade, Patna and my brother-in-law Dr.

P.S.K. Sharma & Smt. Manju Sharma, Librarian U.G.C. of New Delhi who have been incessant sources of inspirations.

I also wish to thank all my friends, well wisher relatives & other persons who helped me in any way in completing the present research project and presenting it in a book form.

I deeply appreciate the efforts of Mr. Sumit Sethi of Ess-Ess Publication, New Delhi for so speedily and efficiently publishing this work in such nice form of a book.

At last but not least, I am thankful to my wife Dr. (Mrs.) Neelima Sinha, Reader, P.G. Deptt. of Philosophy, Magadh University, Bodh Gaya for her valuable co-operation. My three lovely children Tulika, Tusharika and Utkarsh have always been a source of inspiration for me also.

Constructive criticism and suggestions from scholars as well as from the learned readers are invited for the improvement of this book in future editions.

The Republic Day' 1999
Jagdamba Bhawan,
Nagmatia Road, Gaya-823 001.
Telephone No. - (0631) - 423188.

Ashok Kumar Sinha.

Introduction

An attempt has been made to unroll historical setting of Magadh Division from unknown past to the current century before projecting profile of the project. The significance of the project and the contents of various chapters have been depicted. A brief layout of source, data, mapping and field study has been mentioned.

BRIEF HISTORY OF THE DIVISION

Magadh Division is located in the heart of Bihar. Magadh formed parts of Bihar and Ramgarh districts till 1865. When Behar subdivision was transferred to Patna district in that year, a new district known as the district of Gaya was created. Since its inception in the year 1865 Gaya district was intact till 1972. Actually history of the present Magadh Division is the history of old Gaya district and Magadh Division is the history of old Gaya district and Magadh Empire or pre-historic period. On 26th January, 1973 Nawada and Aurangabad subdivisions of the district were separated and given the status of independent districts. Another subdivision Jehanabad has also been given status of independent district on 21st July 1986. Magadh administrative division was created on 18.5.1981.

Gaya is one of the holiest spots for the Hindus and there is a regular flow of pilgrims in the town to offer pindas in the Gaya kshetra or dham as it is called. The flow of pilgrims peaks up during Pitripaksha, the first fortnight of the Hindi month of Ashwin, corresponding to September-October. Bodh Gaya, which is situated about 11 kms. south of Gaya town, is also the holiest place for the Buddhists. Buddhists from other countries visit the spot almost daily. Lord Buddha achieved nirvan or enlightement at Bodh Gaya.

The name Gaya according to the Bhagavata purana has its origin from a Demon king Gayasur who lived in the town. Another legend contained in the Vayu purana suggests that Gaya was the name of a demon who performed rigid penance for thousand years.

EARLY HISTORY

The district of Gaya formed an integral part of the ancient kingdom of Magadh. The history of Gaya is, therefore, the history of a part of Magadh. The city of Gaya is one of the oldest town in the world. It recorded the rise and fall of civilisations. Gaya shared Magadh's history, culture and civilisation. Magadh came into prominence in the sixth century B.C. but legends refer to dynasties ruling much earlier.

Gaya become prominent during the reign of king Bimbisara. It was during this period that both Buddha and Mahavira preached their doctrines. It is said that Gautama Buddha was invited to visit the Brahmayoni Hills by the Brahmins and Kshatriyas then living in Gaya. It was from here that Gautama moved to Bodh Gaya and attained enlightenment. Buddha then went on to Sarnath to 'move the wheel of Dharma'. He came to Gaya again and converted the jatila ascetics, and with them went to Rajgir on the invitation of king Bimbisara. Buddha lived in Gaya district for a considerable time.

With the fall of the Haryankakula dynasty, the Sisunagas came to power and conquerd Avanti (Malva). The Sinsuagas were set aside by Mahapadmananda, who founded the Nanda dynasty. He extended his empire to include practically the whole of northern India. The Nandas were followed by the Mauryas who established their capital at Patliputra or modern Patna. During the reign of Emperor Ashoka, Gaya came into prominence once again, Ashoka embraced Buddhism, and went on a pilgrimage to Bodh Gaya where he built a temple and a monastery. It was during Ashoka's reign that a branch of the Mahabodhi tree was taken to Ceylon, now known as Sri Lanka. Not much is known about the history of Gaya between the end of the Mauryan rule in 184 B.C. and the rise of the Guptas.

The next prominent date in the history of Gaya is about 330 A.D. Samudra Gupta of the Gupta dynasty was the king of Magadh and Meghavarma, the king of Ceylon, built a monastery at Bodh Gaya. A copper plate inscription of Samudragupta's time has been found at Gaya. Gaya was the headquarters (Gayadhistan) of the Gaya district (Visheya) in the Gupta empire. An official seal of Gaya Visheya has been found in Nalanda. Local dynasties came into prominence after the fall of the Gupta empire. In the region of the Barabar Hills a Maukhari feudal dynasty consisting of Yagnavarman, Sardula Varman and Avanti Varman ruled for three generations. Inscriptions of these rulers have been found in the Barbar and Nagarjuna Hills. Later, Gaya was included in the empire of Harsha.

Hiuen Tsang, Chinese traveller who visited India between 630 and 645 A.D. during the reign of Harsha found the district quite prosperous. There were numerous Buddhist shrines in the district. He found a magnificient monastery at Gunamati, which has been identified with a place south of Dharwat. In close proximity to this place was the school of

Sheelbhadra. The Chinese traveller also visited Gaya and found the town well fortified. He offered worship at Bodh Gaya and was highly impressed by the monasteries and the stupas that stood around the temple and by the monasteries.

After the death of Harsha (648 A.D.) the later Gupta King Madhavagupta, a friend of Harsha, restored the fortunes of the later Gupta dynasty. But north-eastern India was soon plunged into anarchy. This ended with the election of Gopala, who founded the Pala dynasty. Bihar (including Gaya) formed a part of the Pala empire. An inscription of the 20th year of the reign of Dharmpala, son of Gopala has been found in Bodh Gaya temple. A large number of images and temples were dedicated in the time of the Pala Kings like Devapala, Surapala and Narayanpala. Some of their inscriptions have been found on images. However, Magadh appears to have passed temporarily under the control of the imperial Gurjara Pratiharas of Kanauj, the inveterate rivals of the Palas. However, Pala King Naryanapala soon recovered the lost Kingdom. The district did not have any important event there after until the Afghans overran Bihar including the district of Gaya.

MUSLIM PERIOD

The District Census Handbook, 1961 further mentions that sometime after 1193 but before 1200 A.D. Mohammad-bin-Bakhtiyar Khilji invaded Bihar. He stormed Oddantapuri (Biharsharif) and Nalanda monasteries. Gaya suffered with other parts of the State. The invaders were intolerant of the monasteries and other non-Islamic religious institutions, and large-scale persecution of the monks and priests ensued. The monasteries and temples were ransaked and destroyed, the monks and priests were slain, and the idols broken. Those monks who could escape fled to Tibet, Nepal and southers India, and Buddhism was practically effaced from the land of its birth. Biharsharif became the headquarters of Muslim Subah of Bihar. There is inscriptional evidence that Emperor Firoz Tughalak visited village Kako in Jehanabad subdivisioin on his way to Bihar.

The control of Biahr passed into the hands of the Sherqui dynasty of Jaunpur from 1394 to 1486, Gaya was thus tagged on with the Kingdom of Jaunpur, whose kings granted jagirs to Pathan Chiefs. Ragput and Bhumihar landlords also acquired some power. Sher Shah also held Gaya during his ascendency to power. After the fall of this dynasty, the Mughals gained control of the district. In the last years of the Mughal empire when the central authority became weak, Gaya was overrun on a number of occasions by the armies of several aspirants to power. During the period of turmoil, the district was split up into a number of principalities, each maintaining its own army. The Raja of Tikari was a very powerful chief in the central part of the district. So was the Raja of Ramgarh in the western region. He openly defined the Viceroys of the Province. This state of affairs continued till the British finally succeeded in establishing their hold over the district.

BRITISH PERIOD

During the British period, there was no event of consequence except when Raja Ram Narayan, the Deputy Governor of Bihar, led an expedition to punish Bishun Singh, the Zamindar of Siris and Kutumba, on his refusal to pay revenue. Gaya became an integral part of the British empire after the battle of Buxar in 1764. Thereafter the East India Company gained full control over the lower provinces of Bengal. Gradually they built up the edifice of the elaborate administrative machinery wherewith the British governed India for two centuries. it was not till almost a hundred years later that the seething discontent over foreign domination found an organised and sustained expression in the Movement of 1857.

THE MOVEMENT OF 1857

Initially, the success of the movement led by the Rajput chief Kunwar Singh of Jagdishput did not have much impact in the district of Gaya. The Collector of Gaya had been assured of assistance by the local people (particularly Gayawals). The news of further successes of the freedom fighters, however, goaded the wavering elements in Gaya and the Collector found a growing support for the national cause. He apprehended open defiance of his authority even from those who had, earlier pledged their support to him. The Collector immediately quite the town with the Government treasure. No sooner had he moved, the town was besieged by the nationalists. Gaya, which had practically forsaken the foreign yoke for a brief spell was restored to the British by a contingent consisting of Captain Rattray's Sikh soldiers and some British troops.

In the years following the 1857 movement, the Government took measures to tighten their grip over the Indians. The participants of the movement were crushed and the loyalists rewarded. The natural and innate yearning of the people for complete political independence could not, however, be suppressed for long. Gaya continued to have a prominent place in all freedom movements in the subsequent period. It also became a very important place in the annals of Freedom Movement on account of the famous session of the Indian National Congress at Gaya in 1922. Since then modern history preserves making of Magadh Division.

Dr. Keshav Prasad Sinha was one of the prominent freedom fighters of Magadh Division. He was a political internee incarcerated in the Cellular Jail on Andman (Kalapani) island in 1937. After independence Dr. Sinha became the first M.L.A. of Gaya town in the first general election of 1952.

PROFILE OF PROJECT

The word 'market' is derived from the Latin meracatus which refers to the place or method of contact between buyer and seller.[1] In the present context, market is a place for the sale and purchase of different types of commodities generally brought from outside the market place and sometimes produced locally. Market centres are of different orders, grades or ranks which vary from the rural market of a hamlet or a village to the urban market of a metropolitan centre. The market is a focus of farming activities over a well defined local area. The village or rural market centres have been the first crude forms of the modern markets. The geography of marketing and rural development is one such theme which directly focusses attention on the uplifting of the society interwoven with it since ages. The society and the economy of India largely operates through rural marketing systems. The market centres can make to the development of the region they serve.

Large rural settlements and small towns are known as rurban centres which perform services of some rural and some urban nature for the people of the areas of their influence. On such centrees, the concentration of service facilities for surrounding hinterland and business proficiency are overwhelmingly of great importance as they serve a levers of regional development. Rurban centres may be a commercial, administrative, transportational, industrial or religious node.

SIGNIFICANCE OF RURAL MARKETS AND RURBAN CENTRES

Rural markets and Rurban centres both have markets with them and a humbel efforts have been made to make a geographical analysis of markets associated with them. Any market work as central place.

Rural market centres play a very significant role in accelerating the process of regional development. In a country like India with her predominantly subsistence agricultural economy and poor mobility of man, his goods and ideas, the markets not only serve as outlets for surplus produce and shopping for their daily needs but also prove a suitable base for social and cultural, contacts of the people. Periodic rural markets have a vital importance in the socio-economic life of the rural people which function as the important collecting and distribution centres of the local rural produce. These markets held not only daily but also once, twice or thrice every week transacting predominantly as wholesale, wholesale-cum-retail and retail centres at fixed places on regular intervals. Moreover these market centres also work as growth centres and growth points which are important tools in the integrated rural area development.

Twentieth century economic development requires both functional and locational specializations. Rural markets and Rurban centres work as catalyst for improvement of the rural environment through the backward and forward movement of technological advances and innovations.

Rural market centres represent the cross profile of rural India. They function not only as exchange of commodities through primitive means of barter to modern methods, but they also form a hub of collecting and distributing centres on a miniature scale. Their distribution seems to shape in harmony with morphology of landscape and economic horizon of the country around the area.

SELECTION OF RESEARCH TOPIC

Keeping in view, the vast rural population which contributes about 80% of total Indian population and about 90% of Bihar and more than 91% of the Magadh Division is the primary consideration for selecting this project for Ph.D. Little study has been done in this branch in our country and particularly in our state. Subsisting on traditional socio-economic structure sincerely replicates the regional organisation of marketing system of the country. The economic structure of the Magadh Division depends mainly upon local marketing pattern in form of one or more shops in every village. The countryside people continue to suffer from poverty, unemployment, under-employment and socio-economic backwardness the transformation of the rural structure can be made through these periodic market centres if new developed technology and improved agricultural innovations are transmitted through them to the countryside.

An indigenous marketing system and retail distribution of commodities in the region, all these market centres exist primarily to provide goods and services for the surrounding area according to their local demand, varying financial capacity, social and cultural status of the population. Trends of consumer travel and periodicity of the market depend mainly upon accessibility and means of transport.

We have accepted village hat or market which assemble at a place in the morning and terminates in the evening. One or more than one shop of permanent structure may remain as relict landscape. Permanent market has been discussed in shape of rurban centre and periodic market associated with the centre. A separate chapter has also been devoted to rurban centres for tracing characteristics of markets.

GEOGRAPHICAL DISTRIBUTION OF MARKET CENTRES

The Geographical distribution of these market centres in the region is determined partly by physical but mostly by the maximum distance the poor consumers are willing to travel. This marketing system is intimately linked to local economy and the village society. Poor agricultural surplus, absence of good transport net work and purchasing capacity of majority of population in the region has resulted in such an indigenous traditional market system.

With the growing realisation of imbalance in the regional development in India and the need to smoothen this disparity has given much importance to the market centres as appropriate means of transformation and balanced organisation of regional economy because these places are one of the most important elemental components in the spatial articulation of economic and social activities. Therefore, spatial integration of market system and regional development have become inevitable in the context of modern regional development and planning in India.

The significance of the study of the central places from a geographers' view-point has been recognised, particularly in the west where it has gained both as an academic descipline, and as a practical planning tool in governmental, business and socio-cultural affairs. In India too, some studies in Marketing Geography have been made, and the subject is advancing a steady step to take its rightful place as a venerable branch of the geographic discipline. The present work is also an attempt to make an humble contribution to the same end. In our country also, it is now being realized that geographers too have their own point of view in the study of a region as a human occupance unit.

URBAN-RURAL RELATIONSHIP

The town and country relationship begins from the finiest 'Urban Core' which is represented by the village shop, forming the bedrock on which stands the magnificant edifice of the urban settlements, ranging layer after layer in inter-locking hierarchical pattern through the small service centres to the city and the metropolis. Distinguish and rather the pioneer works of Galpin Kolb in the United States, Christaller and Dickinson in Europe have recognised the significance of the small service centres in the successful functioning of the rural society, particularly as they are, unlike the city and the metropolis, not divorced from the rural milieu, but are just an inherent part and parcel of the same fabrics, although with a somewhat distinct core of an urban or semi urban setting. In India, essentially a land of villages and agricultural communities, the role of the village 'hats', market villages and small towns is rather more important than in the more urbanized countries of the west. Here too, however, not unlike the west, the growing net of the means of communication and transport has caused the general decay of the small service centrès, and has given rise to a set of multitudinous problems in the context of the country-town relationship. The present study seeks to analyze and interpret, from a geographer's angle, the nature of the growth, morphology, functional structure, behavioural aspect and the changing complex thereof, the centrality and the hierarchy of the centres and the functioning of the rural 'hats' and other centres in their areal context : It will be seen that throughout the study the reciprocal behavioural pattern of relationship of the town and the country runs as an inherent theme.

CHAPTERS OF STUDY AREA

The study falls into eight chapters. Chapter I gives a reconnaissance - type appraisal of the geographic personality of the region, mainly with regard to its bearing and impact, varying even in small facts of land, upon the nature and functioning of the service centres. In this chapter apart from introducing the region-physical landscape with geology, physiography, drainage, climate, soils, natural vegetation and minerals and cultural landscape with landuse, irrigation, agriculture, industries, communication, population, rural market system, rurban centres have been depicted.

Chapter II treats its theoretical bases. In this chapter Central Place Theory, mechanism of theory, modifications, periodic central places, theory of general interaction, assessment, need for verification and hierarchy of rural markets and rurban centres have been reviewed.

Chapter III deals with the spatio temporal characteristics of rural market centres where theoretical background, spatial pattern, temporal aspects, periodicity, chi-squared test, spatiotemporal synchronization and market cycles have been analysed.

Chapter IV makes an analysis of functions and behavioural characteristics of markets. In this chapter aspects of functions data, procedure of sampling, questionnaire, field limitations, functions of the market, behavioural aspects, over view, theoretical dimensions, behaviour of consumer, consumer frequency, behaviour of traders have been defined.

Chapter V deals with rurban centres their nature and development, review of social changes, method, classification, functional hierarchy, rurban index value. Spacing of rurban centres has also been treated.

Micro Geography of Sample Markets has been studied in chapter VI where morphology of Targir, Khemda, Kinjar, Amawan and Sherghati markets has been established. An assessment and zonal arrangement of shops find its place here.

The crux of study of Marketing and Rural Development is marketing located in chapter VII which is a subject of research. Policy of rural development, market days synchronization, establishing new market centres, market regulation, improvement, information networks and other locational strategies have been suggested.

Rural Development is a significant aspect of agricultural India where markets play a dominant role to trace market morphology, rurban progress and spanning strategies. Land policy, ground water, surface irrigation, crop planning, input supply, pesticides, credit, crop insurance, marketing facility, transport, management and organizational reforms, education, drinking water supply, electrification, housing, nutrition, roads health, and unemployment have been analysed in this project.

In the last the study has been summarized and some concluding trends have been given in chapter VIII.

SOURCE MATERIAL, FIELD STUDY OF MICRO RURAL MARKETS

Source-materials have been collected from the diverse sources, published and unpublished, but a vast majority of the maps and the graphs are based on field observation and intensive calculation of the available data. The author has made a special survey work of five selected market places to prepare their morphology, functions and behavioral characteristics. Snaps have been taken by the author to illustrate market centres.

REFERENCE

1. Encyclopaedia Britannica, Vol. 14, p. 912.

1

Geographical Setting

1.1 INTRODUCING MAGADH DIVISION

The objective of the present chapter is to portray the essential features of the Magadh Division under the heads of the physical and socio-economic environment, with a note on existing rural market system. The present study is concerned with the search of a link between the region's resource endowment and economy specially agriculture under the physical setting. A keen observation of the physical background requires an examination of resource utilization and deals with the study of geology, soil, climate and drainage that help in designing the infrastructure of agricultural plan. Potentiality of the development of the region is also judged with these aspects. Planning depends on its geo-physical character.

The Magadh Division of the state of Bihar was created on 18.5.1981 which lies between 24°17' and 25°19' north latitude and 84°0' and 86°3' east longitude. This administrative division comprises four districts of Aurangabad, Jehanabad, Gaya and Nawada. The country is subdivided into fortysix blocks (*Fig. no. 1.1*) and has a sizeable area of 12,344 Sq. Kms. It is bounded in the north by Patna and Nalanda districts, on the easty by Munger, Hazaribag and Giridih districts, on the south by Hazaribag and Palamu districts. The Son river defines its western natural boundary separating it from Rohtas and Bhojpour districts. Magadh division spans over the Magadh Plain except the areas of the districts of Nalanda and Patan. Magadh plain is a plain of deposition. Outliers of Chotanagpur highlands appear like islands in the sea of alluvium in the south of Magadh plain. Magadh plain, in fact, begins when scarps and plunging spurs Project in the south. The natural landscape forms the stage over which man inscribes his activities. He writes several pages of cultural landscape to register his abode and numerous activities. The making of natural landscape is the product of countless process which have obliterated its form.[1] Magadh Division has almost rectangular shape.

Geo-physical Components

Geology, relief, drainage system, climate and soil are the dominent geo-physical components which affect the agriculture and its pattern and

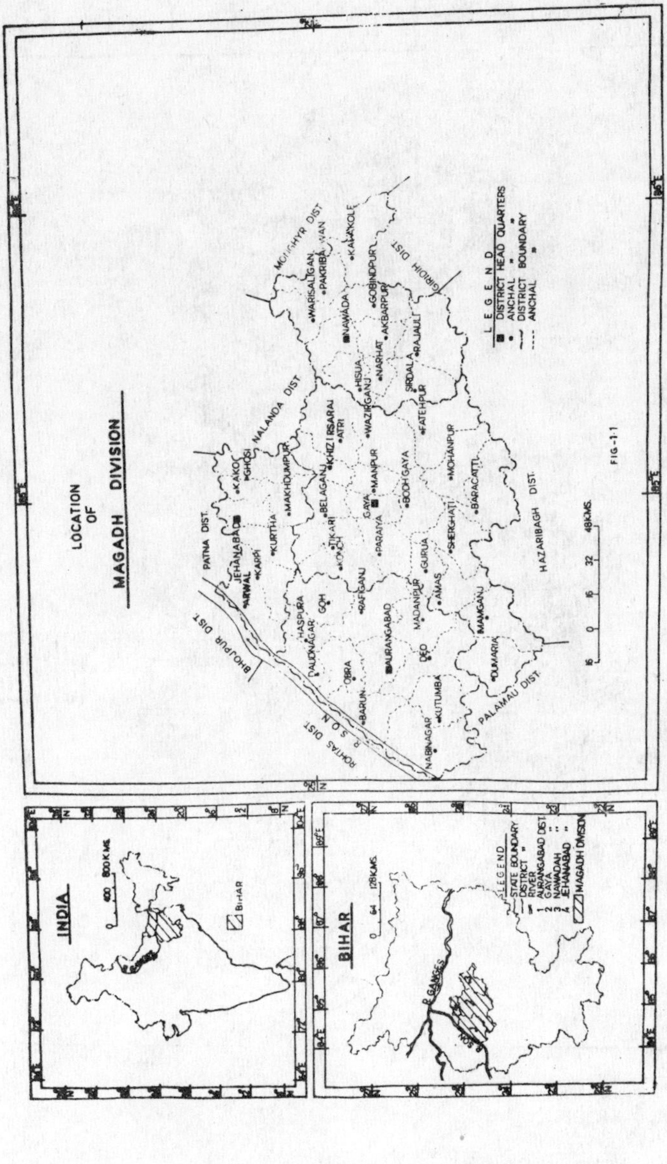
LOCATION OF MAGADH DIVISION
LEGEND
DISTRICT HEAD QUARTERS
ANCHAL
DISTRICT BOUNDARY
ANCHAL
PATNA DIST
NALANDA DIST
MONGHYR DIST
GIRIDIH DIST
HAZARIBAGH DIST
PALAMAU DIST
ROHTAS DIST
BHOJPUR DIST
R. SON
JEHANABAD
ARWAL
KARPI
KURTHA
GHOSI
KAKO
MAKHDUMPUR
BELAGANJ
KHIZIRSARAI
ATRI
TIKARI
KONCH
GAYA
MANPUR
PARAIYA
BODH GAYA
WAZIRGANJ
HISUA
NAWADA
WARISALIGANJ
PAKRIBARAWAN
KAWAKOLE
GOBINDPUR
AKBARPUR
NARHAT
RAJAULI
SIRDALA
FATEHPUR
MOHANPUR
BARACATTI
SHERGHATI
GURUA
AMAS
MADANPUR
DEO
AURANGABAD
RAFIGANJ
GOH
HASPURA
DAUDNAGAR
OBRA
BARUN
NABINAGAR
KUTUMBA
IMAMGANJ
DUMARIA
FIG-1.1
INDIA
BIHAR
BIHAR
LEGEND
STATE BOUNDARY
DISTRICT
RIVER
AURANGABAD DIST
GAYA
NAWADAH
JEHANABAD
MAGADH DIVISION
R. GANGES

Fig. 1.1

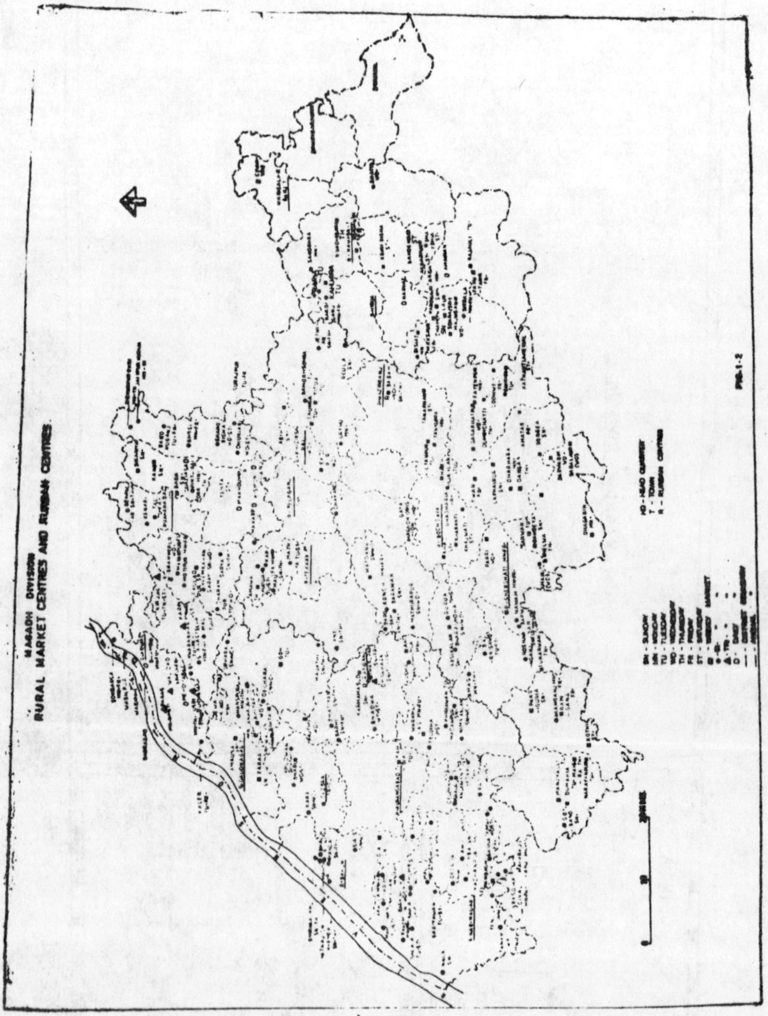

Fig. 1.2

other land uses of the country. The nature of terrain is directly related to the geological formation, relief, river system and the resultant soils where climatic conditions permit types of crops to be cultivated.

PHYSICAL LANDSCAPE

1.2 GEOLOGY

Geology forms the base for analysing its landscape features. Magadh Division is an interesting area for geological and morphological analysis. Rocks of four geological formation crop out in Magadh Division (*Fig. no. 1.3*(*a*)) Magadh Division is primarily an alluvial plain where it has recorded sedimentation of the Pleistocene period. Rocks of Archaean Schists, Granite and Vindhaya sandstone and limestone constitute ancient formation.

These rocks are confined to southern and eastern parts forming plunging spurs, hogbacks, scarps, hills and rolling upland. In fact, outlines of Chotanagpur occur in the southern part of the Magadh Division. Scarps and phunging spurs descend towards the Gaya Plain. Ancient rocks of the south have given rise to regolith, sandy-loam, gravely sand and sandy soils which vary in fertility. The recent formation of Gangetic alluvium spreads over its most of the part and covers more than three fourth of the total area. Alluvium tracts are composed of loam, clay, clayey loam. pH contents of soil in the south is reported 5.6 to 6.5, which indicate soils of moderate and strong acidity. It varies from 6.5 to 8.4 in the north indicating natural and alkaline character of the soils. These pH values are the results of ferruginous rocks in the south and deposited weathered detritus in the north accompanied by organic material. Hence geology controlling soils of the country plays a significant role in agricultural practices.

Archaean Schists

In the southern and eastern parts of the Magadh Division, rocks of pre-Cambrian are popularly known as Dharwar schist. It "consists of a great variety of crystalline rocks forming parallel bands and known in geological nomenclature of India as Bengal gneiss, a subdivision of Archean system which contains the oldest rock of the earth's crust".[2] Amidst the Archaean schists, numerous isolated and disjointed patches of Granite occur.

Granite

A continuous belt of granite, an extension of the formation of Chotanagpur, crops out in the southern part of the region right from

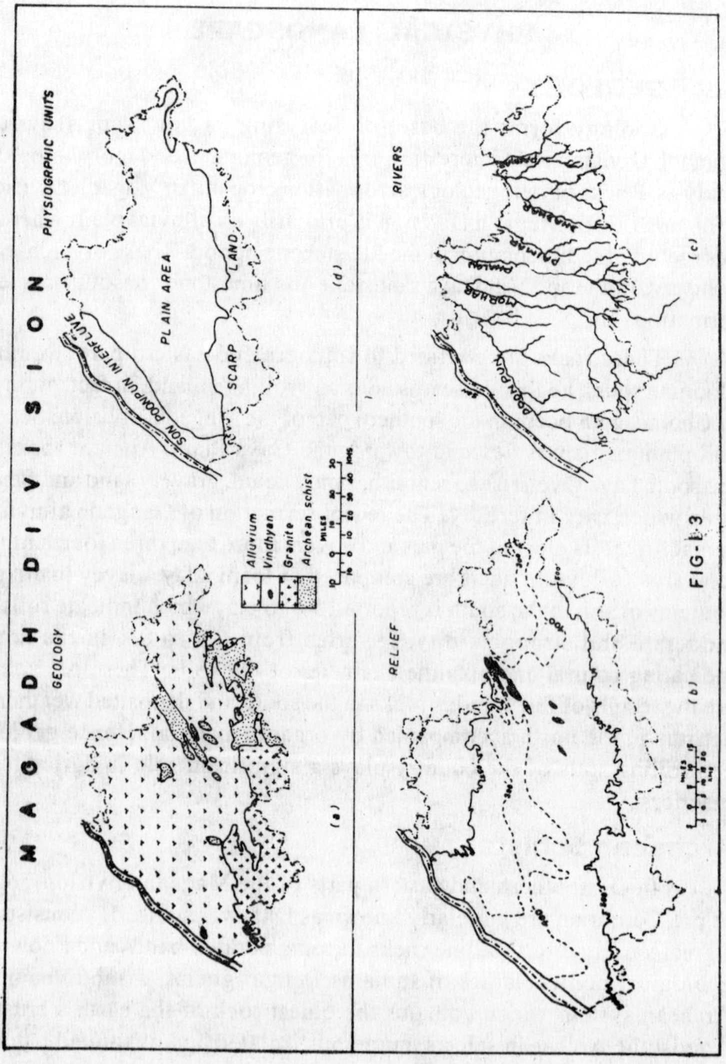
MAGADH DIVISION
GEOLOGY
PHYSIOGRPHIC UNITS
SON POONPUN INTERFLUVE
PLAIN AREA
SCARP LAND
Alluvium
Vindhyan
Granite
Archean schist
(a)
(d)
RELIEF
RIVERS
(b)
(c)
FIG-1.3

Fig. 1.3

Barachatti in the east to east of Nabinagar anchal in the west. The hard and resistent granite blocks, capable of withstanding the onslaught of age old weathering and erosion, have still been maintaining their identity in its topography.

The chain of Rajgir-Munger hills, embedded with quartzite and trending WSW to ENS, show a trend 'which might be a part of the Satpura-Rajgir Orogeny'.[3] Hills of similar formations are found in the vicisnity of Gaya city. Brahmyoni hill is an example of it. The isolation of the ridges and hills and their elongated shape with high dips of strata stand as an evidence of the fact that they have been formed by the greater pressures that have thrown them into close-set of synclinal and anticlinal folds. The intrusion of the great masses of granite and pegmatite have altered the nature and character of the present rocks. The contact effect is noticed in Mahar hill and a detached range near Gaya where idols and utencils are extensively built from soft altered rocks.

The hilly tracts from Bodh-Gaya to Rajgir is composed of quartizite and slate. "This cluster, except along its northern face, consists almost entirely of quartz siliceous hornblande, or Jasper".[4]

Vindhyan Formation

The country records fine patches of Vindhyan rocks in Nabinagar anchal. In fact, Vindhyan rocks project through the bed of the Son to be covered with alluvium in the south western part of Magadh Division. Small out crops of Vindhyan rocks have been registered in Nabinagar anchal of Magadh Division.

Alluvium

The prow of the highlands of Chotanagpur seems to have been down warped where streams from peninsular fringe and Himalaya have spread detritus since Pleistocene period. Magadh Division, lying to the south of the Ganga, is composed of alluvium brought by several streams that have their source in the highland country.

1.3 TOPOGRAPHY

The topography of Magadh Division is almost flat and level dotted with the hills. Chain of hills and high grounds are found all along the southern and south eastern parts of the region forming a compact and continuous belt. The landscape defines the scarp land of Palamu and Hazaribag districts. This is rather a zone of ridges and spurs projecting from the Chotanagpur plateau and merging into the level alluvial tract of south Ganga plain. Durvasahi (671.10M.), Sringirikhi (556 M.) and

Mahabar Hills (558 M.) are the hills of notable elevation in its south eastern part. Other hills of low altitudes are Murgara Pahar (411 M.), Satgharwa Pahar (349 M.), Bazari Pahar (362 M.) Harla Pahar (315 M.), Lohrowa Pahar (339 M.) Thari Pahar (362 M.) and Charkahi Pahar (308 M.) Durvasahi, Lomasgiri, Gotmi and Sringirikhi hills have been named after the legendary saints like Durvasa, Lomas, Gautam and Sringi who it is said, had found their abode in the hills respectively.[5]

This chain of outliers of Chotanagpur plateau begins est of Aurangabad-Daltongang road in the west and ends with the Siyur hills in the east falling in Gobindpur Anchal. Its northern boundary is zig-zag attaining maximum width in the central portion. It extends upto Madanpur. The area falling between 142 M. to 76.2 M. contour lines of the country is dotted with numerous isolated ridges and hills of low heights which break the monotony of the otherwise flat and level topography.

A chain of low hills runs in the north-east from the vicinity of Bodh-Gaya to Giriak marked with gaps and interruptions. This, in fact, defines Rajgir hills. The central part of Rajgir hill is low undulating country while northern and southern rims form scarps. Another group of hills are found in and around the city of Gaya. The highest among these is the Pretshila hill (266 M.). Other hills encircling the holy city of Gaya are Katari hill (138 M.) on the west, Brahmyoni hill (241 M.) on the south and Ramshila hill (218 M.) on the north. A little over 24 kilometres to the north of Gaya is the Barabar hill (312 M.). It is composed of massive boulders piled one upon the other. The rocks scattered over the surface and slopes of the hills appear to carry some ferruginous matter. Close to the Barabar hill is a solitary peak of Kauwadol composed of a huge perched boulder. It has acquaired its name after the legendary saying that it vibrates when a crow sits over its top. In fact, balanced rocks crown its top.

Beyond the northern border of the district of Nawada up to the Ganga in the north in Patna district and Son in the west in Aurangabad district, there is flat and monotonous alluvial tract with imperceptible slope. Almost parallel dry sandy channels of rivers are the noticeable land features in the vast span of level land. The levee of the Ganga present unique feature. The profile of the levee country shows comparatively high land followed by gentle slope and lowland. It is ribbon-shaped country running parallel to the Ganga in the south. After the flood recedes leaving a thine filament of fine sediments, the tract gives a fine yield of rabi crops. All along the western border of the region, there is a comparatively broader band of interfluvial tract in between the river son and river Pun-pun. This elongated tract of flat land sloping north to north-eastward has maintained its separate from rest of the country in the sense that it is devoid of any river channel.

The rivers, debouching from the highland of Chotanagpur and descending down south Ganga plain, form some beautiful waterfalls. The fall at Kakolat, nearly (16 Km.) south of Nawada is the most picturesque waterfall. Other within the southern scarpland are Tamasin, Hariakhal and Mohana.

1.4 RELIEF ANALYSIS

The general slope of the region, as it is evident from the courses of the net work of streams, is from south to north. High lands are found along the southern and south-eastern parts of the country where three distinct relief features are noticed. Lands over (304 M.) altitude are found in Dumaria, Amas and Deo Anchals of Aurangabad district. Similarly, south-eastern part of Rajauli Gobindpur and Kakolat Anchals of Nawada district describe some type of relief.

The area between 152.5 M. and 304 M. of altitude above mean sea level lies between the southern border of Magadh Division. The boundary lies demarcating the limit of scarp land except the portion of the high land above 304 M.

Fig. No. 1.3(b) depicts relief of the detailed country. Interpolated contour lines based on the detailed spot heights have been drawn at an interval of 100' up to 500'. All the contour lines, except 100' run in an east west direction. As one travels from south to north, the counter lines fall apart with their decreasing values. In shows that the gradient of the slope is little rather imperceptible in the areas which fall below 152.5 M (500') of height. Thus the relief map shows four distinct elevations of land surface (i) Land above 152.5 M. i.e. scarpland; (ii) Land above 122 M., (iii) Land above 92 M. and (iv) Land above 60 M.

Water level of the country is outlined by its relief. The depth of water in the south is higher than the north. Rocky southern and eastern parts are not porous, as a result water flows to downwards in the north. Hence it is an added benefit to the ground water in the northern alluvial tracts.

1.5 DRAINAGE

Rivers of the Magadh Division rise in the highlands of Chotanagpur and flow from south to north in almost parallel course.

Rivers are dry in summer due to the seasonal character of rainfall. They are turbulent and devastating during the rainy season. The son, Punpun, Dhowa, Morhar, Phalgu, Paimar, Tilaya are few important rivers, which are utilized for irrigation. Rivers are used up for 'Pyne' or artificial water channels for irrigation purpose. During the scarcity of rainfall these rivers are quite useful. Flood water is diverted to small Pynes and Ahars. The son has its source on the Maikal range in the vicinity of Amarkantak in Madhya Pradesh. It describes the western natural boundary of the Magadh Division and runs straight from S.S.W. to N.N.E. direction covering a distance of about 100 Km. The width of the river varies between three of five kilometres all along its course. Several shallow streams describe braided patterns amidst its wide stretch of sandy bad. Since it traverses a long hills tract of over 484 Kms. before entering into this part of the country. It turns violent in rainy season after collecting water from a large catchment basin in Madhya Pradesh. The river, finding unable to drain the excess water, overflows its bank and flood waters rush down heavily, causing inundation in low lying tract on either side. These floods are, however, of short duration, hardly lasting for more than three to four days. The level of the water in the river recedes to its normal level.

The Son hardly receives any tributary worth mentioning in its entire journey on the western bounds of the Magadh Division. Head of sands along its eastern bank are noticed, forming a sort of natural embankment.

At Indrapuri (Barun), there is a massive masonary dam on the river which supplies water to the canal, known as Patna Canal, which is of immense irrigation value for the farmers of Son-Pun Pun interfluve. The river remains navigable in its lower reaches during rainy season, except when it is in spate. The Son-sands, noted for its large-sized grains are used extensively in construction works, even outside the state also.

The Son is stated to have flowed far east in the region than its present course.[6] The old and abandoned course of the Son is presently occupied by the Punpun, which after uniting with the Morhar merges with the Ganga near Patna. Sandy depressions forming a number of ephemeral lakes are, in fact, the abandoned course of the Son. The river has gradually moved westward to its present position.[7]

The Pun Pun, originating into the hilly tract of Palamu district, enters into the area under study near village Panru. It flows northward upto Nabinagar and takes slightly eastward turn. The Pun Pun flows almost parallel to the Son from this place and finally merges with Ganga near Fatwa. it collects several small feeders all along its right bank like the Ramrekah, Bathane, Adri, Nira, Morhar and Dardha. The terminating stream is the branch of the Morhar which in its upper reaches is called Sorhar. The Pun Pun is the only river which has its source in the highland of Chotanagpur. It retains some water even in the dry season. The river water is extensively used for irrigation purposes. The Pun Pun is a sacred river and those who come to Gaya for 'Pind Dan' shave their heads on its bank and take holydip in its water. Pilgrims offer first 'Pinda' on its bank near Pun Pun railway station on Patna-Gaya branch railway line.

The Morhar river rises in Hazaribag plateau and flows northwards and then takes a turn forwards north-east to reach Sherghati, a subdivisional town on the national highway no. 2 (Shershah Suri Marg formerly G.T. Road) of Gaya district, where it divides into two parts. They re-unite at a short distance in the north. It again bifurcates into branches. The bifurcating branch is popularly known as the Sorhar. The Sorhar further north flows through the district town of Jehanabad with an attribute of Dardha. The Dardha ultimately joins the Pun Pun.

The Phalgu is the name of the united streams of the Mohane and Lilajan. The Mohane has its source in Hazaribag plateau where as the Lilajan has its source in the hilly area of Palamu. The Phalgu carves out its valley through the holy city of the Gaya. It meanders through the central part of Magadh plain. After reaching near the Barabar hill, it is divided into two branches, the Phalgu flowing in the northerly direction while the Mohane takes a north easterly turn. They are divided into numerous branches and their water is taken to several canals and pynes for irrigational purposes. The Phalgu is recognised as Mohane and flows from west to east begane carving out its valley through the levee to merge with the Ganga.

During the rainy season, the Phalgu swells suddenly to the extent that it touches the road and railway bridge across it at Gaya. But the water soon recedes and the river dwindles to an insignificant streams and finally is lost into its sandy bed. To ward off the danger of flood, the river water is diverted into numerous channels called 'Pynes' locally.

The Phalgu is regarded as a sacred river by the Hindus so long it flows through the holy city of Gaya.

The Sakri, like other rivers also finds it origin in Chotanagpur plateau and enters into the region near Gobindpur in Nawada District. After flowing west for some distances, it takes a northerly course in the Nalanda district and then takes a eastward turn before entering into Munger district. Besides the rivers mentioned above, there are a host rivers of which the important rivers are Paimar, Dhadhar, Tilaiya, Khuri and Jati (Fig. No. 1.3(c)).

All these rivers fall into the category of rain-fed rivers. They remain dry for the most part of the year. Even during the rainy season, the water dwindles into slender channels and get dry in their mid course. All rivers meander and their beds are filled with course sands. Other peculiarities of these streams are as follows:

Most of the streams run from south to north excavating parallel channels. Most of them are divided into several branches as they advance northwards and finally unite and form one channel known as Dhowa river which flows in a west to east direction parallel to the Gaya as they are not able to cross the flood bank of the Ganga. The Dhowa flowing eastward acquires a new name of Mohni river.

1.6 PHYSIOGRAPHY

The above discussion under different geo-physical aspects of the region forms three distinct 'physiographic unit' (Fig. No. 1.3(d)) namely (i) scarp land, (ii) plain area (iii) SonPun Pun interfluve. The last two units insignificantly differ in agricultural practice.

(i) Scarp Land

Scrap land forms a distinct physiographic unit of Magadh Division. It lies south of plain area. It covers an area of 2,252 Km^2. Contrary to other units, it is full of hills, ridge, plateau of low height and varieties of undulations. It is rather a region of spurs that project from the northern rim of Chotanagpur plateau. Plain lands with comparatively steeper slopes are found in disjointed pathces. The hills and lands higher than 304 M. are covered with deciduous forest. The trees commonly found in this part are Sal, Kendu, Asan, Khair and a few others. The unscruplous and unsystematic falling of trees and unrestricted grazing in the past have degenerated the once dence forest of Rajauli, Dihra, Bhalua and Sherghati.

The anchals of Dumaria, Imamganj, Amas and Barachatti aprat from parts of the anchals of Deo, Madanpur, Sherghati, Mohanpur, Fatehpur, Sirdala and Rajauli lie within the jurisdiction of scarp land.

(ii) Plain Area

Plain area is the largest of all physiographic units. The entire area is fertile plain except a few exception. The net work of trunk and tributary rivers drain the water of the plain. But, on the contrary, this region is dotted with a number of hills and ridges which are virtually outlines of the Chotanagpur plateau. The Rajgir hills form significant topographic feature of the area. Other notable feature is the ring of hills encircling the city of Gaya. Nearly 24 Km. north of Gaya are the hills of Barabar and Kawakol. The plain, though dotted with a few hills, lacks the coverage of natural vegetation. Most of the weathered hill-tops and slope are barren. Slopes of the hills and ridges present a picture of rugged ravines overlooking the alluvial plains surrounding them. Serpentine courses of dry beds of meandering rivers are the only significant landmarks amidst the flat alluvial plains of the region. The region is well served with a net work of a number of streams of which the Pun Pun, Morhar, Phalgu, Paimar and Sakri are worth mentioning. All these streams flowing northward are directed into several branches which serve as irrigational channels.

This region lies south of Patna district and east of SonPunPun interfluve. Its southern boundary follows approximately the trend of the contour line of 152 M. It separates this region from that of scarp land. Aurangabad, Rafiganj, Konch, Tikari, Paraiya, Gaya, Bodh-Gaya, Belaganj, Khizersarai, Jehanabad, Kako, Makhdumpur, Ghosi, Nawada, Warisaliganj, Pakri Barawan, Manpur, Atri, Wazirganj, Hisua, Narhat, Gurua and Akbarpur anchals fall in this unit. Besides parts of Nabinagar, Barun, Kutumba, Obra, Goh, Fatehpur, Mohanpur, Kurtha, Sherghati, Deo and Madanpur also fall in this unit. Besides Gaya city, the towns of Nawada, Warisaliganj, Pakri Barawan, Manpur, Atri, Wazirganj, Hisua, Narhat, Gurua and Akbarpur anchals fall in this unit. Besides parts of Nabinagar, Barun, Kutumba, Obra, Goh, Fatehpur, Mohanpur, Kurtha, Sherghati, Deo and Madanpur also fall in this unit. Besides Gaya city, the towns of Nawada, Aurangabad, Jehanabad, Warisaliganj, Wazirganj, Hisua. Tikari and Rafiganj are located in this physiographic unit.

(iii) Son-Pun Pun Interfluve

Son-Pun Pun interfluve is a distinct physiographic unit having laveled and fertile tract. It is bounded by the Son in the west, the Pun Pun river in the east, Southern boundary of Patna district in the north. Its southern boundary is the boundary of Magadh division's southern boundary. This linear shaped region has maintained its individuality due to complete absence of any river course and hill or highland worth mentioning. Only a very small patch of rock of Vindhayan origin extending from beyond the Son river valley crops out in Nabinagar anchal, but it loses its significance due to the vast and uninterrupted expanse of alluvium covering the entire area. Dry sandy beds of the abondaned channel of the Son is the only landmark of any significance.

It encompases within its ambit the anchals of Arwal, Daudnagar, Haspura and grater parts of the anchals of Nabinagar, Barun, Obra and Karpi. A fraction of Goh anchal also falls in this region. Only two small towns Nabinagar (5,804), Daudnagar (16,866) are located in this region.

1.7 CLIMATE

Lying between 24°17' and 25°19' north latitude and 84°o' to 86°3' east longitude and falling just north of the tropic of cancer (23½°N) Magadh Division enjoys Monsoon climate for all practical purposes. Since the region is far from the ocean (425 Km.), there is an element of continentality in its climate. Like India in general and Bihar in particular, the year is popularly divided into three broad seasons - (1) Cold weather season (November to mid March), (2) Hot weather season (Mid-March to mid June) and (3) Season of general rains (Mid June to September).

October is a sticky transitional month between rainy season and cold season. Some times last spell of rain occurs in October (Hathia Nakshatra) which is vital both for Aghani paddy and the ensuing Rabi cultivation.

In general the region experiences cool and fine weather in winter and hot and tyring weather summer which is characterised by high temperature, reduces the working efficiency of the people. Dust storm occasionally occurs in summer accompanied with thunder showers and rarely hail storm, rainy season is marked with oppressive heat and high humidity. Isotherm and Isohyet maps (*Fig. No. 1.4*) shows the climatic condition in the region.

Temperature

The isotherm map (Fig. No. 1.4(B)) shows the general pattern of the distribution of temperature. Areas of high temperature lie in the south and south-west and it decreases towards the north and north-east. Towards the north west of the Magadh Division, isotherm are close to each other which indicates the variation of temperature in a limited zone. In a nutshell the temperature increases towards south in the southern part and towards east in the northern part of the country.

Rainfall

The isohyet map (Fig. No. 1.4(A)) portrays the geographic distribution and regional variation of the normal rainfall in Magadh Division. Said map indicates northern part as deficient areas of rainfall, yet these areas are flooded for a good part of the year. Hence agricultural activity remains uninterrupted. The areas of comparatively high normal

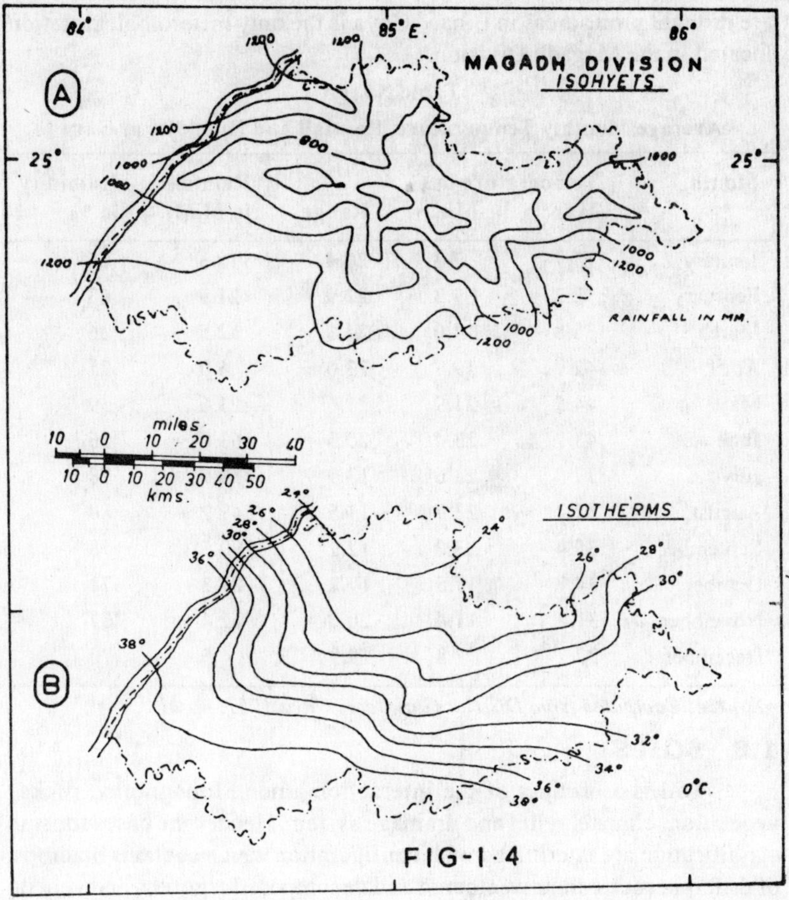
84°
85° E.
86°
MAGADH DIVISION
ISOHYETS
A
25°
25°
1200
1000
800
RAINFALL IN MM.
miles
10 0 10 20 30 40
10 0 10 20 30 40 50
kms.
ISOTHERMS
24°
26°
28°
30°
32°
34°
36°
38°
0°C.
B
FIG-1·4

Fig. 1.4

rainfall (above 1000 mm) are particularly distributed along the border areas of the Division. Though scarpland registers high rainfall, but due to its imporousity and dominent slope towards north, rainwater ultimately goes to plain area. As a result, the southern and eastern parts of the region remain unfavoured for agriculture. The area under cultivation is less in the southern and eastern blocks. All the four districts of Magadh Division are drought prone areas in Bihar.[8] Gaya is the only meterological station located in the Magadh Division.

Table No. 1.1

Average Monthly Temperature, Rainfall and Humidity at Gaya

Month	Temperature in C. Max.	Min.	Range	Rainfall in M.M.	Humidity in %
January	27.7	7.3	20.4	18.3	66
February	32.2	9.3	22.9	21.9	63
March	38.8	14.0	24.8	12.5	36
April	42.7	19.7	23.0	6.0	25
May	44.5	21.9	21.6	23.6	39
June	43.7	23.4	20.3	163.8	56
July	37.5	23.6	13.9	335.5	78
August	35.2	23.7	11.5	349.2	80
September	35.4	23.2	12.2	190.5	78
October	34.7	17.5	17.2	27.3	71
November	31.4	11.4	20.0	12.4	67
December	27.7	7.8	19.9	4.5	70

Source: Computed from District Gazetteer, Gaya 1957, pp.11-15.

1.8 SOILS

Soil is a product of the interaction among topography, rocks, vegetation, climate, relief and drainage system. Hence "the bases for soil classification are interlinked with configuration which contains outcrops of different rocks, their weathered and decomposed regoliths and veneer of drift and residual soils".[9] The parent materials (alluvium), in Magadh Division have been spread over and deposited on its flat surfaces by the Ganga, the Son and all the rivers emanating from the highlands of Chotanagpur "where chemical decomposition of rocks and minerals predominate over their physical disintigration".[10] Thus the grains of the present material become finer as one moves from south to north. To be more precise, soil of the Division may be described by soil association found in the Division. Soil association is based on the pH percentage and soil texture (sand, clay, loam, silt, gravel) Foothill soil' and `alluvium' are the two broad categories of soil association. The later may be defined into two sub-categories the recent alluvium and old alluvium. The division into these soil association group (*Fig. No. 1.5*) are more or less akin to the physiographic units of the Division. `Foothill' soil spreads over almost whole of the scarp land area. This group of soil is yellowiish-red in colour. This soil is usually shellow covering the bed rocks and pebbles. It is moderately to strongly acidic in reaction with poor to moderate fertility status. `Old alluvium' is grey and yellow in colour and heavy to medium heavy in texture. The surface soil reaction is neutral to slightly alkaline. This group of soil being clayey loam and Kewal develops linear creeks after getting dry. The fertility status of this group of varies from medium to high and is suitable for the cultivation of paddy and maize. With an aid of irrigation it is capable of raising second crop of wheat, barley and oil seeds also. `Recent alluvium' is mainly found along the banks of Son, Pun Pun and Phalgu rivers. This Son-calcarious soil is yellowish to redish-yellow in colour. The soils are generally sandy and moderately acidic to neutral in reaction and poor in fertility.

Soil's pH percentage has five categories of soil in the country (i) The soil group with over 8.4% of pH value which are strongly alkaline are found in a very small patches here and there. The anchals of Tikari, Atri, Praiya, Arwal and Kutumba each contain one very small patch of this type of soil. (ii) Similarly, another category of soils of poor fertility having pH value below 5.5 and being strongly acidic occurs insignificantly in small patches in the anchals of Arwal, Belaganj, Tikari and along the border of Atri. (iii) Moderately alkaline soil with pH per cent between 7.4 to 8.4 occupies the area in the east of the central region, apart from these medium to small patches are scattered over rest of the area. (iv) Large segment of Magadh Division is covered with the group of soil which is central in reaction with pH per cent varying between 6.6 to 7.3 Except a few small and isolated patches, nearly the whole of plain area and the Son-Pun Pun interfluve is occupied by it. These soils appear in patches even in the scarpland. (v) Soils between 5.6 to 6.5 pH per cent and slightly to moderately acidic in reaction are well distributed over the entire area in patches of varying size. There, however, are more humerous and extensive in the upper part of the plain and scarp land and few and far between lower part of the plain and Son-Pun Pun interfluves. It covers wider areas in the anchals of Pakri Barawan, Kawakol, Nawada, Fatehpur, Mohanpur, Barachatti and Deo.

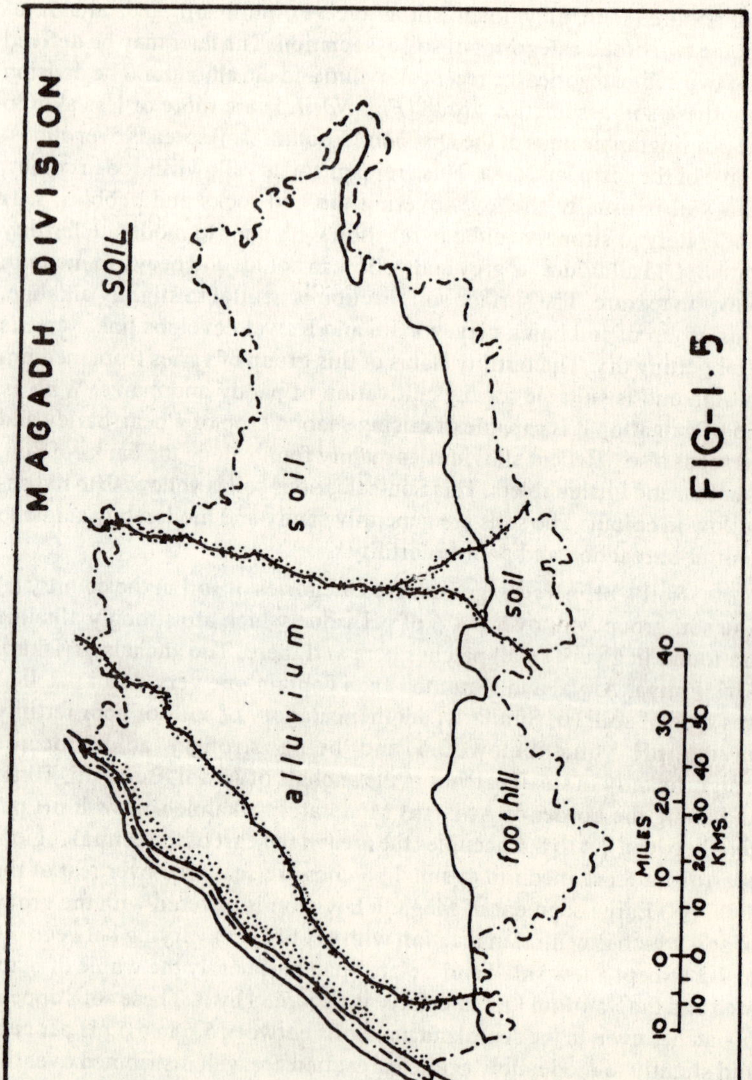
MAGADH DIVISION
SOIL
alluvium soil
foot hill soil
FIG-1.5
MILES
KMS.
10 0 10 20 30 40
10 0 10 20 30 40 50

Fig. 1.5

The surface soils with the reactions ranging from nearly neutral to slightly alkaline and acidic, are termed as fertile soils. Similarly soils of moderate fertility belong to the class of moderately acidic to moderately alkaline in reaction. Thus soils being strongly alkaline and strongly acidic come in the category of poor fertility status.[11]

The more practical, if not more important, basis of the classification of soils is texture. As much as eight categories of soil based on the varying degree of proportion of sand, clay, loam, silt and gravels have been discussed.

1. Soils with overall preponderence of sand over after are found in three small and isolated patches of it lie in the central part.

2. Clay occupies in the northern part of the boundary area of the area under study. This is a good tract of fertile land which gives yield to varieties of food and cash crops.

3. *Loam*. Leaving aside the belt of clay, loam is well represented over the entire length and breadth of the Magadh region. It is more extensive in the central and southern parts of Son-Pun Pun interfluve. Central and southern part of plain is also predominantly occupied by loam. It is best suited to paddy cultivation where the facility of irrigation exists, good yield of wheat, sugercane, maize and gram are harvested.

(4 & 5) Among the soils of loamy sand and sandy loam, sand is in greater proportion than loam in the former where as the loam is in greater proportion than sand in the latter. Both the soil types are found extensively in the all along eastern part of the region in more or less continuous belt stretching from the northern border of the region to border line of the Magadh Division in the south. The soils are rich in fertility and suitable for the production of varieties of crops.

6. Clay-loam a mixture of clay and loam is predominantly found in the western section of plain area. In small and isolated patches it is scattered over the remaining portion of plain specially in upper area. It is very fertile indeed and best suited for the cultivation of paddy. A peculiar feature of this soil is that it opens out, when dry, in gaping fissures becomes hard and stiff. The usual dimension of cracks vary between 5 to 8 cm. wide and 60 to 120 cm. deep, thus allowing very little profile development to take place.

7. *Silty-loan.* This group of soil formed out of greater proportion of loam and smaller proportion of silt is found in small and isolated patches most of which are found in the eastern part of the region, with a wider coverage in Pakri Barawan and Warisaliganj anchals. Small patches also occur in Nabinagar, Arwal and Karpi anchals of Son-Pun Pun interfluve.

8. *Gravely sand.* This soil group in which gravel is found mixed with coarse sand, is exclusively found in the scarp land area. A large belt of it is found extending between Amas, Madanpur and Deo. It also occurs in the southern border of Sherghati and Fatehpur anchals. Naturally this soil is the least fertile one and remains practically idle.

Soil Association Groups[12]

Based on the description of pH percentage and texture of the soils, the area under study has been divided into three broad soil association groups which are more or less akin to the physiographic units of Magadh Division.

1. Recent Alluvium

The broad soil association group of non-calcareous recent alluvium soil is found along the banks of the Son, Pun Pun and Phalgu rivers. It is yellowish to reddish-yellow in colour. The soils are generally sandy and moderately acidic to neutral in reaction and poor in fertility.

2. Old Alluvium

Rest of the portion of Magadh Division excluding the scarp land belt comes under this soil association group. But on the basis of the texture, colour and reactions they have further been subdivided into two groups- (A) Old Alluvium and (B) Old Alluvium.

The first (A) group (old Alluvium) is grey, greyish and yellow in colour and heavy to madium heavy in texture. The surface soil reaction is neutral to slightly alkaline. This group of soil, being clayey loam and 'kewal' developes linear creaks after getting dry. It is spread over the central and northern part of the plain area. The fertility status of this soil varies from medium to high and is suitable for the cultivation of paddy and Maize. With an aid of irrigation it is capable of raising second crop of wheat, barley and oil seeds also.

The second (B) group of this soil association (Old Alluvium) covers a wider area in the east, west and south of the plain region. It encompasses within its limit the Son-Pun Pun interfluve as well.

This soil group is reddish, yellow to yellow-grey in colour, moderately to slightly acidic and neutral to slightly alkaline in reaction. This well-drained and free from riverine flood soil group, generally, contains ferrugenous concretions which have given it a reddish tint. Crops like paddy, maize, wheat gram and arhar are grown depending upon the level of the land. Sugarcane is grown in areas having irrigational facility.

3. *Foot-Hill Soil*

Spread over almost whole of the scarp land area, south of plain, the foot hill soil group is yellowish-red-in colour. This heavily to moderately drained soil is usually shallow covering the bed rocks and pebbles. It is moderately to strongly acidic in reaction with poor to moderate fertility status. Generally maize, millets and pulses are grown. Paddy also finds place but in favoured pockets.

1.9 NATURAL VEGETATION

A vast tract of level land, having fertile alluvium soil which serves as a base for predominently agricultural activity, has restricted the natural vegetation either to the hilly areas, dissected rim of the Chotangagpur plateau in the scarp land region or some revrine tract. The total area under natural vegetation is 40,88,83 acres including pastures, groves trees etc. which is hardly 12.47% of the geographical area of the Magadh Division. It is far below the state level (21.4%) and much below the standard (33%) set under the National Forest Policy.[13]

Map (*Fig. No. 1.6*) shows the areas that are under physical occupation of Natural Vegetation. It is evident that a continuous linear belt occurs all along the south and eastern parts of the scarp land extending over Kawakol (39,845 acres), Gobindupur (17,881 acres), Mohanpur (28,546 acres) Barachatti (45,233 acres), Sherghati (1,321 acres), Imamganj (22,930 acres), Dumaria (26,730 acres), anchals etc. Apart from this continuous belt vegetation occuring in sizeable area in the scarpland region are the anchals of Madanpur, Deo and Amas etc.

Beyond the scarpland regions, the worth mentioning anchals having vegetational cover are Atri (6,000 acres), Wazirganj (4,337 acres) and Belagnaj (1,638 acres) etc.

Map (*Fig. No. 1.7*) shows that areas completely devoid of natural vegetation lie extensively in the northern and western part of the region where not even one per cent of land is under natural vegetation. As we move from north to south the percentage of land under the cover of natural vegetation increases. Areas having less than 10% vegetation are also extensive and continuous belt falling just south of the belt mentioned

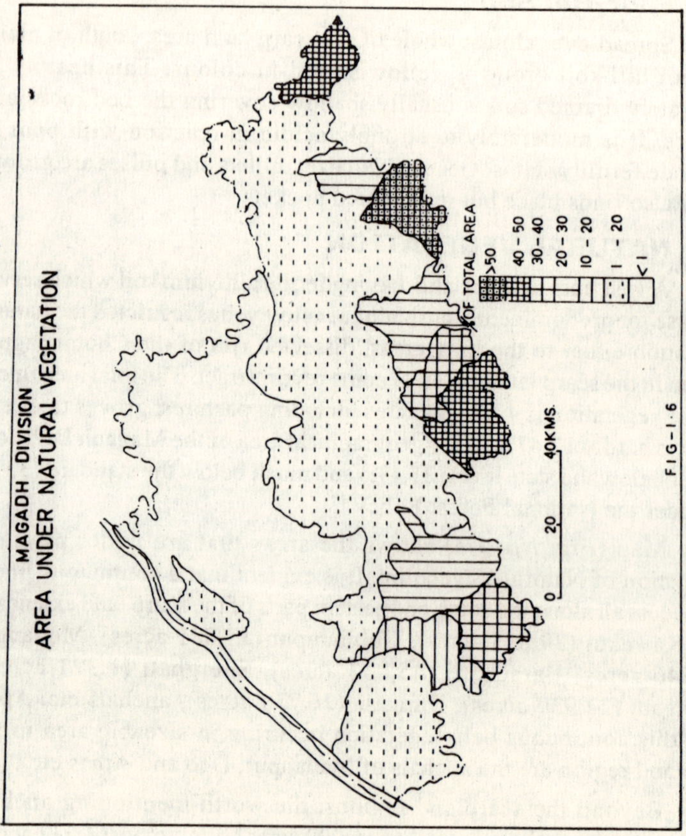
MAGADH DIVISION
AREA UNDER NATURAL VEGETATION
% OF TOTAL AREA
>50
40 – 50
30 – 40
20 – 30
10 – 20
1 – 20
< 1
0
20
40KMS.
FIG-1.6

Fig. 1.6

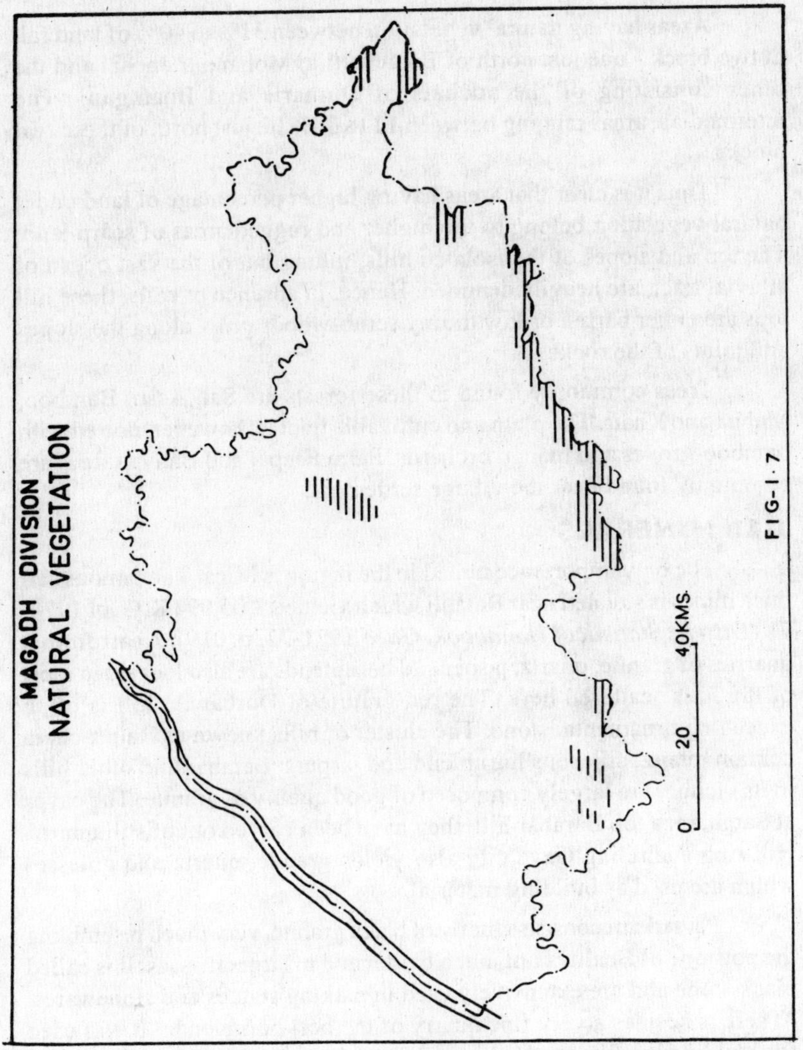

Fig. 1.7

above. On the contrary, Rajauli is the only anchal in this region having more than half of its land (52.95%) under forest. Next in hierarchy are the anchals of Barachatti (49.48%), Kawakol (48.1%) occupying eastern most part of the scarp land.

Areas having natural vegetation between 31% to 40% of land fall in two block - one just north of Barachatti in Mohanpur anchal and the other consisting of the anchals of Dumaria and Imamganj. The intermediate areas ranging between 11 to 30% lie just north of these two blocks.

Thus it is clear that areas having higher percentage of land under natural vegetation belong to the higher and rugged areas of scarp land. The top and slopes of the isolated hills, jutting out of the vast ocean of alluvial tract, are heavily denuded. Hence, in absence of soils, these hill tops are either barren or low thorny scrub-woods grow along the slopes and joints of the rocks.

Trees commonly found in these forests are Sal, Asan, Bamboo, Mahua and Khair. The plain and cultivable tract is, however, dotted with bamboo-groves and mango orchards. Palm Peepal and Banyan trees are commonly found near the village settlement.

1.10 MINERALS

The only importance mined in the region is Mica. The famous safi mica mines is situated near Rajauli which yielded 3,05,094 K.G. in 1970-71 (*District Statistical Handbook, Gaya* 1971-72, p. 019). Apart from it quarries of granite, quartz, jasper and hornblends are also located in most of the hills scattered here. The red granite of Durbanahi hill is of an exceeding ornamental stone. The cluster of hills known as Rajgir chain contain quartz, siliceous hornblend and jaspers. Barabar and other hills in its vicinity are largely composed of good quality of granite. The caves at Satghara, a top Barabar hill, they have been carved out of still quartz. Hill ring encircling Gaya city also yields granite, quartz and gniesses which are used as building material.

Patharkatti consists chiefly of black granite, very much resembling the potstone of Bhaluya but much harder and in larger masses. It is called black stone and are extensively used in making statues and stonewares. "There is besides a very fine quarry of the best hornblende. It was used for building the famous Vishnupad Temple at Gaya".[15]

Sands are extensively excavated from beds of the Phalgu and Son and are of commercial significance.

The total revenue collected by the District Mining Officer at Gaya from stone chips, sands, bricks and reh lime was Rs. 2,86,567 during 1970-71.(*District Statistical Handbook, Gaya* 1971-72, p. 109.)

CULTURAL LANDSCAPE

1.11 LAND USE

Land use is the junction of the interplay of Land which provides platform, and the ingenuity of man, who is the measure of significance of all phenomana in geography. Man although has limited role to play in nature except under the pressure of exigencies, still the biobic potentialities of land - its configuration, drainage, soil, climate etc. offer a permissible limit to man for its utilization. Through viable change in land use pattern, the desired agricultural plan, which is a part of this thesis, may be prepared. This agricultural plan will give the future marketed surplus.

There are nine categories to which the land in Bihar has been classified by the Directorate of Statistics and Evaluation, Government of Bihar. Here also nine categories of land uses are broadly identified in Magadh Division which are presented in the table no. 1.2. This table explain that agricultural intensity in the Magadh Division is 32% i.e. are sown more than once as per cent of the net area sown. The agricultural intensity justifies the harvesting of limited crops two or three times a year, where as it also indicates the traditional way of cultivation. About 17% of the total geographical areas, falling under categories of cultivable waste land. Other fallow land, current fallow land, may be considered as potential area for cultivation.

Table No. 1.2

Land Use Pattern

Sl. No.	Land use categories	Area in acres	Percentage to the total area
1.	Forest	3,69,663	11.24
2.	Barren and uncultivable land	4,32,840	13.17
3.	Land put to non-agricultural uses	3,07,809	9.36
4.	Permanent pasture and other grazing land	30,029	0.96
5.	Miscellaneous trees, crops and grooves	9,191	0.27

Sl. No.	Land use categories	Area in acres	Percentage to the total area
6.	Cultivable wasteland	38,313	1.16
7.	Other fallow land	52,077	1.58
8.	Current fallow land	4,66,144	14.18
9.	Net Area Sown (N.A.S.)	15,80,466	48.08
	Total geographical area	32,86,530	100.00
	Area sown more than once	5,07,988	
	Total cropped area	20,88,452	63.54*

** Figure indicates per cent of total geographical area.*

The proportion of the area not available for cultivation, fluctuation, since the rapid growth of population right from 1931 onward requires more land for housing and allied purposes.

The barren and uncultivable land can not be filled except at a prohibitive cost.

It is the cultivable area alone which falls an easy prey to the growing pressure of population on the otherwise limited land. If, therefore, shows a consistent and accelerated decline in its proportion to the total land.

Cultivated area conspicuously entails the largest proportion of the land, more than half of the total area. The fall in the area under this category in 1951 to 1961 is due largely to the growth in forest area in the corresponding period. It so happened due to the aforestation programme of the government.

Now coming to the figure given in Table No. 1.2. it is obvious that uncultivable area including forest, baren land and land put to non-agricultural uses constitute only 33.77% of the total area of Magadh Division.

Areas under four categories of land are namely (i) permanent pasture and other grazing ground; (ii) miscellaneous trees, crops and groves, (iii) cultivable waste land and; (iv) other fallow land put together and termed as arable land is hardly 3.97% of the total area (*Fig. No. 1.8*). A natural corolary to it is that the normal diet of the inhabitants of the country must be heavily deficient in animal products, fruits and vegetables so vital for the up keep of their health.

The net area sown, with a largest proportion of land 48.08% of the geographical area of Magadh Division, coupled with the areas under

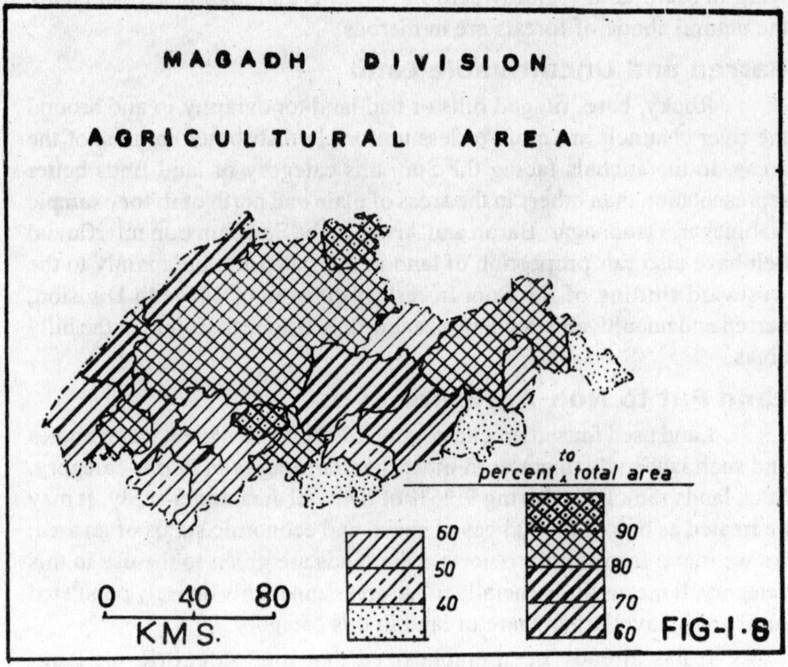
MAGADH DIVISION
AGRICULTURAL AREA
percent to total area
60
50
40
90
80
70
60
0 40 80
KMS.
FIG-I·8

Fig. 1.8

current fallow (14.18%), exuberantly display the predominance of agriculture over others. An extensive plain land endowed with fertile alluvial soil with a net work of river system and long tradition of farming has facilited bring maximum land under plough.

In the region the predominance of net area sown is apparent. This category of land use dwarfs all other categories in almost all the anchals, except that of Kawakol, Rajauli, Mohanpur, Barahatti and Dumaria where the land under forest has the upper most position.

Forest land occurs in significantly higher proportion in the anchals lying in scarp land region where ridges, hills and high lands which are the natural abode of forests are numerous.

Barren and Uncultivable Land

Rocky, bare, rugged hills or bad land topography in and around the river channels are more or less uniformly distributed in most of the areas. In the anchals facing the Son, this category of land finds better representation than others in the areas of plain and north of it, for example Nabinagar, Daudnagar, Barun and Arwal in the Son-Pun Pun interfluvial belt have also fair proportion of land in this category due mainly to the westward shifting of the Son. In rest of the area of Magadh Division, barren and uncultivable land, in sizeable dimension, are found in the hilly areas.

Land Put to Non-Agricultural Use

Land used for settlement, communication, permanent water bodies and such lands which are used other than farming falls in this category. Such lands rank fifth sharing 9.96% of the total area under study. It may be treated as one of the indices of social and economic status of an area. As we move from south to north mere lands are given to the use in this category. It means that generally urban areas and highly densely populated rural areas have larger share of land in this category.

It has already been emphasized that four categories of land-cultivable waste, permanent pasture and other grazing grounds, miscellaneous trees, crops and groves and other fallow land even put together, stand on the lowest pedestal, so far the average and its proportion to the total area is concerned.

Since, the land under Net Sown Area, in this predominently agricultural region, is disproportionately large (48.08% of the total land). The highest proportion of net sown area lies extensively in the belt of well irrigated agricultural tract in the densely populated part where more intensive agriculture is practiced.

Impact of topography is apparently seen in the scarp land belt where majority of the anchals belong to the categories which have less than half of the land given to farming. Rajauli anchal deserves special mention for the fact that the blade of the plough turns only over 19% of its land.

1.12 Irrigation

Topography, soil and scatiness of total rainfall with its irregularity are the major causes which have led the people of the Magadh Division to devise a system of which the natural course of water in the river is impeded and utilized for cultivation. The Division is characterized by a scanty rainfall, a rapid slope off which the water quickly runs and a soil which is either a still clay or a loose sand and equally unretentive of moisture. Rapid slope also prevents the land from gaining the full benefit of the rainwater where it is allowed to flow unchecked, and the cultivation of rice on which the people almost entirely depend, would be impossible, if the water were not impounded in expensive reservoirs called 'Ahara', which are formed by constructing a series of retaining embankments across the line of drainage. The whole indeavour forms a most remarkable and ingenious system of artificial irrigation which is admirably supplemented by the manner in which the water is distributed from field and retained in them by a network of low banks. In the cold weather again, when the 'Ahars have dried up and 'Pynes' no longer contain water, the people of the area go back on their wells, and thus the crops are protected from failure throughout the year. People have a small advantage of canal irrigation. In the north-west, an ample and regular supply of water is due to Son canals. The acreage and percentage of irrigated land through these different sources of irrigation are described in the following table.

Table No. 1.3
Sources of Irrigation and Areas

Sources	Irrigated areas (in acres)	Percent of total irrigated areas	Irrigated area as percent to total cultivated areas
Canals	2,61,502	26.74	12.52
Tubewells	1,73,467	17.74	8.30
Other wells	68,610	7.04	3.28
Other sources	4,74,019	48.48	12.70
Total	9,77,598	100.00	46.80

The maximum area is irrigated by indegenous method or irrigation, which is described under the other sources in table no. 1.3. Canal is the next means of irrigation. It is remarkable in the above table that only about 47% of the total cropped area has been benefit of irrigation facilities. Among other sources of irrigation 'Ahars' and 'Pynes' are the most important (*Fig. No. 1.9*).

Canals

The western part of Son-Pun Pun Interfluve is served partially by Son-Canal system. An ancient across the Son at Barun was constructed in the year 1875,[16] and canals were dug out east of it, known as eastern canal. The Patna canal branches off the main eastern canal 6.4 Km. (4 metres) from the Son in north direction. The canal along with its distributaries command a total area of over 400,000 acres.[17]

Tanks and 'Ahars'

'Ahars' in an U shaped or rectangular embankment, of which one side is either left open or slightly raised. It is a device to collect rain water by blocking a small rivulet. It irrigates paddy field and itself during winter becomes a good field for rabi cultivation.

'Pynes' (a sort of narrow inundation canal) are dug from the convenient point of the river to carry water to paddy fields. Taking an advantage of the 'fit-feel flow' of the swollen torrents debouching from the highlands of Chotanagpur, 'Pynes' are filled up intermittently and the water conveyed to the paddy fields.

Tube Wells and Wells

With the rapid pace of rural electrification after the independence, Tube Wells operated both by electricity and mineral oil have become a potential source of irrigation (17.74%) of total irrigated land. Wells both (Kacha and Pakka) tap the sub soil water and by employing intensive manual or animal labour, farmers use them to irrigate vegetables, cash crops and to some extent rabi crops as well.

Taking all the sources of irrigation together we find that the peasants have to travel a long way to cover up the remaining (about 53%) portion of the fields which are under their plough. But even among the irrigated areas, a great regional variation is found. There are altogether three anchals of Gobindpur, Konch and Arwal which have a large area under irrigation. Gobindpur anchal located in the eastern part of the plain area has hardly 38% of its total area under irrigation where as Arwal has the highest proportion of irrigated areas (93%).

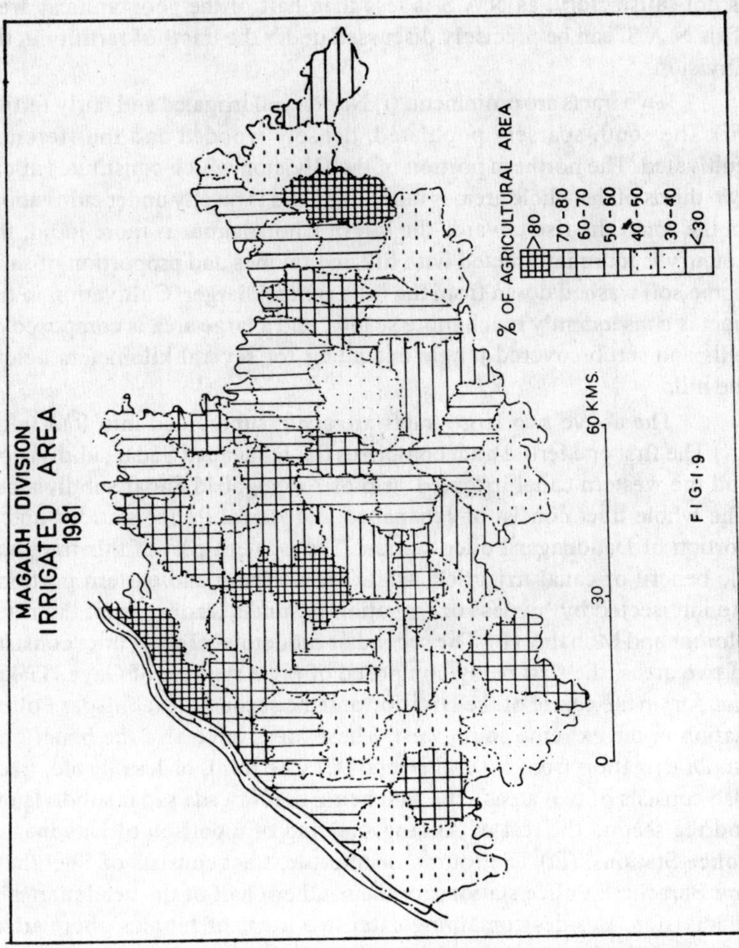
MAGADH DIVISION
IRRIGATED AREA
1981
% OF AGRICULTURAL AREA
>80
70-80
60-70
50-60
40-50
30-40
<30
0
30
60 KMS.
FIG-1·9

Fig. 1.9

1.13 AGRICULTURE

It has already been stated that approximately 48% of the total geographical areas of the Magadh Division is under net area sown. It directly indicates that physical requirement for cultivation in the Division is not satisfactory, as N.A.S is less than half of the geographical area. This N.A.S. can be precisely discussed under the tracts of fertility in the Division.

Two tracts are prominent: (i) North-well irrigated and fairly fertile, (ii) The south-sparsely populated, densely wooded and indifferently cultivated. The northern portion of the Division which constitutes about two thirds of the whole area, is fairly level and is mostly under cultivation. In the south the rise towards the hill of Chotanagpur is more rapid, the country is more intersected with hill and ravines and proportion of sand in the soil washed down from the hills is much larger. Cultivation in the tract is consequently much more scanty, and a large area is composed of hills and scrub covered jungle extending for several kilometers below the hills.

The above two large tracts are again subdivided into four units (A) The first one fertile tract comprises the Jehanabad Sadar subdivision and the western canal irrigated strip of Aurangabad Sadar subdivision. The whole tract consist of Jehanabad and Arwal Police stations and a portion of Daudnagar Police station. The western part of this tract has the benefit of canal irrigation, while the northern and eastern portions are intersected by 'pynes' or irrigation channels leading from the river Morhar and Mohabe; (B) The second or moderately fertile tract consists of two areas, the first being composed of plice stations of Gaya, Tiakri and Atri in the centre of the Division and the second of Nabinagar Police station in the extreme south west. These areas have also the benefit of ample irrigation from several rivers; (C) The third, or less fertile, tract also consists of two areas - the first being the Nawada sadar subdivision and the second the rest of Aurangabad and of a portion of Daudnagar Police Stations; (D) The fourth, or infertile, tract consists of Sherghati and Barachatti Police stations, or the southern half of the headquarter's subdivision. Besides containing extensive tracts of Jungles, there are a few 'pynes' and only 10% of the villages are irrigated.

Area sown more than once falls in the northern fertile tract, relatively more than that of southern tract. Nearly 15.45% of the total area is being used for multiple cropping. Though the fertility also decides the area sown more than once, but one of the reasons may be increasing number of persons, which has forced farmers, to raise more than one crop, on the same piece of land, other manifestation of the growing population, on the limited land resources, is that most of the available land is being used for raising the cereal crops. The table given below reflects the relative importance of the crops raised in different seasons.

Table No. 1.4

Type of Crops and Percent of Total Cropped Area

Crops	Percent of total cropped area
Bhadai	4.20
Aghani	46.00
Rabi	46.49
Garma	3.31
Total	100.00

It is apparent from the table that Aghani and Rabi occupying more than 90% of the total cropped area are equally important. Bhadai though occupying a meager proportion of acreage is important in the sense that it is harvested at the time when stock of farmer's grain is virtually depleted. Maize is the important Bhadai crop 'Garma' crop is grown in summer with the help of irrigation.

Area occupied by different crops is quite apparent from the table given below (No. 1.5).

Table No. 1.5

Seasonal Crops and Percent of the Total Area

Crops		**Percent of the total cropped area**
Autumn paddy		0.15
Winter paddy	-	50.17
Summer paddy	-	0.98
Wheat	-	23.33
Autumn maize	-	2.75
Summer maize	-	0.23
Gram	-	3.30
Sugarcane	-	1.08
Potato	-	1.37
Pulses	-	12.42
Fruits and vegetables	-	2.22
Others	-	2.00
Total		**100.00**

The above table reveals that more half of the total cropped area is occupied by the cultivation of rice, which is staple food of the people. Wheat is grown over a little more than 23 per cent of the total cropped area. Pulses, including mainly Masoor, Arhar, Khesari cover more than 12% of the total cropped area. Gram and maize are the third crop of the Division. Here the areal pattern of their distribution is being discussed.

1. *Rice*. (*Fig. No. ,1.10(b)*) shows the area distribution the percentage of acreage under rice. Two categories of areas average on the map, namely (a) Areas of high percentage of acreage (about 60%). The areas of low percentage of acreage, i.e. less than 30% is not available in the Division. The areas of medium percentage are concentrated in southern, eastern and some of the west central parts in pockets of small disjointed belts. Rest parts of the Division is characterized with high acreage.
2. *Wheat*. The second most important cereal crop of the division comes next to rice. (Fig. No. 1.10(a)) displays the geographical distribution of wheat in the Division. The areas having highest proportion of acreage are mainly found in Obra, Manpur, Sirdala and Kawakole anchals lying in different parts of the Division. The area under the low percentage of acreage (less than 15% of the Net Area Sown) under wheat are Haspura, Nabinagar, Sherghati, Pakri-barawan and a belt consisting of Fatehpur, Wazirganj, Atri and Khizirsarai anchals. Rest parts of division's come under medium category (15.1% - 30%).
3. *Maize*. It is a third important cereal crop. (Fig. No. 1.10(c)) reveals that areas having relatively high proportion of acreage under maize are found in four southern anchals namely - Dumaria, Barachatti, Mohanpur and Rajauli. Areas having medium percentage of acreage under maize are contiguous, whereas areas having low percentage of acreage are wide spreaded.

The distribution of acreage under different crops give rise to the arrival of particular crop in a market, or the market deals with these commodities, which are covering more acreage in the surrounding region.

1.14 INDUSTRIES

Magadh Division can be reckoned as an industrially backward country. Since only 1.65 per cent of its total population is engaged in the activities of manufacturing, processing, servicing and repairs, all taken together. (*District Statistical Handbook, Gaya*, 1971-72, p. 109.) Even

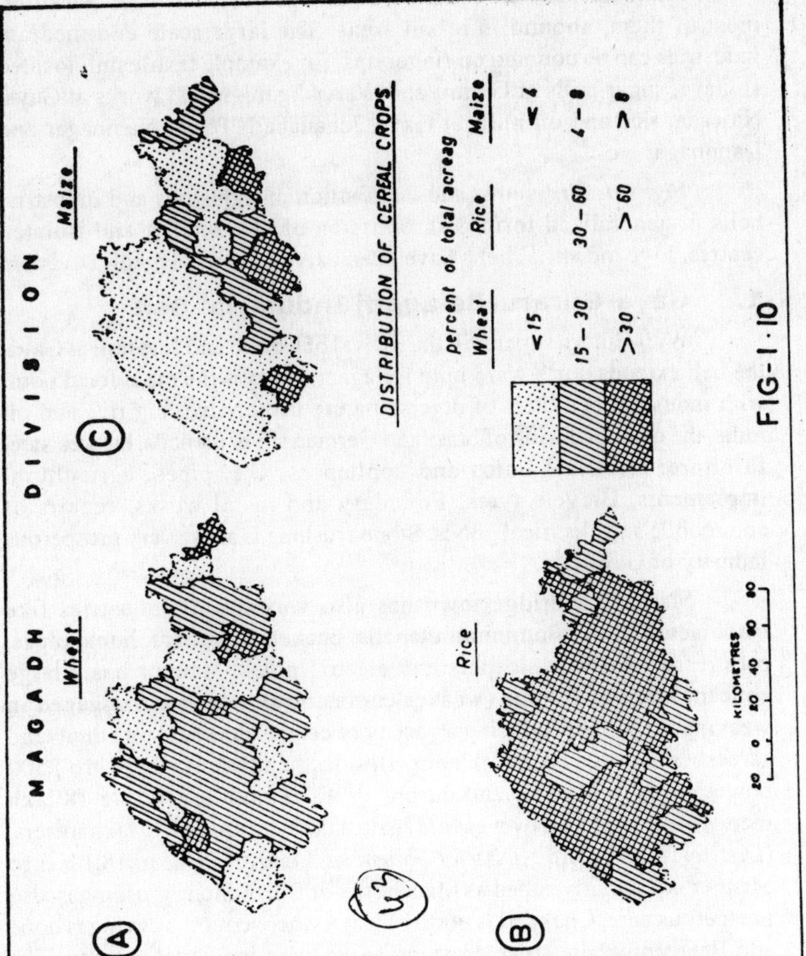
MAGADH DIVISION
A
Wheat
B
Rice
C
Maize
DISTRIBUTION OF CEREAL CROPS
percent of total acreag
Wheat
Rice
Maize
<15
<4
15 — 30
30 — 60
4 — 8
>30
>60
>8
KILOMETRES
20 0 20 40 60 80
FIG-1·10

Fig. 1.10

among the active population the percentage figure of this category of workers is only 5.59 percent [*As per planning commission's notification issued in 1975, Old Gaya District (Present Magadh Div..) has been categorised as industrially backward district*].

Although there are a number of cottage and small scale industries, most of them, abound in urban areas. The large scale and medium industries can be counted on finger tips, for example textile mill located at Gaya, sugar mills at Guraru and Warisaliganj, Metal works at Gaya, Nawada, rice and oil mills at Gaya, Jehanabad, Tehta, Nabinagar and Daudnagar etc.

Fig. No. 1.11 shows the distribution of industries and industrial belts in generalized form with omission of few smaller and isolated centres. Five industrial belts have been carved out in Magadh Division.

1. Gaya-Guraru-Belaganj Industrial Belt

With Guraru sugar mill the revival of Cotton and Jute mill at Gaya, the belt extends north ward upto Belaganj. Gaya is the main focal point with industrial activities of diverse nature namely two big rice and oil mills, the manufacturing of brass and German silver utencils, bucket, steel furniture, electrical bulbs and appliances, G.I. pipes, agricultural implements, Bicycle tyres, Foundary and metal works, repairs of automobile and electrical goods. Stone crushing is also a very prosperous industry of Gaya city.

Manpur, a bridge town has also varieties of industries like manufacturing of alluminium utencils, bucket, iron, bare, hume pipes, prestressed Railway sleepers and electric poles. Manpur has a large concentration of Patwas (weaver community), which are engaged in weaving activities producing a variety of coarse clothes (Janta dhoti and sarees) in an organiased manner. Besides handlooms, there are 3500 powerlooms in Manpur and during 1978-79 cloth measuring 18 lakh metres were produced by weavers against the state total of 40 lakh meters. (*District Action Plan : District Industries Centre, Gaya,* p. 18.) Hence Manpur is popularly called as Manchester of Bihar. Stone crushing is also prosperous here. Chakand is north of Gaya where cotton weaving is done and Belaganj where stone crushing is the main industrial activity. The sources of raw materials is Barabar hill for stone crushing.

This belt has also an excellent Transport facility, the region is served with Garand Chord line of eastern railway, connecting it to important centres of the country, Patna-Gaya and Gaya-Kiul railway lines along with a net work of roads, provide a good industrial base.

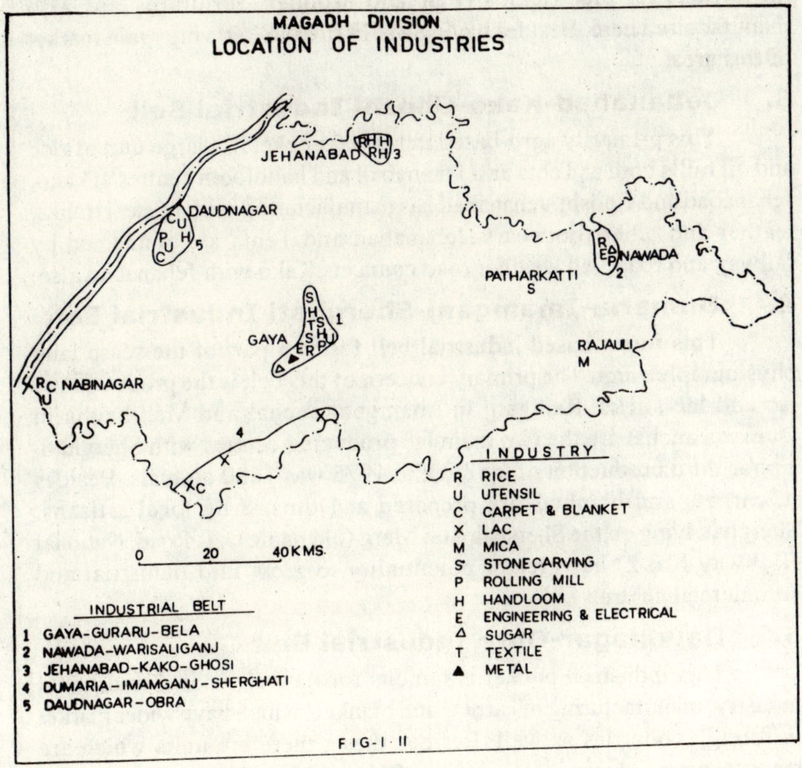
MAGADH DIVISION
LOCATION OF INDUSTRIES
JEHANABAD
DAUDNAGAR
NAWADA
PATHARKATTI
GAYA
RAJAULI
NABINAGAR
0 20 40 KMS.
INDUSTRIAL BELT
1 GAYA-GURARU-BELA
2 NAWADA-WARISALIGANJ
3 JEHANABAD-KAKO-GHOSI
4 DUMARIA-IMAMGANJ-SHERGHATI
5 DAUDNAGAR-OBRA
INDUSTRY
R RICE
U UTENSIL
C CARPET & BLANKET
X LAC
M MICA
S STONE CARVING
P ROLLING MILL
H HANDLOOM
E ENGINEERING & ELECTRICAL
Δ SUGAR
T TEXTILE
▲ METAL
FIG-1 11

Fig. 1.11

2. Nawada-Warisaliganj Industrial Belt

This one is the second industrial belt of Magadh Division. This belt is served with Gaya-Kiul railway line and Nawada has a facility of National Highway No. 31. Nawada has re-rolling mills and a number of small scale industries manufacturing steel truncts, wooden furnitures, footwears and general engineering and repairing centres. Cloth weaving is done in Warishaliganj which is just east of Nawada. Warisaliganj is well known for its sugar mill (Mohni Sugar Mill) and a big oil and rice mill. Bakelits electrical switch and wooden furnitures are also manufactured here. Besides having a cold storage it is a big grain market of this area.

3. Jehanabad-Kako-Ghoshi Industrial Belt

This primarily agro-based industrial pocket has large unit of rice and oil mills both at Tehta and Jehanabad and handloom centres at kako, Jehanabad and Ghoshi. Jehanabad has manufacturing units of steel trunks, leather and other footwears. Jehanabad and Tehta are connected by railway and road. All weather road connects Kako with Jehanabad also.

4. Dumaria-Imamganj-Sherghati Industrial Belt

This forest based industrial belt forms a part of the scarp land physiographic unit. The primary concern of this belt is the production of lac and lac-sticks. Raniganj in Imamganj anchal and Manjhaulia in Dumaria anchal are the two main lac producing centres with Sherghati, a poor third production of lac stick in 1975 was 1680 quintals. Besides it, carpets and blankets are prepared at Dumaria by local artisans. Sherghati lying on the Shershah Suri Marg (old name G.T. Road, National Highway No. 2) has greater potentiality to grow into industrial and commercial centre.

5. Daudnagar-Obra Industrial Belt

This industrial pocket is famous for its well known traditional industry, manufacturing of carpets and blankets which have wider market in foreign countries as well. Besides these, there are units which are manufacturing brass utencils both at Obra and Daudnagar.

Daudangar is a prosperous centre having Brass rolling mill, Brass and Bell metal Industry, Rice and oil mill and handloom units.

Among the important centres which fall out side the above mentioned industrial belts are Nabinagar which has oil and rice mill and manufacturing units of Brass utencils, carpets and blankets, Rajauli lying in the south eastern part of the Magadh Division is the only mica mining and processing centre, through presently in a decadent stage.

Patharkatti also deserves special mention for its unique activity of stone-carving and manufacturing of articles like mortars, pestless, crude lamps, bowls and vases. The articles, apart from being marketed in Gaya, are also exported to Varanasi, Allahabad, Mathura Haridwar, Delhi and elsewhere. The trade is being practiced by workmen of Jaipur who were brought in connection with the construction of famous stone built Vishnupad Temple at Gaya nearly over 200 years ago.[14]

Thus the map (fig. no. 1.11) depicts distinctly the inadequary of industries in Magadh Division. The industrial belts look like tiny patches over the vast expance of agricultural landscape.

1.15 COMMUNICATION

Railways and roads are the main means of communication in the Magadh Division. The famous Shershah Suri Marg (formerly Grand Trunk Road) which is the National Highway No. 2 runs through Magadh Division for a length of 111 kms. On the otherhand grand clord railway line of eastern railway connects the different parts of the Division.

The Shershah Suri Marg or the National Highway No. 2 is the most important interstate artery. It enters Magadh Division from the Hazaribag district near Bhalua and leaves it by a great causeway in the bed of Son at Barun. The road passes through important places of Barachatti, Dobhi, Sherghati, Madanpur and Aurangabad. The last two places Sherghati and Aurangabad are townships. The National Highway No. 31 is Bihar-Nawada-Rajauli Singrawan section of Patna-Ranchi road with a length of 52 Kms. in the region. The total length of all categories of roads in the Division is 1,495 Kms. and it is well served with a net work of roads of various categories.

The Division is served by three most important railway lines lying in the Grand Chord section of eastern railway.

(i) Grand Chord Railway Section

The grand chord railway line enters the region near Barun in the west after crossing the Son bridge and leaves it near Dalwa in the east after traversing a distance of 198 kms. Direct daily mail express trains are available from Gaya Jn. through this line for three metropolitians of the country i.e. Calcutta, Delhi and Bombay.

(ii) Gaya-Patna Railway Line

It connects the state capital city Patan in the north and covers a distance of 92 Kms. Double broad gauge of this branch line is the need of the hour.

Table No. 1.6

Means of Communication, Length, Area, Population and Market.,

Means of Communi cation	Length (in kms.)		Area (km^2)		Population		Kms. per market of Magadh Div.	
	Magadh Div.	Bihar	Magadh Div.	Bihar	Magadh Div.	Bihar	Regu-lated	Perio-dical
Road	1490	94032	8.28	1.85	3673	742	186.25	5.98
Railways	348	4606	35.47	37.4	15729	15159	43.50	1.39

(iii) Gaya-Kiul Railway Line

This line serves the region up to Warisaliganj, a commercial town, for a distance of 58 Kms.

Another Barun (Son Nagar) - Daltonganj (H.Q. of Palamu district) railway line has a distance of 38 kms. in the region, is of local importance. The following table reveals the means of communication and areas, population as well as market.

Table No. 1.6 reflects per kilometer rail line in length serving an area of 35.47 Km^2 and 15,729 persons of the Division. The man-road and area ratio are 3,673 persons and 8.28 Km^2 of per kilometer of road respectively. Compared to the similar figures for the state of Bihar, the defficiency of the road in the Division becomes apparent. There is no great difference in case of area per kilometer of railway. Rather the Division position is better than that of the state as a whole. Again the population served by railway in the Division is less than that of state, which is a positive remark.

The last column of the table shows the length of road and railway per market. The one regulated market is served by 186.25 Kms. length of road, whereas low figure of railway market ratio indicates the importance of road with regard to market. Periodical markets, more in number (216) in the Division as a whole, is served by 6 Km. of road length. There is no significance of railway in this respect. The detail study on market transport relationship will be carried out in latter chapters, while discussing the catchment areas of agricultural markets and identification of socio-economic texture of the regional economy. Ultimately whole problem i.e. location-allocation of markets is going to be solved by market-distance (from blocks) relationship.

In spite of the engineering and technological development, the control of topography and resource geography is evident. *Fig. No. 1.12* clearly indicates that part of the Son and Patna-Gaya railway line, is full of net works of roads, whereas most of scarp lands lack in transportation paucity of road building materials in the flat land is a contributory factor.

Fig. No. 1.13 shows the areas which do not find easy access to roads. (*Areas 5 Km. away from the motorable road approach have been regarded as an in accessible area.*) Such areas of larger dimentions find place south of the railway line running between Barun-Gaya and Warisaliganj. Other belt of in accessible area, though smaller in dimension, is found between Patan-Gaya railway line. All such in accessible areas put together stretch over several square kilometrs.

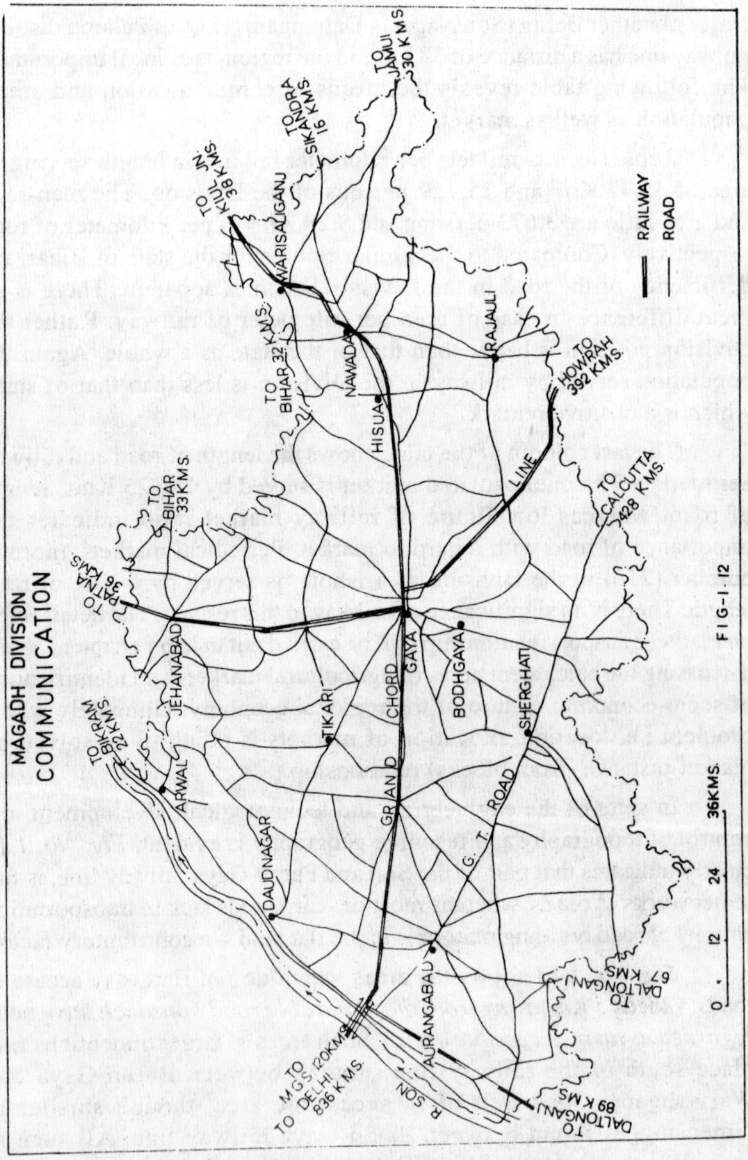
MAGADH DIVISION
COMMUNICATION
TO BIKRAM 22 KMS.
TO PATNA 36 KMS.
TO BIHAR 33 KMS.
TO BIHAR 32 KMS.
TO KIUL JN. 38 KMS.
TO SIKANDRA 16 KMS
TO JAMUI 30 KMS
TO HOWRAH 392 KMS.
TO CALCUTTA 428 KMS.
TO DALTONGANJ 67 KMS.
TO DALTONGANJ 89 KMS.
TO M.G.S. 120 KMS.
TO DELHI 836 KMS.
ARWAL
JEHANABAD
DAUDNAGAR
TIKARI
GAYA
BODHGAYA
SHERGHATI
AURANGABAD
HISUA
NAWADA
WARISALIGANJ
RAJAULI
GRAND CHORD LINE
G. T. ROAD
R. SON
RAILWAY
ROAD
0 12 24 36 KMS.
FIG-1.12

Fig. 1.12

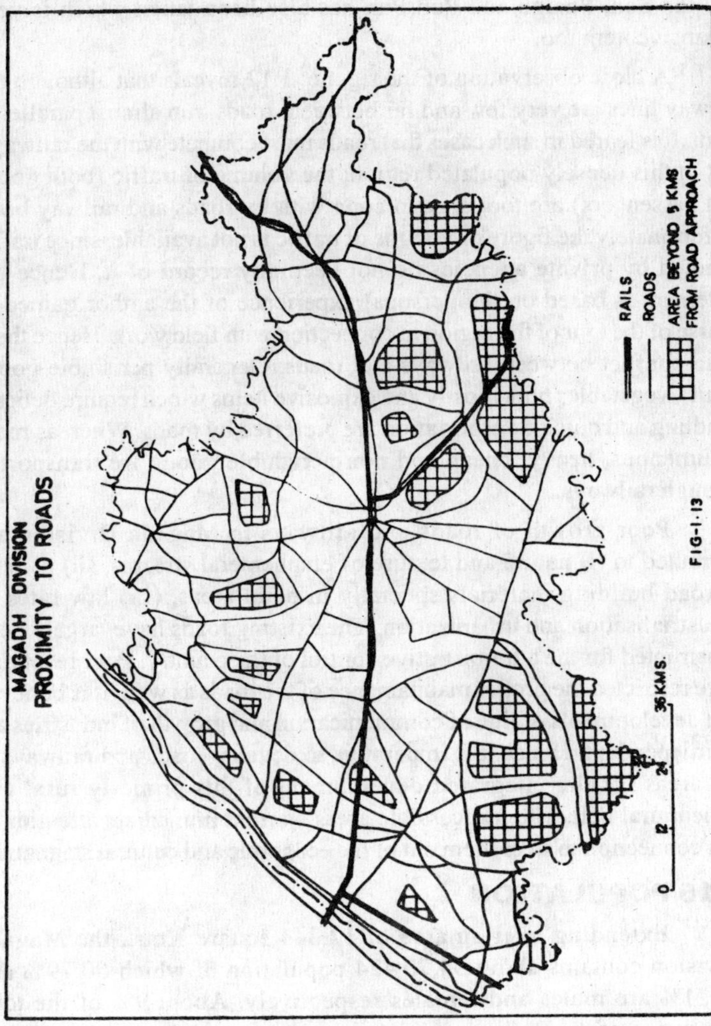
MAGADH DIVISION
PROXIMITY TO ROADS
RAILS
ROADS
AREA BEYOND 5 KMS FROM ROAD APPROACH
0 12 24 36KMS.
FIG-1-13

Fig. 1.13

The role of topography is also seen in the lay out of railway and roads. The grand chord line of eastern railway and the highway running in the region occupy a good area. It has also facilitated to protect the life line from the revages of floods. Construction of bridges over a few rivers like the Son, Phalgu and Pun Pun has also been taken which is very expansive item too.

A close observation of the fig. no. 1.12 reveals that although the railway lines are very few and far between, roads, run almost parallel to them. It is feared in such cases that roads must compete with the railways. But in this densely populated region, the volume of traffic (both goods and passengers) are too large to cope with by roads and railway both. Unfortunately the figure of volume of traffic is not available, since traffic handled by private agencies do not keep any record of it. Hence the statement is based on the personal experience of the author gained in course of the tour of the region in connection with field work. Hence there is no conflict between railways and roads. Generally perishible goods (fruits, vegetables milk) costly and explosive items which require delicate handling and quick transportation are preferred by roads. Whereas more volumenous, heavy, cheap and non-perishible goods are transported through railways.

Poor growth of roads and railways in Magadh Division are attributed to (i) nature and texture of emphemeral streams, (ii) paucity of road-building materials specially in plain areas, (iii) low rates of industrialisation and urbanization. The existing roads have largely been constructed for the administrative control of the country. Poor resources have restricted the proper maintainence of the roads as well. It is believed that developments of line of communication and growth of industries are interdependent. Hence it is imperative to develop roads and railways in the areas for the integrated development of this primerly rural and agricultural belt. The inaccessible areas warrent immediate attention in this connection to steer them out of the economic and cultural stagnation.

1.16 POPULATION

Extending over an area of 12,344 square Kms., the Magadh Division contains about 54,70,424 population of which 50.79% and 49.21% are males and females respectively. About 9% of the total population of the Division is in twelve urban centres.

The table (no. 1.7) shows the area and demographic structure of Bihar as well as the Magadh Division is in 1981.

Table No. 1.7

Demographic Structure of Bihar and Magadh Division, 1981*

	Bihar	Magadh Div.	Per cent of Bihar
Area (in sq. Kms.)	1,73,877	12,344	7.09
Total population	6,99,14,734	54,70,424	7.82
Rural population	6,11,95,744	49,71,472	8.12
Urban population	87,18,990	4,98,952	5.72
Male population	3,59,30,560	27,78,895	7.73
Female population	3,39,84,174	26,91,529	7.91
Working population	2,07,12,215	16,50,257	7.96
Primary population	1,64,05,738	13,63,376	
	(79.20)	(82.70)	
Secondary population	6,22,988	54,614	
	(3.00)	(3.3)	
Tertiary population	3,68,34,89	230,361	
	(17.80)	(14.00)	
Density (Persons perSq. Km)	402.00	443.44	
Females per thousand males	946.80	968.56	

Figures in bracket indicate the percentage of total workers.
* *Appendix - I for more details of data.*

The above table shows the following:

1. 7.09% of the total area of Bihar support 7.82% of the population.
2. There is little difference in the percentage of male, female total population working population to that of Bihar in the Magadh Division.
3. Percentage of Bihar's Urban population living in Magadh Division is about 5% and 9% of the total population being urban in the division indicates rural domination.
4. Predominence of agricultural economy is reflected by the fact the primary population of the Division accounts 82.7% of the total working population.
5. Dependency ratio, i.e. non working population per working population of Magadh Division (2.31) corresponds with that of Bihar (2.37).

6. Males of Magadh Division support less females than that of Bihar.
7. The density of population per Sq. Km. in the Division (443.44) is higher than that of Bihar (402.00). The higher density of the population has its obvious bearing on per capital share of land, where nearly 82.7% of the working population derives their sustenance form soil.

Distribution and Density of Population

The *Fig. no. 1.14* shows the areal pattern of the distribution of population including urban centres. The proportionate size of transparent circles indicate the size of urban population. The pattern is not uniform, but map portrays that in the south scarp land, distribution of population is sparse. It gradually increases towards the north. The intensity of peopling in the Division seems to be closely associated with the fertility of land and more with the dominence of rice crop.

The density map indicates higher density in northern part of the Division and relatively low in the south (Fig. no. 1.14(b)).

Density of Rural Population

The distributional aspect of population is inseparately linked with that of population density, expressed in terms of the number of people per unit area. It serves as a quantative tool for assissing the degree of human concentration. It also reflects the impact of size as well as the spacing of village in the unit area concerned.

The average density of population in Magadh Division is 443.44 persons per Sq. Km. which is decidedly high as compared to that of Bihar 402 as per 1981 census. The main factors contributing to its high density are intensive system of agriculture with emphasis on food crops, relatively higher degree of urbanization and long history of human occupance.

Out of the total population of 5,470,424 approximately 4,971,472 constitute rural population of Magadh Division. Density of rural population is significantly higher than the rural density of the state of Bihar as a whole.

There are four groups of density of population (*Fig. No. 1.15*).

Urban-Rural Ratio

In the Magadh Division, there are thirteen urban centres, each being located in individual anchals except Aurangabad anchal.

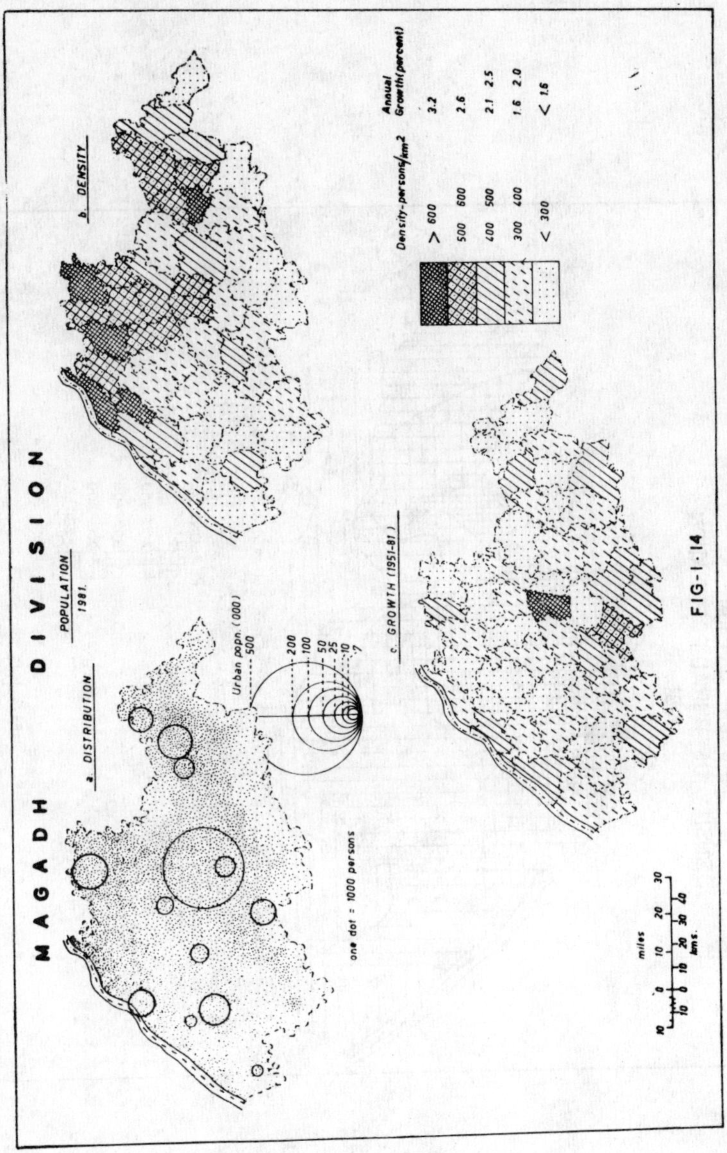
MAGADH DIVISION
POPULATION
1981.
a. DISTRIBUTION
b. DENSITY
c. GROWTH (1951-81)
Urban popn. (000)
500
200
100
50
25
10
one dot = 1000 persons
Density-persons/km2
Annual Growth(percent)
> 600
500 600
400 500
300 400
< 300
3.2
2.6
2.1 2.5
1.6 2.0
< 1.6
miles
kms.
FIG-1-14

Fig. 1.14

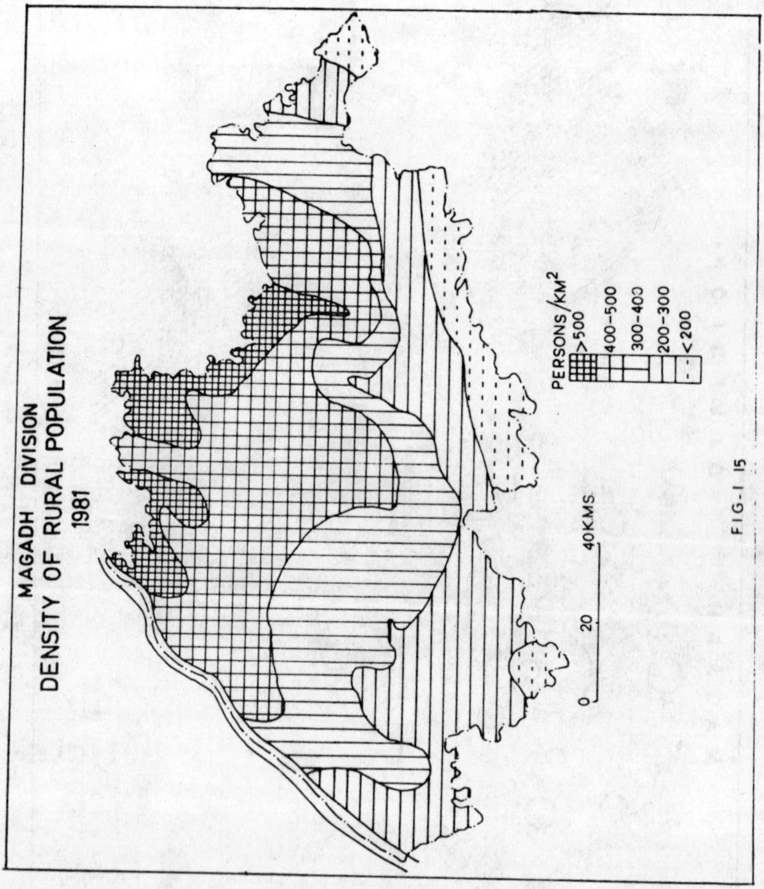
MAGADH DIVISION
DENSITY OF RURAL POPULATION
1981
PERSONS/KM²
>500
400–500
300–400
200–300
<200
0 20 40KMS
FIG-1.15

Fig. 1.15

Aurangabad anchal has two urban centres, the anchal headquarter itself and other is Jamhaur. The table no. 1.8 given below shows the urban-rural ratio of the twelve anchals. Rest have no urban centres.

Table No. 1.8

Urban-Rural Population Ratio in Twelve Anchals, 1981

Sl. No.	Anchals	Urban Population	Urban-Rural Ratio
1.	Tikari	12,280	0.08
2.	Gaya Town	2,46,778	2.55
3.	Bodh Gaya	15,724	0.01
4.	Sherghati	20,290	0.20
5.	Jehanabad	44,647	0.41
6.	Nawada	38,750	0.22
7.	Warisaliganj	18,872	0.17
8.	Hisua	15,422	0.14
9.	Aurangabad	39,185	0.26
10.	Daudnagar	24,515	0.23
11.	Refiganj	14,628	0.08
12.	Nabinagar	7,473	0.05

Growth of Population and Projection of Population for 1991 and 2001

The Annual Growth Rate (AGR) of population of all forty six anchals (blocks) are given in table no. 1.9. These annual growth rates have been worked out with the population variation between 1951 and 1981 census. The annual growth rates have been mapped. The AGR of urban population (table no. 1.10) has been worked out on the basis of decadal variation between 1971 and 1981 population.

Table No. 1.9

Growth of Population and Projection of Populatoin for 1991 and 2001.

Sl. No.	Anchals (Blocks)	1951	1981	GR	1991	2001
1	2	. 3	4	5	6	7
1.	Manupur	42,330	67,817	1.58	79,354	92,854
2.	Paraiya	59,584	105,209	1.91	127,163	153,698
3.	Koch	68,463	114,280	1.72	135,563	160,810

1	2	3	4	5	6	7
4.	Tikari	79,873	129,369	1.62	151,928	178,422
5.	Belaganj	62,899	112,555	1.958	136,648	165,899
6.	Khizirsarai	51,907	92,203	1.93	111,665	135,235
7.	Gaya	37,946	97,713	3.20	133,931	183,573
8.	Bodh Gaya	57,441	91,072	1.54	106,195	123,830
9.	Sherghati	43,355	94,129	2.61	121,885	157,826
10.	Barachatti	48,151,	91,921,	2.17	124,029	141,455
11.	Mohanpur	50,479	94,129	2.09	115,858	142,604
12.	Atri	82,627	137,091	1.70	162,294	192,132
13.	Wazirganj	86,629	147,059	1.77	175,428	209,271
14.	Fatehpur	72,102	129,742	1.97	157.808	191,941
15.	Amas	53,694	96,496	1.97	117.319	142,637
16.	Gurua	45,221	88,781	2.27	111,168	139,200
17.	Imamganj	57,127	104,130	2.02	127,200	155,381
18.	Dumaria	31,278	60,657	2.23	75.641	94,328
19.	Arwal	101,700	171,161	1.75	203,594	242,173
20.	Karpi	83,277	137,511	1.68	162,533	192,108
21.	Kurtha	64,087	159,684	1.77	190,475	227,203
22.	Jehanabad	47,869	88,502	2.10	109,003	134,253
23.	Kako	59,787	91,330	1.42	105,183	121,139
24.	Ghosi	99,050	157,323	1.53	183,557	214,166
25.	Makhdumpur	84,852	138,733	1.65	163.437	192,541
26.	Nawada	69,009	130,694	2.15	161,698	200,057
27.	Warisaligang	63,607	105,623	1.70	125,076	148,113
28.	Akbarpur	66,555	110,224	1.69	130.409	154,290
29.	Rajauli	42,214	84,804	2.35	107.004	135,017
30.	Gobindpur	62,569	109,887	1.89	132,579	159,957
31.	Kawakole	49,942	93,889	2.12	115,877	143,014
32.	Pakribarawan	63,663	103,840	1.64	122.233	143,885
33.	Sirdala	65,201	112,743	1.84	135.321	162,422
34.	Narhat	51,967	79,936	1.44	92,274	106,517
35.	Hisua	55,157	94,383	1.50	112,890	135,027
36.	Aurangabad	45,981	80,618	1.80	97,211	117,219
37.	Barun	52,009	97,052	2.10	119,484	147,103

1	2	3	4	5	6	7
38.	Obra	64,973	116,998	1.97	142,339	173.171
39.	Daudnagar	44,376	84,144	2.15	104,147	128,906
40.	Haspura	52,821	81,466	1.45	94.123	108,748
41.	Goh	68,177	110,386	1.61	129,620	152,205
42.	Rafiganj	83,350	133,799	1.59	156,663	183,435
43.	Nabinagar	83,379	144,871	1.85	174,163	209,378
44.	Kutumba	64,122	110,604	1.83	132,645	159,079
45.	Doe	56,499	86,375	1.42	990.503	114,626
46.	Madnapur	59,681	104,410	1.88	125,808	151,593

GR = Annual Growth Rate In (%).

ı991-2001 = Projected Population.

Table No. 1.10

The Annual Growth Rate of 12 Anchals Urban Population

	Urban Centres	**Populatinon 1971**	**1981**	**AGR**	**Projected 1991**	**2001**
1.	Gaya	179,884	246,778	3.71	338,548	464,445
2.	Bodh Gaya	6,968	15,724	8.48	35,483	80,070
3.	Sherghati	15,047	20,290	3.03	27,359	36,893
4.	Tikari	8,700	12,280	3.51	17,333	24,466
5.	Jehanabad	29,198	44,647	4.33	68,270	104,393
6.	Nawada	23,746	38,750	5.01	63,234	103,189
7.	Hisua	11,256	15,422	3.20	21,130	28,450
8.	Warisaliganj	15,004	18,872	2.32	23,737	29,857
9.	Aurangabad	18,714	33,189	5.90	58,860	104,388
	Jamhaur*	-	5,996	4.00	8,875	13,138
10.	Nabinagar	5,804	7,473	2.56	9,622	12,389
11.	Daudnagar	16.866	24,514	3.81	35,645	51,818
12.	Rafiganj	8,818	14,628	5.19	24,266	40,255

**The Population of Jamhaur has been projected on the basis of average AGR (4.00)*

Projection of population has been done by the Geometric method and projected values are given in the above table no. 1.10.

Spacing of Villages

Magadh Division contains altogether 6,856 villages out of which 6,229 are inhabited and remaining 759 are uninhabited. The average spacing of inhabited villages comes out to be 2.10 Km^2 of net rural area. But villages are not uniformly spaced in all parts of the country.

Villages are very vlosely spaced (1-2 Km^2) over a large territory covering more than half of the total area of the country. On the contrary, sparcely spaced villatges over 4 Km^2 are localised in Kawakol. Villages ranging between 3-4 Km^2 are found in the anchals of Parkribarawan, Rajauli, Imamganj and Daudnagar. Rest villages falling in the category of 2 to 3 Km^2. The notable feature of the special pattern of the spacing of village is that densely spaced village occupy the central part of the country extending from north to south. A small belt of this category projects in south-western part.

A comparison of the areal distribution of size and spacing of inhabited villages in Magadh Division shows a broad relationship of inverse variation between the two with a few exception. The areas, with a fairly good number of large size villages are characterised by sparsely spaced villages and the vice versa. That is, croweded rural areas have larger number of small size villages. Notable exceptions to these general pattern are Rajauli and Imamganj anchals in the south where inspite of the larger proportion of small size villages, they are sparsely spaced (*Fig. No. 1.16*).

1.17 RURAL MARKET SYSTEM

The Magadh Division is served by a net work of rural markets dealing mainly in grains and vegetables. These market centres have evolved along the transportation lines and are located in different parts of the Division. The linkage between market centres and farms, from where the supply of grain is expected, through the transpowtation line gives a spatial dimension to agricultural market system. In the Magadh Division two broad types of market centres make the system.

(1) Primary Markets

These are held once, twice or thrice a week in or near the village or villages and are colloquially known as 'hats'. Goods transacted are : - food grains, fruits, vegetables, cloth, earthenwares and other commodities of daily need. The days on which these hats are held in the region, are generally so fixed as to enable the itinerant dealers to visit these in succession in a particular places. These are usually called periodical markets.

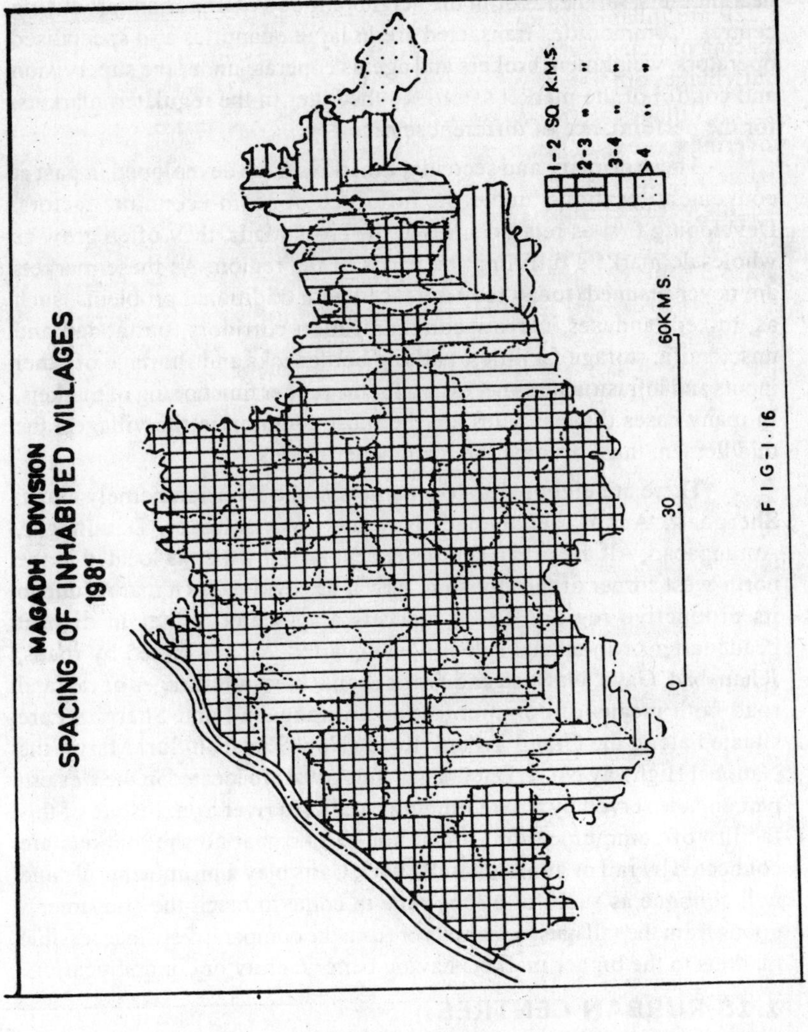
MAGADH DIVISION
SPACING OF INHABITED VILLAGES
1981
1-2 SQ. K.M.S.
2-3 "
3-4 "
>4 "
0
30
60 K M S.
F I G - I. 16

Fig. 1.16

(2) Secondary Markets

It is also called 'mandis' and held at places where business is transcted daily. Usually these are situated in district or subdivisional headquarters, rail heads or in the neighbourhood of important producing centres. Commodities transacted are in large quantities and specialised operators, weighmen, brokers and agents coperate under the supervision and control of the market samities - the latter in the regulated markets, for the performance of different services.

These primary and secondary markets have deveoloped in past at convenient locations. under the influence of socio-economic factors. Developing first as retail centres at the cross roads, they often grow as wholesale markets fulfilling the needs of the region. As these markets are never planned, today they are faced with traditional problems, such as, mixed landuses, narrow communication corridors, outmoded and unscientific storage facilities, parking bottlenecks and shortage of other inputs and infrastructures necessary for the proper functioning of markets. In many cases distress sales are the most common in the villages, the middlemen, thus, become the main beneficieries.

There are eight regulated markets in the Division namely Gaya, Sherghati, Arwal, Jehanabad, Nawada, Warisaliganj, Daudnagar, Aurangabad. All are urban centres except Arwal which is located in the north-west corner of the Division. Arwal has evolved as a market due to its productive region. These markets are located either in district headquarter or in anchal (block) headquarter. All are linked by roads, Jehanabad, Gaya, Nawada and Warisalignaj have advantages of rail and road both means of communication. Aurangabad and Sherghati are situated along the Grand Truunk Road (Now Shershah Suri Marg), the National Highway No. 2. Daudnagar and Arwal are located in the western part and are served by a road running parallel to river Son. Inspite of this facility of communication, it can not be said that all the markets are connected by rail or good roads. Bullock Carts play a prominent role and will continue as such for a long time to come to reach the consumer's goods from the villages to markets or from the comparatively inaccessible markets to the bigger markets having better facility or communication.

1.18 RURBAN CENTRES

One part of the study is also concerned with the relationship among rural centres wherein activities often than agriculture assume significant proportions. Such places have been referred to as 'service centres' because the facilities such as retial shopping, entertainment, cultural, professional and similar services provided from these are, sought by people from the surrounding areas.[18] The range of importance of these centres vearies from places of very limited local significance to those with considerable regional importance. The less important a centre is, the great is its dependence upon other more important service centres. Large rural settlements and small towns are known as 'Rurban Centres' which perform services of some urban and some rural nature for the people of the areas of their influence. Geometrical planning being idealistic may indeed be valied in the case of distribution of neatfare or information or other institutional activities of non-central significance. But hierarchical and development considerations in general have got to be necessarily related to the regional characteristics of area development. This perhaps has got a much greater relevance in the case of rurban centres, which as differentiated from urban centres, are predominently associated with rural areas in very diverse conditions of developement.

Keeping in view that a preliminary regional appraisal is imperative in all considerations of rurban centres growth and planning, the Magadh Division region was stuided with a objective of knowledge in this field of study.

REFERENCES

1. Singh, Dr. J.N. (1981) : Population Geography of Magadh Plain. Unpublished Ph.D. Thesis. M.U., Bodh Gaya.
2. Roy Choudhary, P.C. (1957): Bihar District Gazetteers, Gaya, p. 3.
3. Singh, Dr. R.P. and Kumar, Anil (1970) : Monograph of Bihar, Bharti Bhawan, Patna-4.
4. Buchanan Francis (1811-12) : An Account of the District of Bihar and Patna, Book III, p. 464.
5. Roy Chaudhary, P.C. (1957) : Op. cit., p. 5.
6. Kumar, N. (1970) : Bihar District Gazetteers, Patna, p. 7.
7. Roy Chaudhary, P.C. (1957) : Op. cit., p. 8.
8. Sinha, Ashok Kumar (1988) : Planning Strategies for Drought Prone Areas of Bihar: A Case Study of Palamu District, Indian Journal of Landscape Systems and Ecological Studies, Calcutta, June, 1988, Vol. II No. 1, pp. 105-111.
9. Singh, Dr. R.P. and Kumar, A. : Opcit, p. 25.
10. Jha, P.P. (1969) : Soils of Bihar 'Fertiliser News' Vol. 14, No. 10, October 1969, pp. 63-67.
11. Agricultural Research Institute: 'Soil Survey Report' Technical Report No. 10, Sabour (Bihar), pp. 76-77.
12. Jha, P.P. (1969) : Op. cit.

13. ——— (1981): District Census Hand Book, Gaya, Bihar.

14. Roy Chaudhary, P.C. : Op. cit., p. 147.

15. Buchanan Francis : Op. cit., p. 481.

16. O. Malley (1906) : District Gazetteer of Gaya, 1906.

17. Kumar, N. : Patna District Gazetteer, Op. cit.

18. Carruthers, Ian (1958) : A Classification of Service Centres in England and Wales, "Geographical Journal, Vol. CXXIX, p. 371

2

Theoretical Bases

The study of this branch of the subject is based on the methods of explanation and of theory evolved in economically advanced countries. It is significant to review the relevance of such methods and theories while they are being applied to under developed area like this. Walter Christaller's (1933) Central place theory, in so far as it aims at developing a primary net of central places on which the phenomenon of industrialization may be superimposed, is one of the basic theories applied to market place studies. The theory and its modification may be analysed here.

2.1 CENTRAL PLACE THEORY

The inherent assumption of central place theory is that there is an apparent order in spatial distribution of human settlements. By order is meant that the sizes and spacing of those settlements which provide goods and services to the population of their complementary areas are governed by a set of principles. Such settlements are called central places and hence the theory is known as central place theory. Fundamentally, the theory is concerned with explaining the regularities in the location of tertiary activities. It is, however, important to note that the theory is not concerned with urban growth arising due to industrial or other productive forces. It assumes that there exists an isotropic plane where population densities and the purchasing capacity of people are uniform.

2.2 THE MECHANISM OF THE THEORY

The theory is based on two premises. One is a set of economic constraints operating on the nature and fixation of market centres. Another is related to the structural regularities found in the optimum location of settlements which provide central functions. The economic constraints are based on what it may be called the threshhold and range of goods. There must be a minimum level of demand for a supplier to survive, secondly, the maximum distance that the consumers are willing to travel to come to a central place or the maximum distance over which goods and services can be sent and still be sold at a profit, which determines the size of the trade area of market place. Following this, centres dealing with good of daily needs tend to be more numerous and consequently more frequently distributed as they can survive on the more frequent visits of a few consumers. On the other hand, centres dealing with specialised goods are less numerous and sparsely distributed as they can survive on visits of a larger number of people with less frequency. Gradually, if optimum conditions prevail, markets of similar type become equally spaced.

Table No. 2.1

Characteristics of Size for Central Places and Areas of Trade in Agricultural Regions.

Type	Theoritical Centres	No. of Trade Areas	Types of Goods Offered No.	Typical Centres 000	Population Trade Areas
Landstat	1	1	2000	500	3500
Provinzestudt	2	3	1000	100	1000
Gaustadt	6	9	600	30	350
Bezirkstadt	18	27	350	10	100
Kreisstadt	54	81	180	4	35
Amtsort	162	243	90	2	11
Marktort	486	729	40	1	3.5

Source: Christaller, W. (Translated by C. Baskin), Central Places in Southern Germany, Prentice Hall, 1966.

Regarding the question of structural regularities, Christaller follows the development of hexagonal market areas. With this shape the precise locations of the largest centres in relation to the smaller ones may be precisely determined. The hexagone is the nearest geometrical equivalent of a circle.[1] If the locations of the single most dominant centres are known the locations of next larger centre will be exactly at the midpoint between three such centres, or the aprices of their hexagonal trade areas (*Fig. no. 2. 1-A, B. and C*). The hexagone of the next larger central places will be equal in size to those trade areas for the same type of lower order goods in the largest centres. Locations of successively smaller central places will be determined at the mid-point between three larger centres. Following this, every central place will be surrounded by six less important central places.

Thus the mechanism of growth processes and structural regularities lead to specific rules about the frequencies in occurrence of different sizes of centres and trade areas (Table No. 2.1). This consistent

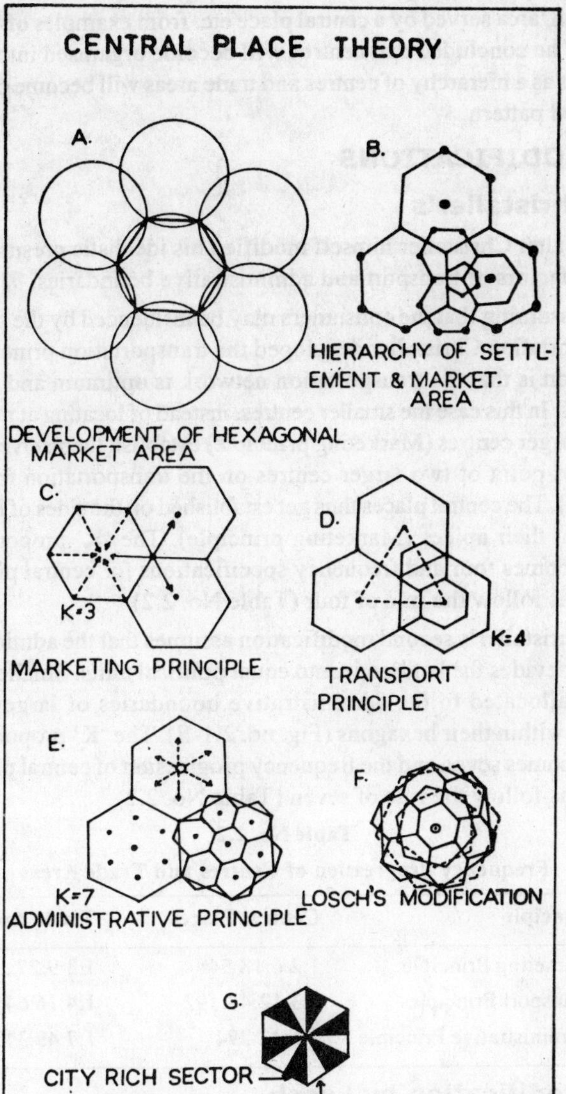
CENTRAL PLACE THEORY
A.
DEVELOPMENT OF HEXAGONAL MARKET AREA
B.
HIERARCHY OF SETTL-EMENT & MARKET-AREA
C.
K=3
MARKETING PRINCIPLE
D.
K=4
TRANSPORT PRINCIPLE
E.
K=7
ADMINISTRATIVE PRINCIPLE
F.
LOSCH'S MODIFICATION
G.
CITY RICH SECTOR
" POOR "
FIG-2·1

Fig. 2.1

progression by three, in case of trade area size relationship, is known as the 'K' proportionality factor. Christaller calculated the distance, population, area served by a central place etc. from examples of Southern Germany he concluded that centres will become organised into discrete size levels as a hierarchy of centres and trade areas will become organised in a nested pattern.

2.3 MODIFICATIONS

(i) Christaller's

Walter Christaller himself modified his idealistic presumption in terms of factors of transport and administrative boundaries.

Assuming that the consumers may be influenced by the provision of transportation Christaller developed the transportation principle. The assumption is that the transportation network is optimum and connects all centres. In this case the smaller centres, instead of locating at mid points of three larger centres (Marketing principle) establish themselves exactly at the mid-point of two larger centres on the transportation route (fig. no. 2.1-D). The central places thus get established on the sides of hexagons and not at their apices (Marketing principle). The 'K' proportionality factor becomes four and frequency specifications for central places and trade areas follow the rule of four (Table No. 2.2)

Christaller's second modification assumes that the administrative network devides the landscape into equal political units. Smaller centres become allocated to the administrative boundaries of larger centres enclosed within their hexagons (Fig. no. 2.1-E). The 'K' proportionality factor becomes seven and the frequency progression of central places and trade areas follow the rule of seven (Table No. 2.2)

Table No. 2.2

Frequency Progression of Centres and Trade Areas

	Principle	Central Places	Trade Areas
1.	Marketing Principle	1:2:6:18:54	1:3:9:27...
2.	Transport Principle	1:3:12:48:192	1:4:16:64:256...
3.	Administrative Principle	1:6:42:294	1:7:49:343...

(ii) Modification by Losch

Losch[2] re-examined central place theory from the point of view of multiplicity of goods and their varying trade areas. He demonstrated that different goods commanded different areas and these would than dictate the location actually occupied by centres. Thus alternatives trade areas become possible for the complex activities of settlements a single optimum pattern should be determined from the average of such alternative trade areas. Losch geometrically titled and swivelled the entire range of different trade areas about a base set of smallest centres till a maximum coincidence in location was achieved (Fig. no. 2.1-F). This resulted in city-rich and city-poor sector of the landscape (fig. no. 2.1-G). The stepped hierarchy of central places, as shown by Christaller, changes to a size continum. Lastly it is not necessary that the centres of similar type will provide similar type of goods.

Losch demonstrated that the following relationship holds where the hierarchic distribution of functions can be summarised by a Pareto curve with a slope of unity.

$$P_1 = \frac{S_1 r_1}{1 - s_1} C(i-1)$$

where r_1 = rural population required to support a first order urban function at the lowest level of the hierarchy, S_1 = proportionality constant relating the population of a central place (at level 1) to the total population it serves, C = nesting factor indicating the number of market areas at the (i - 1) at level included in a market area at the i-th level. Since C is raised to a power, city size increases exponentially in relation to the level of urban function.

For example if r = 1800, $S_1 = 0.1$ and C = 4, then the population of a city with first order function (P_1) is 200; then $P_2 = 800$, $P_3 = 3200$, $P_4 = 12{,}800$ and so on.

(iii) Modifications of Berry and Garrison

Berry and Garrison[3] observed that the central place theory also operated in areas where isotropic conditions do not prevail. A settlement hierarchy could be observed in areas of unequal population distribution density and unequal purchasing power, secondly, hierarchies are observed inside individual urban areas.[4] These observations have broadened the horizon of the central place theory and it becomes a theory of tertiary activity based on the concepts of range of a good and threshhold.

2.4 PERIODIC CENTRAL PLACES

Central place theory of Christaller was developed under the assumption that the central places are permanent and they provide goods and services on a regular basis. This holds goods for economically advanced areas with a high proportion of urban population. In predominantly agricultural areas of the developing nations, central functions are very often provided by periodic market centres which are held once, twice or thrice a week. These three types of central places stand in contrast to each other in so far as their space-time relationship is concerned. Periodic market centres form a market cycle i.e. time and market ring in space to make a hierarchical system.[5] They are coherently linked to central place system developed by permanent central places. Christaller did not include such areas in his basic premises. Therefore, conventional central place studies do not account for periodicity of central places and thus leave a gap in such studies.

Periodic central places idea was first discussed by Skinner[6] in his paper on marketing and social structure in rural China. Basing his ideas on Christaller and Losch both, he has emphasized the role of administrative and economic functions in the formation of hierarchic levels. He has found central place theory applicable in rural China where periodic central places exist. However, the only work that has seriously dealt with the problem of the extension of periodic central places into the study of permanent central places was that of Shrivastava.[7] This attempt has given a new dimension to central place theory.

The theory is rigid and deterministic in nature.[8] It describes a mainly static set of locational relationship. The process of centralization of mass around a nucleus is the main basis of the theory. The presumption is that retail functions which serve the surrounding population of a place keep on concentrating in and the concerned settlement develops to the status of a central place. However, in reality, agglomerative force may also play a role. Agglomeration as a process different then centralization means the association of productive activities in close proximity to the one another at a place. Such activities do not serve the population of the surrounding areas of the place at which the activities grow. Hence such a place does not develop into a central place. In other words agglomeration of secondary activities at a place may be useful for an area far away from it. Thus activities may or may not be centralised and it will be difficult to differentiate between the two. However, the organizational aspects of systematic structural regularities in settlements and shopping centres is a very useful concept of this theory. The theory provides an underlying strategy of settlements.

Marketing geography goes a bit further as it deals with interaction among settlements and consumers. Two more theoretical dimension in the context of marketing geography may, therefore, also be examined.

2.5 THEORY OF GENERAL INTERACTION

Theory of General Interaction deals with the controls which affect the interaction between central places. Its bases and postulates are not as strong as those of the central place theory. They are linked to the gravity concept analogous to Newton's law in physics. General interaction theory is based on Reilly's law of Retail Gravitation[9]. This law states that two cities attract trade from an intermediate town in the vicinity of the breaking point approximately in direct proportion to the population of the two cities and in inverse proportion to the square of the distances from these two cities to the intermediate town'.

$$\frac{T_a}{T_b} = \frac{P_a}{P_b} = \frac{d^2\ b}{d^2\ a}$$

where T_a T_b = the proportion of trade drawn to cities a and b. P_a P_b = the population sizes of cities a and b. d_a d_b = the distance from the intermediate town to cities a and b.

The applicability of the gravity model to urban shopping centres has been made more specific.[10]

The population size and distance relationship are known as attraction and deterrence factors respectively. The concept of 'distance-decay' accounts for a decrease in frequency of trips away from centres. Interaction is measured within a system of centres and not only between two centres.

Reilly's model leaves the problem of delimitation of trade area dimensions. The 'break point' model determines the exact position within an intermediate area where trade becomes split between two competing centres.[11] It may be examined as under:

$$D_b = \frac{d_{ab}}{1 + \sqrt{\dfrac{P_a}{P_b}}}$$

where P_a P_b = the sizes of centres a and b; D_b = the break point distance of trade to centre b; and d_{ab} = the distance between centres a and b (the centres a, b, c, d, e, ... n are of different sizes).

When applied to a system of centres this law yields a number of break points. By joining them trade areas may be delimited.

Human interaction is not as simple as the law intends to investigate. Overlapping of trade areas is a common feature of rural marketing which the law does not explain.[12] Huff's model gives greater scope to such considerations.[13] The market potential model and the Lakshmanan and Hansen model[14] and Stewart[15] have been developed to predict growth potential of centres and sales volumes. The discussion of these models is left out here for want of such empirical work in this project.

2.6 ASSESSMENT

It may thus be reviewed that central place theory is basic to the study of Marketing Geography. The viability of this theory has been increased following two conditions. One is the extension of the factor of periodicity of central places at par with permanent centres. The second is the development of general interaction theory in so far as it allows much greater viability in the directions of consumer movements. Gravity models represent aggregate behaviour of consumers. The question of qualitative controls such as the impact of non-economic factors like social and religious belief on consumer movements still remains unsolved.[16] These theories are applicable upto regional or subregional levels and may thus serve the need of the present study. However, they provide only a few guidelines for micro-studies.

2.7 THE NEED FOR VERIFICATION

Against the mise-en-scene of the theories developed in the western world comes the question of the relevancy of methods of explanation and of theory evolved in economically advanced countries to the developing ones. It has been observed that the basic assumptions of central place theory need modification when confronted with reality in parts other than those of the western world by Bromlay[17] and Bhole[18]. These modifications are necessitated due to the differing cultural and economic conditions in different areas. The need for theoretically examining the applicability of central place theory in the present oriental context is further realised by the incongruity of results arrived at in certain Indian Case Studies by R.L. Singh,[19] Kar,[20] Mayfield[21,22,23] Neale,[24] Mukherji[25], Berry,[26] Sen,[27] Wanmali,[28] Harriss,[29 & 30] K. Shrivastava.[31]

None of the above mentioned studies, however, have either clearly confirmed or denied Christaller's theory. One of the inconsistencies in results has been that the test applied were not rigrous enough to produce reliable results. As Also observed by Harris[32] in the case of growth centre and service centre ideology in India, such studies are based on untested assumption or assumptions that are verified by gathering supportive evidence. It has also been commented that the discrepancy between intention and actual results of developing country research arise because the researcher takes up problems which arise in alien countries and tries to solve them from empirical examples of developing countries.[33] Among other reasons have been a lack of interest of the researchers of developing nations in regional characteristics, which exhibit a great variety. Christaller himself predicated in 1933 that there will be deviations in his scheme of central places due to factors like the distribution and the density of population industrial location, transportation conditions and the regulators of economic system. Obviously a relevant account of the regional characteristics should be a pre-requisite for any central place study. What is needed in a resume of the regional variants oriented to the specific needs of the study which could serve as a mise-en-scene to illustrate the deviations from the theoretical norms. For example, it may be observed that in developed economies as well planned network of central places is normally found. These places develop mostly on account of the natural development of economic activities. Besides, a broad economic cohesiveness of the society in terms of demand for goods is noted in developed societies. This brings a regional and even sub-regional uniformity in terms of demand for goods and services due to economic rationality dominating the movement. Among the less developed and developing economics, on the other hand, one deals with a predominantly rural organization which is dominated by indigenous farmers and is less commercially based. Generally, in such areas economic rationality is often overpowered by traditional conservatism, religious heterogeneity and its staunncheners, object poverty and great disparity in the living standards of the population. The influence of these complex socio-cultural phenomena is reflected in the demands being made on central places. The regional and sub-regional heterogeneity, produced in this way influences the initiation, development and spatial distribution of central places.

While emphasizing the need of an appropriate evaluation of the regional variants, caution should also be taken with respect to the available data and their authenticity. This is highly important, particularly in the field of pointer research, as the conclusions based on unauthentic and unspecified data can produce misleading results. Coming back to the debate of developed and developing economies, it may be said that most central places of a developed economy normally perform daily commercial functions. The units like shops, warehouses etc. performing these activities are housed in permanent structures. Such units and functions are officially enumerated and data are readily available. Data regarding the other goods and services are also available up to the lowest functional level. Agencies providing information are much more conscious of the need, and responsibility of a researcher. In such a situational, the researcher's task is to evaluate the data in the light of his requirements and make the reader conscious of their weakness, if any.

In the less developed and developing economies the published sources of realiable data regarding central place activities are, however, limited. Of these few sources, census records are more easily available. The census records mainly cover information about administration and amenities like education, transport, communication, public health, public security. This information is available down to village level. In such record a central place researcher may get rather incomplete information about commercial activities, and that too related to higher order central places only. At lower levels, say up to market village level, the existence of commercial activities (market) may only be indicated with a very superficial information about the main items of business and average attendance of buyers and sellers at the market places. Motivated by the demands of central place research, one has to do one's own data collection upto the lowest required level of the central places and to check it against the record of local authorities, if available. If the study area is large, a sampling procedure is also necessary. Thus the census information is to be duly supplemented by field-work to remove the weaknesses of the data. But the question of reliability and comparability of data over larger areas still remains. Consequently, one has to take much trouble in outlining these limitations.

While this nature of data is easily understood, much more caution is needed in identifying and defining variables in order to make explicit their nature and functions, Due to regional heterogeneity in the social, economic and religious characteristics of the population identification of variables becomes important before their enumeration starts. The list of variables used in one region may have to be modified in other regions. For example, in 1963 Mayfield has identified 129 variables in the case of the Indian Punjab. He seems to have taken all precautions and great pains in finalising the list of 'entries' but there is no mention of 'entries' like the mosque, the church, arms and ammunition, manihari (rurul cosmetic shop), bhuja (made of baked rice) etc. Such items are found in the Magadh Division markets.

This cautionary approach needs strengthening in areas where indigenous conditions are typical of a particular country or region. For example, periodicity of markets is a typical feature of developing economies. The periodic market activity may be of an 'inclusive' or 'exclusive' nature. By inclusive we mean those central places where, in addition to a daily market, a periodic weekly or bi-weekly surge of people, goods and services is experienced, 'Exclusive' means sites where only periodic markets are held and which are otherwise deserted. Thus, in some areas temporary selling points are also set up to complement the permanent ones. The periodic surge may be noted in small towns and big cities both. Periodicity, however, is not only confined to the developing nations. In developed economies as well, periodic market activity exists, though its spatial frequency may be limited. This element of periodicity adds new dimensions to central place activities. A fair consideration of this factor is inescapable, and methodology for its inclusion in central place research needs to be developed on lines suggested recently by Dr. Shrivastava.[34]

It is only through evolving a comparable framework of investigation, on similar lines as suggested above, that we can example the question of the relevancy of methods of explanation and of theory question of the relevancy of methods of explanation and of theory evolved in economically advanced countries and applied in developing or less developed countries.

Most of the service centres in the present study area owe their growth to the village origins, peripheral growth is exhibited by many, but lateral growth is the most vigorous. The lateral growth exhibits the multi-nuclear pattern of structure.

Gaya is the only central place which form a well defined hexagone of second order. It is obvious that the observed pattern does not fit in with the theoretical pattern because of administrative, transport and economic limitations as also the influence of centres lying outside the study area.

As is to be expected the towns generally occupy a higher place in the hierarchy of central places than the villages. All central places in second and third groups are towns or cities. In the fourth fifth and sixth groups some are urban and rest are rural settlements and a few are rurban centres.

A lower number of smaller centres indicates that there has been a lack of development of central functions in the rural areas of the Magadh Division. Due to economic backwardness, overdependence on subsistence agriculture and lack of transport facilities, many centres with a potential location as central places have refused to grow Christaller's theory was proposed as a rational scheme of general economic theory or the most favourable state.[35] It was not considered applicable to a backward area like the Magadh Division of Bihar by Christaller himself.

If we consider the pattern of network than the absolute centrality values calculated, it would appear that the hierarchy of central places is well established and closely corresponds with the theoretical model. In actual location of the central places indicate a close correspondence with each other, and considering the distortion affected by transport routes mountains and rivers, no closer correspondence can be expected.

In the study area which is dominated by agricultural plains, the development of central places has been dependent upon minor points of focus that initially were not associated with retail trade. Cross-roads, flour mills, post-offices, railway stations and police stations were some of these. They provided a meeting place for the farmers. Enterprising businessman took advantage of these facilities to open retail shops at such centres. This, in turn, led to the establishment of grain collecting centres, electric lines, telephones and other similar facilities, Combination of these elements led to greater centrality for some of the places, while competition between the growing centress created the pattern of a central place hierachy.

The smallest central place in the study area is a village with basic utility services such as an allopathic doctor, middle school, post-office and a metalled road connection. Villages of this category are closely spaced and may or may not have a retail marketing centre. They do, however, have a weekly or bi-weekly market known as a 'hat'.

Rural central places of a higher order generally provide services like a high school, telegraph office, dispensary, retail market, block development office and a bus stop or a railway station. Such centres are located on the main transport routes between towns and are, therefore, inter-spread between towns and rurban centres.

Further development of these facilities and addition of a telephone exchange, bank, cinema, wholesale market, etc. led to the evolution of a rurban centre. We will discuss the characteristics of rurban centres in the Magadh Division which include both smaller towns and larger villages. Villages which have grown into rurban centres are potential towns. A rise in their population coupled with functional segregation in land uses and increase in employment in tertiary services would make them eligible for classification as towns.

In the Magadh Division the evolution and spacing of rural central places largely depends upon economic prosperity and transport facilities.

2.8 HIERARCHY OF RURAL MARKETS AND RURBAN CENTRES

The hierarchy of market centres consists of several smaller places, overlaid by successively smaller numbers of larger places. The higher an urban area stands in this pyramidal structure, the more numerous and diversified are its business establishments and the more complex its relationship with other places in the system. The principle trade centres in the Magadh Division are normally the headquarter towns of four districts. These are served by a subsidiary trade centres represented by the subdivisional headquarter towns or other towns of similar size or block headquarter places, down to rurban centres and market villages.

To measure the hierarchy of market centres, the number of central function at a centre seems to be the most suitable criterian.

The objective of this thesis is to study rural markets and rurban centres of the Magadh Division. A detailed study of rurban centres of this area has been done in a separate chapter (no. 5) on rurban centres and hierarchy of rurban centres have been determined on the basis of the functions of central places.

Small villages or rural market centres are also central place but are of lowest order. These centres with basic public utility services such as an allopathic doctor, middle school, post office and a metalled or unmettaled road connection. Villages of this category are closely spaced and may or may not have a retail marketing centre. They do, however, have a weekly, bi-weekly, Tri-weekly or daily market known as 'hat'. It is apparent that the evolution and spacing of rural central places largely depends upon economic prosperity and transport facilities. Sale of durable goods, non-vegetarian food, ubiquitous goods, vegetable and fruits, agricultural inputs, food stuff, animals and special goods and provision of certain services are the main function which almost all the rural markets of the Magadh Divison provide to the people of the division. In most of the rural markets the number of shops is less than 100 and hence their identification and classification for determining hierarchy of rural markets is tedious and without much justification, importance and use.

REFERENCES

1. Hagget, P. et al., (1979) : Locational Models, Arnold Heinemann.
2. Losch, A. (1954) : The Economics of Location, Translated by W.H. Woglom and W.F. Stopler, Yale University Press.
3. Berry, B.J.L. and Garrison, W.F. (1958) : Recent Development of Central Place Theory, Papers and Proceedings of the Regional Science Association, 4, pp. 107-20.

4. Jones, Ronald (1967) : Central Place Theory and the Hierarchy and Location of Shopping Centres in a city, Edinburcgh Institute of British Geographers Study Group in Urban Geography, Durban Conference.
5. Haggett, P. et al., (1979) : Opt. cit.
6. Skinner, G.W. (1964-65) : Marketing and Social Structure in rural China : Journal of Asian Studies, 24, pp. 3-43; 195-228; 363-399.
7. Shrivastava, V.K. (1976) : Market Periodicity and Centrality: A Methodological Approach, Mainzer Geographiches Studien, 10, pp. 33-38.
8. Davies, R.L. (1976) : Marketing Geography with Special Reference to Retailing, Methuen and Co., London.
9. Reilly, W.J. (1931) : The Law of Retail Gravitation, Knicker Bocker Press.
10. Cordey-Hayes, M. (1968) : Retail Location Models, Centre for Environmental Studies, working paper 16.
11. Converse, P.D. (1949) : New Laws of Retail Gravitation, Journal of Marketing, 14, pp. 379-84.
12. Shrivastava, V.K. and Udhaw Ram (1982) : Nature and Demarcation of Market Area Regions of the Lower Ganga-Ghagra Doab, Uttar Bharat Bhoogol Patrika, 18, pp. 97-107.
13. Huff, D.L. (1963) : A Probability Analysis of Shopping Centre Trade Areas, Land Economics, pp. 5381-89.
14. Lakshmanan, T.R. and Hansen, W.G. (1956) : A Retail Marketing Potential Model, Journal of American Institute of Planners, 31, pp. 134-43.
15. Stewart, J.Q. and Warntz, W. (1958) : Physics of Population Distribution, Journal of Regional Science, 1, pp. 99-123.
16. Davies, R.L. (1970) : Variable Relationship in Central Place and Research Potential Model, Regional Studies, 4, pp. 49-61.
17. Bromley, R.G. (1971) : Markets in Developing countries : A Review, Geography, 56, pp. 124-32.
18. Bhole, H.G. (1983) : Role and Potentiality of Traditional Market Systems in the Third World Urbanization, International Asian Forum, 14, pp. 345-362.
19. Singh, R.L. (1955) : Evolution of Settlements in the Middle Ganaga Valley, National Geographical Journal of India, 1, pp. 69-114.
20. Kar, N.R. (1960) : Urban Hierarchy and Central Functions Around Calcutta, Lund Studies in Geography B. 1960, pp. 146-53.
21. Mayfield, R.C. (1960) : Conformations of Service and Retail Activities: An Example in Lower Orders of an Urban Hierarchy in a Lesser Developed Area, Lund Studies in Geogrpahy, Series B, pp. 77-86.
22. Mayfield, R.C. (1962) : A Central Place Hierarchy in Northern India, in Garrison, W.L. (ed.), Quantitative Geography, New York, Atherton Press, pp. 120-66.

23. Mayfield, R.C. (1963) : The Range of a Central Good in the Indian Punnjab, Annuals of the Association of American Geographers, 53, pp. 38-49.

24. Neale, W.C. et al., (1965) : Kurali Market : A Report on the Economic Geography of Marketing in Northern Punjab, Economic Development and Cultural Change, XIII, pp. 129-68.

25. Mukherji, S.P. (1968) : Commercial Activity and Market Hierarchy in a part of Eastern Himalaya, Darjeeling, The National Geographical Journal of India, XIV. pp. 189-99.

26. Berry, B.J.L. (1969) : Policy Implications of an urban Location Model for the Kanpur Region in Desai, P.B. (ed.), Regional Perspective on Industrial and Urban Growth, Bombay, pp. 205-19.

27. Sen, L.K. and Wanmali, S. (1971) : Planning Rural Growth Centres for Integrated Area Development: A Study in Miryalguda Taluka, Hyderabad.

28. Wanmali, S. (1972) : Ranking of Settlemets : A Suggestion, Journal of Behavioural Sciences and Community Development, 5, pp. 97-111.

29. Harriss, Barbara (1974) : The Role of Punjab Wheat Markets as Growth Centres, Geographical Journal 140, pp. 52-71.

30. Harriss, Barbara (1976) : The Indian Ideology of Growth Centres, Area, Institute of British Geographers, 4, pp. 263-69.

31. Shrivastava, V.K. (1980) : Central Place Theory in an Indian Context, Indian Journal of Regional Science, XII, pp. 195-206.

32. Harriss, Barbara (1976) : Opt. cit.

33. Bronger, Dirk (1977) : The Dilemma of Developing Country Research, Inter-economics, Nos. 9/10, pp. 245-50.

34. Shrivastava, V.K. (1976) : Opt. cit.

35. Davies, W.K.D (1967) : Centrality and the Central Place Quoted in Hierachy, Urban Studies, Vol. 4, p. 77.

3

Spatio Temporal Characteristics of Rural Market Centres

3.1 INTRODUCTION

The study of rural markets presumes that the periodic markets have played an important role in the development of central places. The central places, however, are not an end product of the process of urbanization. The complexity of human activity increases from periodic markets to central places and the mutual interaction between the two is interminable. There exists a fundamental unity among the social, political economic and spatial aspects of the development of human civilization and market centres do represent one such stage of human civilization and market centres do represent one such stage of development. Market centres are viewed not only as places where economic functions are performed but as places of social interaction as well. Markets of urban centres do not grow for economic purposes alone. The political necessity for town-making arose earlier than the economic need.[1] The political or religious edifices of the ruling elite dominate the urban landscape in developing countries.[2] Market originates around centres of political power as secondary outgrowth, dependent upon the favour, if not the outright subsidy of the ruling elite. The formation of markets was thus a reflex of state control. Every ruler or Zamindar considered it his duty to create a market for his people and to develop the town or city. Thus the role of extra-economic factors in the process of urbanization and in the initiation and development of market centres has been more important in the oriental context. Such extra-economic factors are not unique in Bihar only but in Uttar Pradesh and in Maharashtra also where evidences of the role of historical and religious factors have been found.[3] This is in contrast to the urbanization of the Euro-American nations. Therefore, but for the universal aspects of human beings, the models of evolution of central places developed in the western world may not wholly fit in the present study.

It has already been emphasised that the market centres perform socio-cultural functions. Besides performing exchange activity, markets act as community centres for people of different cultures and religious sects[4] and are also related to local administration. In developing and backward areas, like the one under study, daily or permanent markets do not thrive well. Such areas are often dominated by periodic or temporary markets holding monthly, tri-weekly, bi-weekly or weekly meetings. The needs of a backward society are small and, therefore, are met by periodic markets.[5] Such markets then also become central points for socio-cultural activities because human congregation on fixed days is guaranteed at such centres. The peasants wait for market days when they are able to dispose of their surplus and can buy what they need. They also exchange information of family welfare and also about functions like marriage, mundan, janeu with relativies and are able to enjoy the get-together. Some visit markets for entertainment but they do buy some thing simply because they have visited the market. The custromers thus augment the utility of their time and money spend on market trips. This may partly account for the continuity of periodic markets almost all over the world.

The evolution and developmental growth of market centres has a bearing on the spatio-temporal characteristics of such centres in any area. However, the spatio-temporal characteristics evolve simultaneously with the growth of market centres provided inter-market exchange takes place. Only when the market areas are parcelled out inside territorial units that the spatio-temporal traits get distorted and anomalous evidence are met with. For example, in the days of erstwhile rulers and Zamindars, market centres were initiated and patronized by the rulers. Market territory used to be the territory belonging to the ruler/Zamindar. The markets were established to maintain or regain one's prestige or in competition with the neighbouring ruler. The place and the day of the market were selected not by economic considerations but by considerations of competititon.

3.2 THEORETICAL BACKGROUND

The evolution and development of market centres has been investigated in detail. Christaller proposed a hexagonal network of central places according to his ordering principle.[6] The idea has been applied with a predominantly agricultural area in mind such as the one under study. The implications of this theory are then more applicable to the Magadh Division. But it is to be noted that this theory is basically related to the development of permanent central places where as the Magadh Division is predominated by periodic markets.

J.H. Stine[7] has developed the concepts of threshhold and range of a good in the development of market centres. "There is a minimum amount necessary for any firm to stay in business. It is known as threshhold".

Maximum range is that area from which customers come to buy a certain good. This type of relationship do exists under normal conditions (*Fig. No. 3.1-A*). Wherever movement is restricted for want of means of transport and communication the minimum and maximum ranges become inverted (Fig. No. 3.1-B). It is because the lack of the means of transport restricts movement of a larger segment of the population of an area. Similarly, the lack of knowledge of the existence and functioning of market centres also makes people less mobile. Only few people are able to move long distances. The trader starts moving from one market to the other to obtain a threshhold value. Skinner[8] in his work on rural China, has also described such a situation. Berry[9] has also emphasised the role of periodic markets in local trading system. Similarly Hodder[10] and Saxeana[11] have emphasised the role of transportation in the development of markets. The sequential model developed by Eghimy[12] traces the development of new markets near older ones. Bromley[13] brings out the role of factors of competition and integration in the process of market development. Similarly, Tinkler[14] proposed that a four-day market cycle could ensure to avoid conflicts between adjacent markets. This four-day periodic system could be superimposed on the basic Christaller K = 4 lattice. This system can accommodate both a closed and an open system (Fig. No. 3.1-II). It may further be modified to a six-day cycle by including new markets inside the triangles in the lattice structure (Fig. No. 3.1-D). The primary square pattern of market centres (Fig. No. 3.1-IV), as identified by Shrivastava[15] may or not become a hexagonal pattern in the process of evolution. The consideration of the factor of periodicity has broadened the avenues of central place-theory.[16]

Further to these dimensions is evidence of the role of factors like local regional feelings, personal prestige and religious outlook in the development of market centres.[17] These developments in the theoretical field regarding the origin and evolution of market centres explain the mechanism which operates in the real world situation. The origin and development of markets in the Magadh Division may now be discussed.

The origin and development of markets of the Magadh Division may be explained according to factors like competition, integration, religion, social prestige and local history.

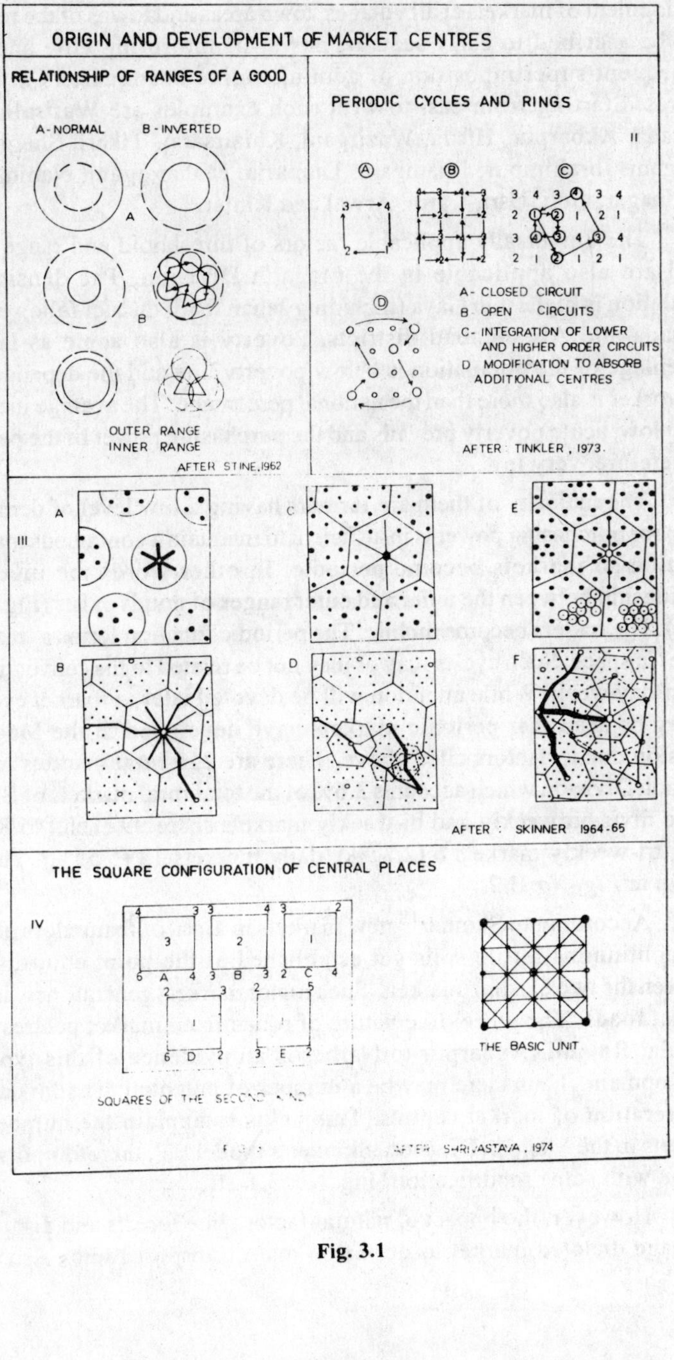
ORIGIN AND DEVELOPMENT OF MARKET CENTRES
RELATIONSHIP OF RANGES OF A GOOD
A-NORMAL
B-INVERTED
A
B
OUTER RANGE
INNER RANGE
AFTER STINE, 1962
PERIODIC CYCLES AND RINGS
II
A- CLOSED CIRCUIT
B- OPEN CIRCUITS
C- INTEGRATION OF LOWER AND HIGHER ORDER CIRCUITS
D- MODIFICATION TO ABSORB ADDITIONAL CENTRES
AFTER : TINKLER, 1973.
III
AFTER : SKINNER 1964-65
THE SQUARE CONFIGURATION OF CENTRAL PLACES
IV
THE BASIC UNIT
AFTER SHRIVASTAVA, 1974

Fig. 3.1

Regarding the local historical factors first, The initiation and development of markets at all villages, town areas and towns of the region may be ascribed to early seats of power of the ruling elite and the consequent superimposition of administrative headquarters at such centres. Starting from east to west such examples are Warisaliganj, Nawada, Akbarpur, Hisua, Wazirganj, Khizirsarai, Tikari, Sherghati, Rafiganj, Ibrahimpur, Imamganj, Dumaria, Maharajganj, Nabinagar, Daudnagar, Goh, Usri, Karpi, Arwal and Kinjar.

The universally applicable factors of threshhold and range of a good are also applicable in the Magadh Division. The density of population is highest in Gaya (including Jehanabad) district followed by Nawada and Aurangabad districts. Poverty is also acute as larger percentage of the population is below poverty line and the dependency per worker is also more than the national percentage. The average income being low, acute poverty prevails and the purchasing power of the people is, therefore, very low.

The majority of them are farmers having a low level of demand. The poor purchasing power is insufficient to maintain a continuous market function so markets become periodic. In other words the inverted relationship between the inner and outer ranges of goods exists (Fig. No. 3.1-I). The traders become mobile. The periodic function forms a 'market cycle' in space. Such cycles may or may not be related to the conventional seven-day week. While attention will be devoted later to market cycles, it may be seen that periodic markets have developed in the Magadh Division due to factors cited above. There are 216 rural markets in the Magadh Division which accounts 3.6% of the total rural markets of Biahr. In the division weekly and bi-weekly markets share 99 each (45.83%) each, tri-weekly markets 6 (2.77%), daily markets 12 (5.55%). This is shown in *Fig. No. 3.2.*

According to Skinner[18] new markets in areas of featureless plains and continuous fertile soils get established at the point equi-distant between the two existing markets. Such minor markets generate new inter-market roads. The wheel like nature of roads from market centres like Sirdala, Rajauli, Akbarpur to Narhat is an evidence of this type of development. Thus there may be a number of potential cites favouring proliferation of market centres. This helps to explain the number of markets in the Magadh Division. Skinner's model 'B', therefore, fits this region with some modification (Fig. No. 3.1-III).

However, the impact of natural factors like forests and disturbed drainage dictated market locations on main transport routes also. For

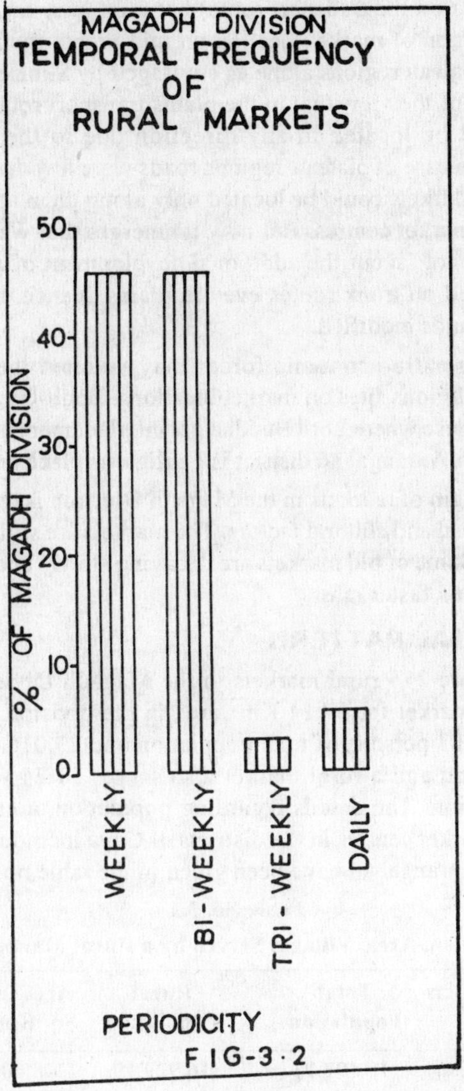
MAGADH DIVISION
TEMPORAL FREQUENCY
OF
RURAL MARKETS
% OF MAGADH DIVISION
50
40
30
20
10
0
WEEKLY
BI-WEEKLY
TRI-WEEKLY
DAILY
PERIODICITY
FIG-3·2

Fig. 3.2

example there is a resemblance between the observed and expected distances (the expected distance being the mid-point of two existing market centres on the transport route) between inter-market locations. The phenomenon of market location on mid-points trunk routes is not confined to plateau regions alone as envisaged by Skinner in his model A. Skinner is of the view that in the plains transport routes and market centres could be located in any direction due to the suitability of topography. In case of plateau-regions roads were few due to unsuitable topography. Markets could be located only along them at mid-points of two existing market centres. But now it emerges that wherever natural conditions do not favour the additional development of roads, markets become located on trunk routes even in plains. Hence, now Skinner's model thus stands modified.

Among extra-economic forces may be cited the influence of ancient and religious sites on market locations. Bodh-Gaya, the famous international place where Lord Buddha got inlightenment have developed market. Deo in Aurangabad district is a religious place and a market.

The origin of markets in the Magadh Division is related to a host of socio-political and cultural factors. The markets are still in the process of evolution. Some of old markets are decaying slowly and new ones are springing up at a faster rate.

3.3 SPATIAL PATTERN

There are 216 rural markets in the Magadh Division of Bihar. There is one market for 57.14 Km^2 area in the division. Each market serves 25,326.03 persons of total population and 23,016.07 persons of rural population and a rural market also serves 31.74 villages in the Magadh Division. The details regarding population, area and villages served by a market centres in the districts of Gaya including Jehanabad, Nawada and Aurangabad have been given in the table no. 3.1.

Table No. 3.1

Population, Area, Villages Served by a Rural Market 1981

Name of Districts & Division	Total Population	Rural Population	Area in Sq. Km.	No. of Villages
Aurangabad Dist.	18,192.23	16,929.19	48.60	27.70
Gaya District including Jehanabad	26,118.12	23,284.75	54.54	32.27
Nawada District	39,256.32	36,647.00	89.07	39.25
Magadh Division	25,326.03	23,.16.07	57.14	31.75

The above noted table (No. 3.1) clearly indicates that the maximum total and rural population and area are being served by a rural market in Nawada district and minimum in Aurangabad district where Gaya including Jehanabad district stands in middle (*Fig. No. 3.3*)

3.4 TEMPORAL ASPECTS

Rural markets are generally of two types. Some of them perform central functions on each day of the week; such rural markets are called daily or permanent markets. On the other hand, some rural markets are held on one or more fixed days of the week. They may provide central goods and services once, twice or three times a week. These types are called periodic markets. Any study of the marketing system of a rural area must make a close enquiry into the temporal aspects of the market centres in question.

3.5 PERIODICITY

The Magadh Division is characterised by a predominance of periodic rural markets. Nearly 95% of its total markets are held on some fixed days of the week (Table No. 3.4). Rural markets which transact business on each day of the week are confined to the districts of Jehanabad (7 daily markets) and Nawada (5 daily markets). These markets are only 12 in number. Among periodic markets weekly and bi-weekly markets constitute equal no. of 99 each (45%.83% each) with a percentage of 91.66% of the total rural markets of the Magadh Division. Markets held three times a week are negligible in number i.e. only 6 (2.77%). Daily markets accounts for 5.55% of the total market of the division. The intra-district analysis shows that the Gaya district has the maximum no. of weekly market i.e. 54 which is 54.54% of the total markets of this category followed by Nawada district 21 number (21.21%), Aurangabad district 17 number (17.17%) and Jehanabad 7 number (7.07%).

So far the no. of bi-weekly markets is concerned Aurangabad stands on the top having 50 bi-weekly markets which accounts 50.50% of the total markets of this class in the Magadh Division which is followed by Jehanabad district 24 number (24.24%), Gaya dist. 23 number (23.23%) and Nawada 2 number (2.03%). Jehanabad district tops in tri-weekly markets which is 5 in number and which accounts 83.34% of the total markets of this type in the Magadh Division followed by Aurangadad district one market (16.66%).

There are 7 daily markets in Jehanabad district which accounts 58.44% of the total market of this class in the Magadh Division followed by Nawada district which has 5 daily markets (41.66%). Aurangabad,

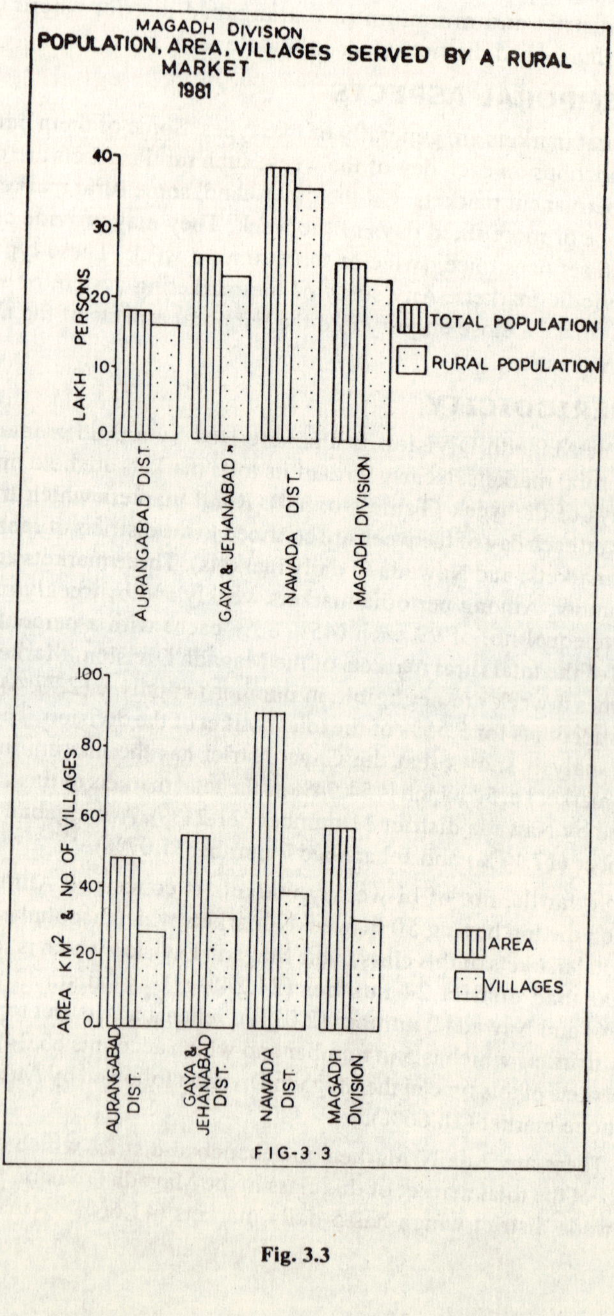
MAGADH DIVISION
POPULATION, AREA, VILLAGES SERVED BY A RURAL MARKET
1981
LAKH PERSONS
40
30
20
10
0
AURANGABAD DIST.
GAYA & JEHANABAD
NAWADA DIST.
MAGADH DIVISION
TOTAL POPULATION
RURAL POPULATION
AREA KM² & NO. OF VILLAGES
100
80
60
40
20
0
AURANGABAD DIST.
GAYA & JEHANABAD DIST.
NAWADA DIST.
MAGADH DIVISION
AREA
VILLAGES
FIG-3·3

Fig. 3.3

Jehanabad and Gaya district have much fertile land and better irrigation and agricultural facilities than Nawada district and hence prosperity is less in this district resulting in less purchasing capacity of the people which restricted the marketing activities other than three districts of the Magadh Division. Always occurrence of severe droughts is one of the most important reason for the backwardness of the district.

The table no. 3.2 given below show the percentage of different types of periodic markets in the Magadh Division (*Fig. No. 3.4*).

Table No. 3.2

Percentage of Different Types of Periodic Markets in the Districts of Magadh Division.

Sl. No.	District	% of Daily Markets	% of Weekly Markets	% of Bi-weekly Markets	% of Tri-weekly Markets
1.	Aurangabad	Nil	25.00	73.53	1.47
2.	Jehanabad	16.28	16.28	55.81	11.63
3.	Gaya	Nil	70.13	29.87	Nil
4.	Nawada	17.86	75.00	7.14	Nil

The above table no. 3.2 indicates that only Jehanabad district has the all types of markets in which maximum 55.81% is of Bi-weekly markets and minimum 11.63% is of Tri weekly markets and has 16.28% each of daily and weekly markets. Auranagabad district has the maximum 73.53% is of bi-weekly markets, 25% of weekly markets and 1.47% of tri-weekly markets and has no daily market. Gaya district has its 70.13% is of weekly markets and 29.87% of bi-weekly markets and has no daily or tri-weekly markets. Nawada district has the maximum 75% of weekly markets followed by 17.86% of daily markets and 7.14% of bi-weekly markets and has no tri-weekly market in the district.

The below table (No. 3.3) indicates the percentage of rural markets in different districts to the total no. of rural markets of the Magadh division. Gaya district has the lowest types (only two) of rural markets but has highest percentage (35.64%) of the total markets of the division of which it has 25% of weekly markets and 10.64% of bi-weekly markets followed by Aurangabad district stood second which has 31.48% of total markets divided in weekly 7.8%, bi-weekly 23.15% and tri-weekly 0.46%. Jehanabad district has third position with 19.90% of total markets. It has all types of markets i.e. daily and weekly 3.24% each, bi-weekly - 11.11% and tri-weekly -2.31%. Nawada district has a total of 12.96%

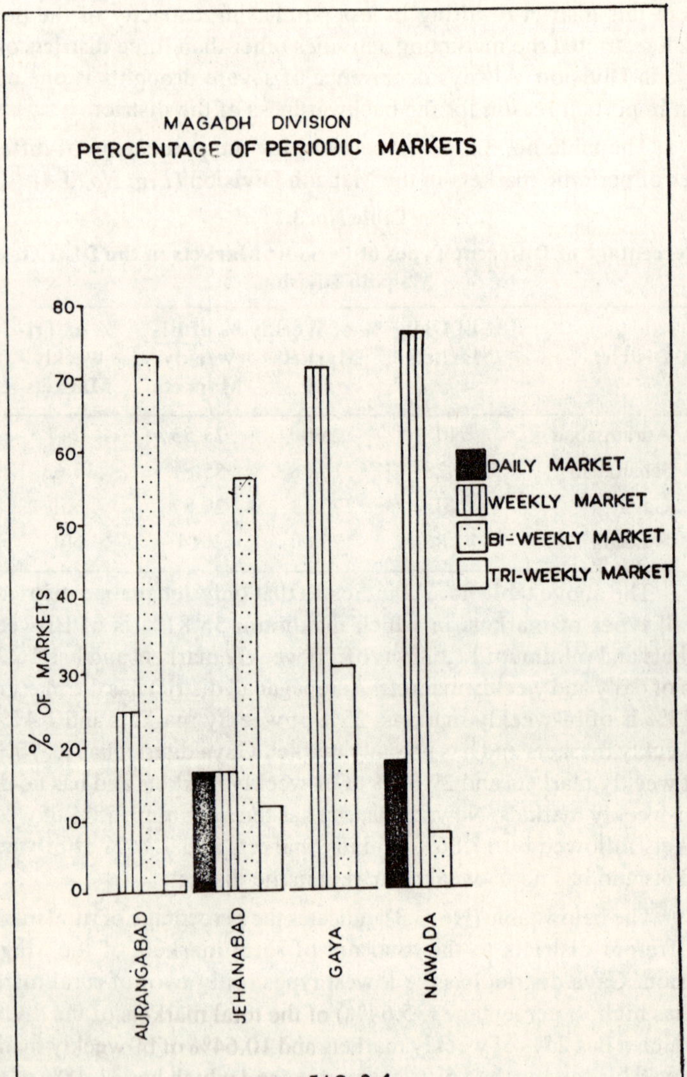
MAGADH DIVISION
PERCENTAGE OF PERIODIC MARKETS
% OF MARKETS
80
70
60
50
40
30
20
10
0
DAILY MARKET
WEEKLY MARKET
BI-WEEKLY MARKET
TRI-WEEKLY MARKET
AURANGABAD
JEHANABAD
GAYA
NAWADA
FIG-3·4

Fig. 3.4

which is lowest in the division and distributed in 2.31% daily markets, 9.72% of weekly markets and 0.93% of bi-weekly markets, (*Fig. No. 3.5*). Thus periodicity is a common feature all over the Magadh Division but intra-district variations do exist. It has been also observed earlier that periodic markets play an important role in the process of urbanization. As market frequency increases the potential for continuous urban functions is propagated.

Table No. 3.3

Percentage of Rural Markets in Different Districts to the Total no. of Rural Markets of the Magadh Division.

Sl. No.	Name of the District	Periodicity				% of the total Rural Markets of the Magadh Division
		Daily	Weekly	Bi-weekly	Tri-weekly	
1.	Aurangabad	X	7.87	23.15	0.46	31.48
2.	Jehanabad	3.24	3.24	11.11	2.31	19.90
3.	Gaya	X	25.00	10.64	X	35.64
4.	Nawada	2.31	9.72	0.93	X	12.96

3.6 PERIODICITY BY DAYS

A deeper analysis of temporal aspects of market centres may be attempted by accounting for the days of a week on which periodic markets are held. In the Magadh Division markets are held on all days of a week. It is in contrast to Bromley's observation in Highland Ecuador where there are major and secondary market day at bi-weekly markets.[19 & 20] Except 69 (18.04%) Sundays, all days of the week hold markets almost an equal number (50 to 58) of markets on each day of the week (Table No. 3.4) in the whole Magadh Division. So far the market frequency by days of the Magadh Division is concerned, Sunday has the maximum number of 69 (17.29%) followed by Thursday 58 (14.53%), Tuesday and Wednesday 56 each (14.03%) each, Monday and Saturday 55 each (13.78% each) and Friday has the lowest number of 50 (12.53%). In Aurangabad district Sunday is the most important with 28 (23.33%), Days of Monday to Thursday have almost the equal importance where Friday and Saturday have a little less importance. This district has the second position in total markets 68 (31.48%) and a maximum total 120 (30.07%) market days in the division after Gaya and Jehanabad respectively (*Fig. No. 3.6*)

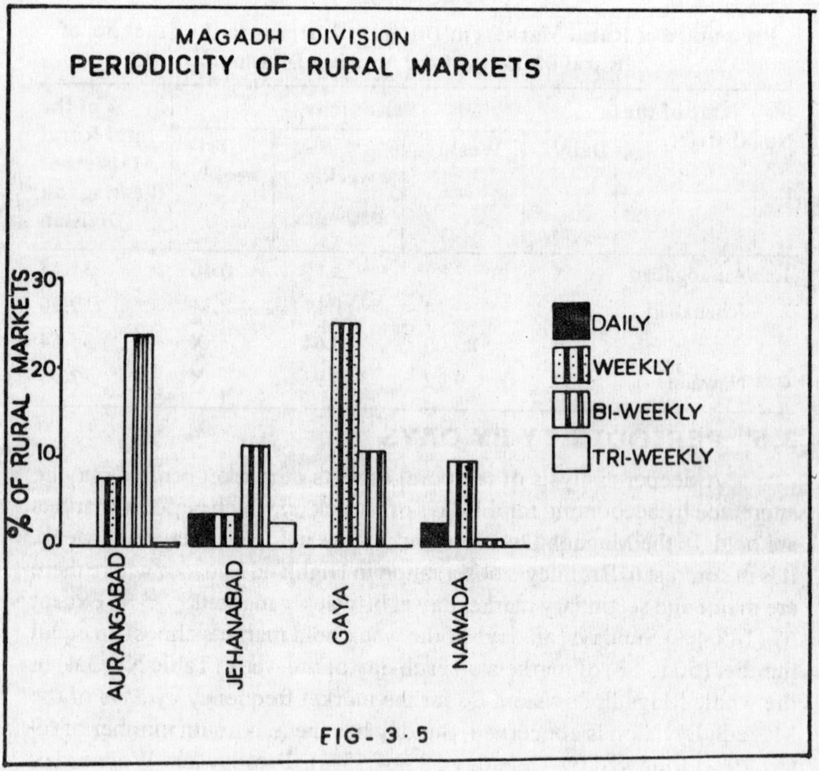
MAGADH DIVISION
PERIODICITY OF RURAL MARKETS
% OF RURAL MARKETS
30
20
10
0
DAILY
WEEKLY
BI-WEEKLY
TRI-WEEKLY
AURANGABAD
JEHANABAD
GAYA
NAWADA
FIG - 3 · 5

Fig. 3.5

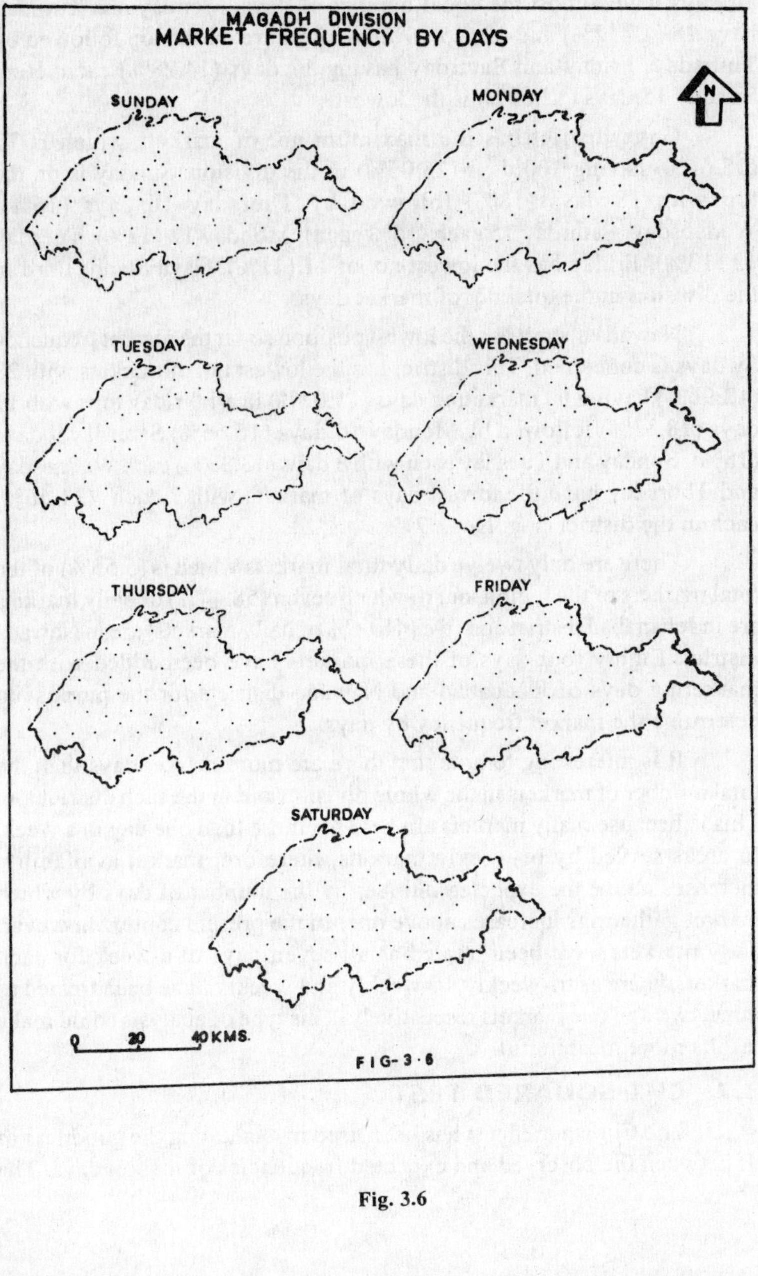
MAGADH DIVISION
MARKET FREQUENCY BY DAYS
N
SUNDAY
MONDAY
TUESDAY
WEDNESDAY
THURSDAY
FRIDAY
SATURDAY
0 20 40 KMS.
FIG-3·6

Fig. 3.6

Jehanabad district has also a 119 days (29.83%) of markets with 43 markets (19.90%) in the division standing third position in respect to no. of markets and second position in total market days. In this district all days have almost the equal number of days. Monday and Tuesday have 18 (15.12%) and 19 (15.96%) markets are on the top followed by Thursday, Friday and Saturday having 17 days (14.28%) each. Here Sunday 15 days (12.60%) is the lowest.

Gaya district has the maximum no. of markets which is 77 (35.64%) having 100 days (25.06%) in the division. Sunday is on the top with 18 days (18%) followed by Thursday 16 days (16%), Wednesday, Saturday 15 each (15% each), Monday 12 (12%), Tuesday 13 (13%), Friday has the lowest no. of 11 (11%). Gaya Stands third in the division in the total no. of market days.

Nawada district has the lowest position so far the market frequency by days is concerned. This district has the lowest no. of markets with 28 (12.96%) having 60 marketing days (15.03%) in all. Friday tops with 11 days (18.33%) followed by Monday 10 days (16.66%) Saturday 9 days (15%), Sunday and Tuesday each with 8 days (13.33%) each Wednesday and Thursday have the lowest days of markets with 7 each (11.66%) each in the district (Fig. No. 3.7).

There are only twelve daily rural markets which is (5.55%) of the total markets of the region, out of which seven (58.44%) of daily markets are in Jehanabad district and five (41.66% of daily markets) are in Nawada district. Eighty four days of these markets have been added with the marketing days of Jehanabad and Nawada districts for the purpose to determine the market frequency by days.

It is interesting to note that there are more market days than the total number of markets in the whole division and in the each district too. This is because many markets are held for more than one day in a week. In areas served by bi-weekly markets, therefore, market availability increases above the expected number by the number of days by which market gatherings increases above one. In the present context however, daily markets have been treated as all seven days of a week for each market, where as tri-weekly, bi-weekly and weekly have been treated as three, two and one markets respectively. This type of analysis could make results more meaningful.

3.7 CHI-SQUARED TEST

The Chi-squared test has been used in evaluating the goodness of fit between the observed and expected frequencies of market days. The

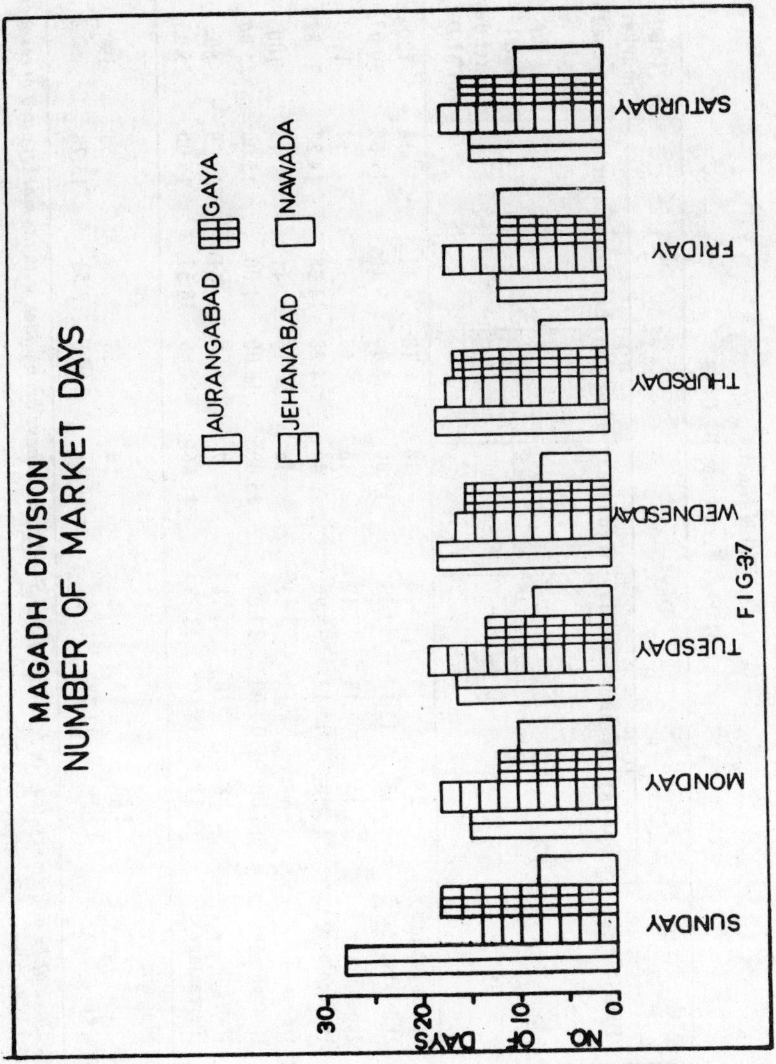
MAGADH DIVISION
NUMBER OF MARKET DAYS
AURANGABAD
GAYA
JEHANABAD
NAWADA
SATURDAY
FRIDAY
THURSDAY
WEDNESDAY
TUESDAY
MONDAY
SUNDAY
FIG-37
NO. OF DAYS
30
20
10
0

Fig. 3.7

Table No. 3.4

Market Frequency By Days

Sl. No.	District	Days							Total market days with their % of the total market days of M.D.	Total markets with their % of the total no. of markets of M.D.
		Sunday	Monday	Tuesday	Wednesday	Thursday	Friday	Saturday		
1.	Aurangabad	28	15	16	18	18	11	14	120	68
	(Percentage)	23.33	12.50	13.33	15.00	15.00	9.16	11.66	30.07	31.48
2.	Jehanabad	15	18	19	16	17	17	17	119	43
	(Percentage)	12.60	15.12	15.96	13.44	14.28	14.28	14.28	29.82	19.90
3.	Gaya	18	12	13	15	16	11	15	100	77
	(percentage)	18.00	12.00	13.00	15.00	16.00	11.00	15.00	25.06	35.64
4.	Nawada	8	10	8	7	7	11	9	60	28
	(Percentage)	13.33	16.66	13.33	11.66	11.66	18.33	15.00	15.03	12.96
Total of Magadh Division		69	55	56	56	58	50	55	399	216
(Percentage)		17.29	13.78	14.03	14.03	14.53	12.53	13.78		

N.B. : 84 Daya of 12 daily markets (7 in Jehanabad and 5 in Nawada) have been added with the market daya of respective districts.

(Source : District Census Handbooks, 1981).

expected frequency, in this case, is an equal proportion of the total market meetings in a district divided by the number of market days of the week. For example if there are 35 market days (meetings) in a week in a district then the expected number of market meetings per day will be 5. The expected values of the number of periodic in market days each week were arrived at by using the following formula:

$$E = \frac{D_a}{T_a} N$$

Where D_a = area of the district

T_a = total area of the division.

N = total number of markets in the district.

E = expected value of the number of periodic markets days each week.

The table no. 3.5 which is given below shows the expected values of the number of periodic market days each week.

Table no. 3.5

Expected Values of the Number of Periodic Market Days Each Week.

Sl. No.	Name of District	Area of the District in Sq. Km.	Total No. of Markets in District	Expected Value Each Weak
1.	Aurangabad	3,305.00	68	18.20
2.	Jehanabad	1,569.30	43	5.46
3.	Gaya	4,975.70	77	31.03
4.	Nawada	2,494.00	28	5.65

The total area of the Magadh Division is 12,344 Sq. Km. Gaya district has the highest expected value (31.03) of the number of periodic market days each week in the Magadh Division followed by Aurangabad district (18.20), Nawada district (5.65) and Jehanabad district (5.46). Nawada and Jehanabad have almost equal expected values (*Fig. No. 3.8*)

The below table no. 3.6 shows that the Aurangabad district and Jehanabad district has almost the equal no. of periodic market days each week with 120 and 119 respectively followed by Gaya district with 100 and Nawada district with 60.

Gaya district covers the maximum average are 49.75 Sq. Km. by each market days followed by Nawada district (40.81), Aurangabad district (27.54) and Jehanabad district (13.18). *Fig. No. 3.9* shows all data.

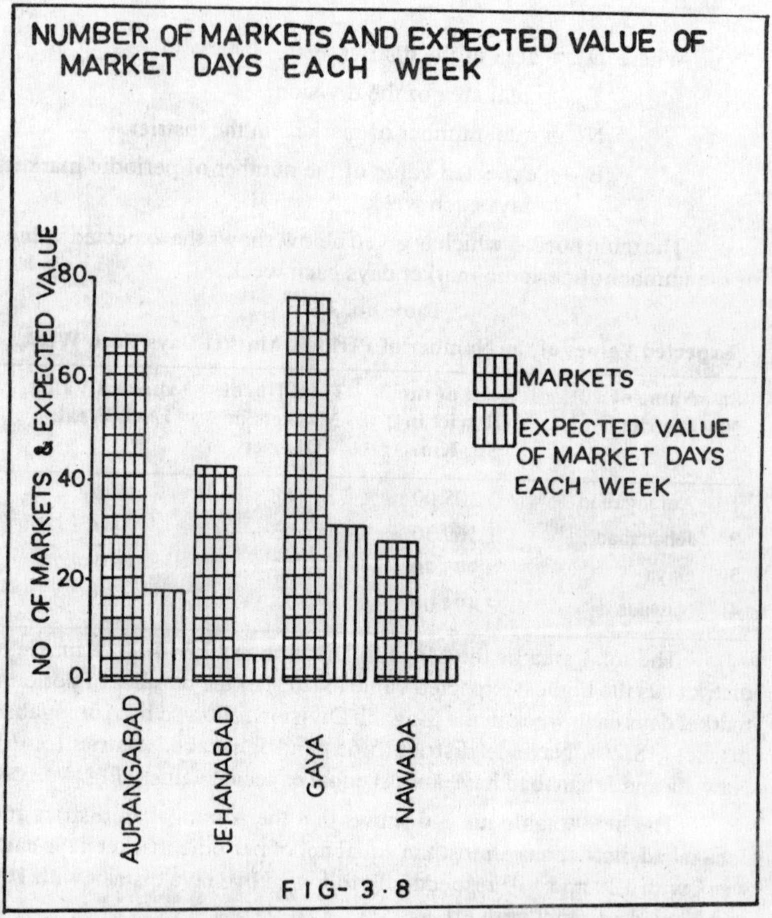
NUMBER OF MARKETS AND EXPECTED VALUE OF MARKET DAYS EACH WEEK
NO OF MARKETS & EXPECTED VALUE
80
60
40
20
0
MARKETS
EXPECTED VALUE OF MARKET DAYS EACH WEEK
AURANGABAD
JEHANABAD
GAYA
NAWADA
FIG- 3.8

Fig. 3.8

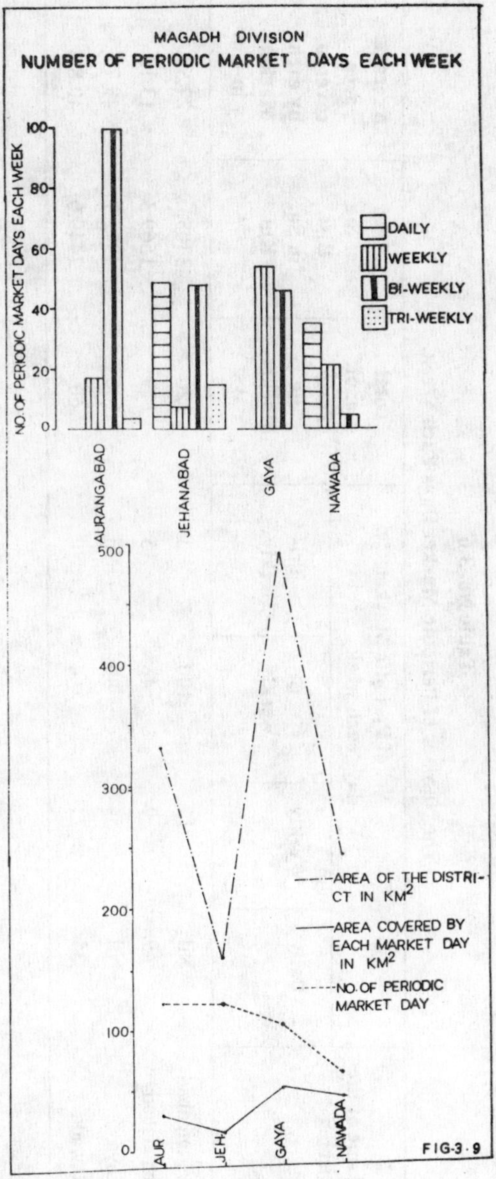
MAGADH DIVISION
NUMBER OF PERIODIC MARKET DAYS EACH WEEK
NO. OF PERIODIC MARKET DAYS EACH WEEK
100
80
60
40
20
0
DAILY
WEEKLY
BI-WEEKLY
TRI-WEEKLY
AURANGABAD
JEHANABAD
GAYA
NAWADA
500
400
300
200
100
0
AREA OF THE DISTRICT IN KM^2
AREA COVERED BY EACH MARKET DAY IN KM^2
NO. OF PERIODIC MARKET DAY
AUR
JEH.
GAYA
NAWADA
FIG-3·9

Fig. 3.9

Table No. 3.6

The Number of Periodic Market Days Each Week.

Sl. No.	Name of the District	No. of Periodic Market days each week				Total no. of Periodic Market days	Area of the Dist. in Sq. Km.	Average area covered by each Market day in Km^2
		Daily	Weekly	Bi-weekly	Tri-weekly			
1.	Aurangabad	Nil	17	100	3	120	3305.0	27.54
2.	Jehanabad	49	7	48	15	119	1569.3	13.18
3.	Gaya	Nil	54	46	Nil	100	4975.7	49.75
4.	Nawada	35	21	4	Nil	60	2449.0	40.81

Periodic markets occur either on the some days or one or two days apart.

Rural markets of the Magadh Division in their temporal aspects reflect a number of significant factors:

(i) The rural population can not support continuous urban functions hence the multiplicity of periodic markets. This is in accordance with the hypothesis that the development of daily markets is usually associated with urban growth.[21]

(ii) Market activity occurs on each day of the week with little variation. This is because the farmers of the region seem to have no concept of 'weekend' or holidays. They can spare any day for marketing depending either on the availability of market or the money to spend.

(iii) Market openings of large and small market centres are arranged in such a manner that traders can plan their itinerary in advance.

3.8 SPATIO-TEMPORAL SYNCHRONIZATION

In area where the purchasing power of population is poor the minimum range of a good exceeds the maximum and trading institutions become mobile in order to service. By rotating market meetings among a group of market places on different days each one can attract a sufficient number of people to justify holding a market.[22]

This chapter presumes that periodicity and locational spacing are two more or less fundamental characteristics of the markets of Magadh Division. A measure of the efficiency of market cycle is, therefore, needed to test whether the spatial pattern and timing of markets are integrated or not. Smith has advanced a method of such measurement.[23 & 24]

Smith implicity assumes that all market centres have only one periodic market day per week and of them are equal in importance. Spatial distances between market centres are measured by a straight line. It is hypothesised that an inverse relationship between spatial and temporal locations exists in a well integrated marketing system. In a poorly integrated system a direct relationship would exist.

Bromley[25] modified Smith's method taking examples from Highland Ecuador. Spatial distances between market centres are over - the route distances in kilometers. These distances are multiplied by an index of between 1.0 and 5.0 to take account of the varying fraction of distance resulting from different types of routes. Thus spatial distances are given in distance units. In this method all markets are treated according to their relative importance. Over the route distances are measured from each periodic market to the nearest periodic market that is of the same size or larger. The temporal distance between periodic markets is measured in days, using a terminology distinct from Smith's. Almost the same method has been used in this study in order to measure spatio-temporal integration.

It may be observed that spatio-temporal patterns of market activity generally correspond to Smith's hypothesis of an inverse relationship in the Magadh Division. There is also a tendency of neighbouring markets to occur on adjacent days is similar to Bromley's observations in the highland Ecuador.

There are some facts which may be summarised in so far as the spatio-temporal synchronization is concerned.

The Magadh Division has not a strong integration in its periodic market system.

Integration is better in a district where the number of market is highest. This confirms the hypothesis that areas with a high density of market centres have better integrated market systems than areas with lower densities of market centres.

There has been an increase in the number of markets and market days in the past. The market system is thus gradually evolving and may develop better integration.

3.9 MARKET CYCLE

In the analysis of spatio-temporal characteristics of market centres the existence of market cycles and market rings must be taken into account. The concept of market cycles is related to time where as that of a market ring in related to space according to Stine[26] Good[27] and Tamaskar.[28] It has been observed that the market activity is dominantly periodic in the Magadh Division. The market days, therefore, must be spread in such a manner over space that consumers in all parts are able to visit the markets conveniently. Under an integrated system of market days over space the consumer fulfils his needs from the nearest market centers. A market ring thus needs from the nearest market centres. A market ring thus consists of a few such markets whose days are systematically spread over the week in a limited area. The consumers visit them on different days of the week at different places.[29]

The market cycles are of two types - complete and incomplete. A complete market cycle means that marketing opportunity is available on all days of the week within the reach of the farmer. In a seven-day week there may be seven markets in a cycle, or less, depending on the frequency of periodicity. For example there may be a weekly market, one bi-weekly market and a daily market to complete the cycle. An incomplete cycle means that on one or more days of a week marketing activity is not available. People in areas of incomplete cycles will then have to depend on a couple of available markets or may be inconveniently located with respect to some consumers. Incomplete market cycles create social inequality of territorial justice on the one hand and provide potential market sites or days on the other.[30] Complete market cycles reduce unhealthy competition among neighbouring markets and promote development. The market cycles may be independent or inter-related to more than one market cycle.[31]

In such areas the superimposition of an additional market or market day in the existing cycles becomes unviable. It has been observed that in the developing societies social tensions and political rivalry at local level leads to the establishment of a new market or an additional market day deliberately ignoring the space-time relationship. It is because holding markets at one's seat of power was a measure of social prestige. In an already developed and synchronosed system of periodic markets the incidence of such attempt is checked. Only a competition which leads to further development of market centres will prevail. The market cycles may be independent in the sense that all the seven days of a week market activity takes place among the market centres occuring in a cycle. For example three weekly markets and two bi-weekly markets will make one complete and independent market cycle. On the other hand, market cycles may be inter-related as well. In this case one or two market days of a market cycle, on which no market is held in that cycle, may be shared with an adjacent market cycle.

In the Magadh Division evidence of complete and incomplete market cycles has been observed. The following cycles have been identified using data collected from field-work and personal knowledge of the area.

3.10 COMPLETE MARKET CYCLE

Complete market cycles have evolved in a scattered fashion, wherever there is a large daily market in the vicinity of periodic ones market cycles are generally found to be complete. In the eastern part of the Magadh Division in the such east part of the district of Nawada we find such a complete market cycle in Sirdala and Rajauli blocks starting from Bisiat to Makesaur, Sonar Majhgawan, Sirdala, Taukatnar, Rajauli, Amawan, Targir, Laun and Parona.

In the northern part of the division on the border area of Gaya and Jehanabad districts, we find a complete market cycle comparising of Tikari (Gaya) and Kurtha (Jehanabad) blocks starting from Mau to Math, Kapea, Sarya, Dharampur, Amawa and Aupur. Just north to this cycle there is one more complete cycle and another market cycle is in the western part of Jehanabad district comprising of tri-weekly, bi-weekly and weekly markets these are inter related market cycles.

Again in the southern part of Gaya district in Fatehpur and Mohanpur blocks we find a market cycle starting from Itwan to Lakhanipur, Dharhara, Dangaa, Bongea, Amatar, Gamhri, Lodhwe, Dumarichatti, Fatehpur and Gagarhatpur.

Aurangabad district has also complete market cycle in the northern part of the district in Haspura, Jakhaura, Ahiyapur, Bihta and Sihrikalan. In the south western part of the district on the bank of river Son in Nabinagar block has evolved a market ring with the help of Mahuawan to Barem, Salaia, Baria, Thumba, Barkiregani, Cherankalan and Akroha.

3.11 INCOMPLETE MARKET CYCLE

There are evidence of incomplete market cycles which outnumber the occurrence of complete market cycles. Thus gaps have been created in areas where weekly area less frequent. For example in the north-western part of Nawada district we find an incomplete market cycle in Hisua and Nawada blocks comparising Nadriganj to Pararia, Sandohra and Kahuara.

We find some incomplete market cycles in Gaya district too, such as in Sherghati sub-division in Dumaria, Kothi, Imamganj and Raniganj area.

In Aurangabad district we again find an incomplete market cycle. In Rafiganj blocks there is also an incomplete market cycle around Rafiganj.

Thus the market system of the Magadh Divison is in the process of evolution both over space and time. Spatio-temporal organizatino is such that territorial inequalities in market availability have been created. The development of market systems is directed towards integration, though at a slower pace. Creation of new market centres at potential sites or addition of new market days to an existing weekly market center are evidences of the process of integration as has been cited above. But such attempts are taking time and initiative is in private hands. Public intervention in the creation of new market centres or market days can accelerate this process well.

REFERENCES

1. Mumford, L. (1945) : The Culure of Cities, Secker and Warburg.
2. Richard, Fox (1969) : From Zamindar to Ballot Box, Cornell University, Press, Itaha.
3. Jain, N.G. (1964) : The Emergence of Urban Centres in Eastern Districts of Vidarbha (Maharashtra), National Geographical Journal of India, X, pp. 148-49.
4. Bromley, R.J. (1976) : Contemporary Marketing Periodicity in Highland Ecuador, Regional Analysis 1, pp. 91-122.
5. Bhole, H.G. (1983) : Role and Potentiality of Traditional Market Systems in the Third World Urbanisation, International Asian Forum, 14, pp. 345-362.
6. Christaller, W. (1933) : Central Places in Southern Germany, Translated by C.W. Baskin, Prentice Hall.
7. Stine, J.H. (1962) : Temporal Aspects of Tertiary Production Elements in Korea in F.R. Pitts (eds.), Urban Systems and Economic Development, University of Orgon, School of Business Administration, Engene, Oregon, pp. 68-88.
8. Skinner, G.W. (1964) : Marketing and Social Structure in Rural China, Journal of Asian Studies, 24, pp. 195-228.
9. Berry, B.J.L. (1967) : Geography of Market Centres and Retail Distribution, Englewood Cliffs, New Jersey.
10. Hodder, B.W. (1965) : The Distribution of Markets in Yorubaland. The Scottish Geographical Magazine, 81, pp. 48-58.
11. Saxena, H.M. (1975) : Geography of Transport and Market Centres : A Case Study of Hadoti Plateau, New Delhi.
12. Eighmy, T.M. (1972) : Rural Periodic Markets and Extension of an Urban System : A Western Nigeria Example, Economic Geography, 48, pp 299-315.
13. Bromley, R.J. (1973) : The Spatial Pattern and Temporal Synchronization of Periodic Markets, Swansea Geographer, II, pp. 15-25.
14. Tinkler, K.J. (1973) : The Topology of Rural Periodic Market Systemes, Geographiska Annaler, 55, pp. 121-33.
15. Shrivastava, V.K. (1974) : The Square Configuration of Central Places : An Indian Case, Oriental Geographer, 18, pp. 105-24.
16. Shrivastava, V.K. and V. Nath (1981) : Rural Marketing and Social Structure in North India : A Case Study Proceedings International Conference on Urbanization and Regional Changes in Developing Countries, Kharagpur.

17. Shrivastava, V.K. and H.P. Nayak (1980) : Origin and Development of Markets, Uttar Bharat Bhoogol Patrika, XVI, pp. 115-26.
18. Skinner, G.W. (1964-65) : Op. cit.
19. Bromley, R. and Bromley, R.J. (1975) : The Debate on Sunday Markets in Nineteenth Century Ecuador, Journal of Latin American Studies, 7.
20. Bromley, R.J. (1976) : Op. cit.
21. Hodder, B.W. (1971) : Periodic and Daily Markets in West Africa, in C. Meillassum (ed.), Development on Indigenous Trade and Markets in West Africa London, Oxford University Press, pp. 347-58.
22. Nanel, S.F. (1942) : A Black Byzentium : The Kingdom of Nupe in Nigeria. (For the International African Institute), Oxford University Press, London.
23. Smith, R.H.T. (1971) : West African Market Places : Temporal Periodicity and Locational Spacing, in Claude Mei Massoux (ed.), The Development of Indigenous Trade and Markets in West Africa, Oxford University Press, London, pp. 319-46.
24. Smith, R.H.T. (1972) : The Synchronization of Periodic Markets, in Adams, W.P. and F.M. Helleiner(eds.), International Geogrpahy, University of Toronot Press, Toronoto, pp. 591-93.
25. Bromley. R.J. (1976) : Op. cit.
26. Stine, J.H. (1962) : Op. cit.
27. Good, C.M. (1975) : Periodic Markets and Travelling Traders in Ugenda, The Geographical Review, pp. 50-72.
28. Tamaskar, B.G. (1983) : Trader Travel Behaviour and Periodic Market Cycles in the Arvi Upland, the Indian Journal of Marketing Geography, l, pp. 22-27.
29. Alao, N.A. (1968) : Periodic Markets in Western Nigeria; Theory and Emprical Evidence, North-Western University, Department of Geography, Research Papers No. 42, pp. 2-3.
30. Shrivastava, K.R. (1983) : Periodic Markets and Central Places in Baghelkhand Region of Madhya Pradesh, Ph. D. Thesis Accepted by Rani Durgawati Vishwa Vidyalaya, Jabalpur (Unpublished).
31. Hodder, B.W. (1969) : Markets in Yoruba Land, in Hodder, B.W. and Ukwu, U.I. (eds.), Markets in West Africa, Ibaden.

4

Functions and Behavioural Characteristics of Markets

4.1 ASPECTS OF FUNCTIONS

Market systems of the Magadh Division have evolved under a variety of socio-ecomonic-cultural bases. Market functions are reflections of the patronage that the markets receive from market place participants. Since the participants here consists of people of different classes and of variable socio-economic and cultural status, their needs will naturally vary greatly.

4.2 THE DATA

The data regarding the functional character of market centres were collected during field work. Initially a list of 86 variables consisting of shops of various types, services, entertainment etc. was drawn up. The supporting components were manufacturing activity, transport and communication, finance, storage, educational institutions, the administrative status of the market place and cultural features like church, temple, mosque, gurudwara, library, community hall etc. The list of 86 variables was expanded upto 115 on the basis of existence of such variables in sampled markets (Appendix III).

In addition, the locational characteristics of various establishments were analysed and classified under clustering, linear and scattered grouping. These locational aspects will be explained in the analysis of the morphology of individual market places to follow.

4.3 PROCEDURE OF SAMPLING

Random sampling was the basis for sample survey of the markets of the study area. Ten per cent of the total markets were randomly selected. Thus about 22 rural markets and a rurban centre were selected taking in account of all types of rural markets and markets of every area and direction.

4.4 THE QUESTIONNAIRE

Altogether four questionnaires were prepared for the field work. Two contained questions pertaining to consumers and traders respectively and the third referred to the characteristics of the market place itself. The fourth questionnaire was related to the shop activity type survey. This questionnaire contained a detailed account of each of the shop types expected to be present in the area of study. Along with the type of shops expected the questionnaire had provision for noting the locational character of the shop type concerned, i.e., clustered, linear, scattered etc. If the shops of one or more type cluster at a particular location they are given the status of 'clustering' Similarly, shops located along a road, railway line, tank, boundary of the market are called 'lineating', whereas shops which do not exhibit any pattern and may be seen everywhere have been called 'scattering'. The field-work was conducted during 1989-90. A team of four to five investigators visited the markets on normal market days and systematically filled in the proforma. About 2,515 proforma were filled in.

4.5 FIELD LIMITATIONS

Field condition were somewhat different than normally expected. In the first instance, in spite of a careful verification of maps, some markets in southern part of the region were found to be unapproachable by normal means. In others the reluctance of local people to reveal the facts of trade hampered field-work a little.

Another difficulty was that in some markets questions about consumer movements were not answered by the people. In some cases the traders refused information about their trading behaviour. In spite of all these, data regarding consumer/trader behaviour were collected for 23 markets and those concerning functional aspects were collected for 15 markets. Due care was taken in accepting each and every questionnaire. The criteria of such acceptance was that at least 75% of the questions were answered.

4.6 FUNCTIONS OF THE MARKET

For the purpose of discussion, the variables identified in enumerating the market functions are divided into groups. The first group consists of durable items like kirana, cloth, hosiery, utensils, general goods, sports goods, manihari etc. (Appendix III). The second group consists of ubiquitous items like betel leaves. cold drinks, tea stall etc. Fruits and vegetables, meat, fish and poultry occur in separate groups. Agricultural input items like seeds, fertilizers, pesticides, Agricultural machinery etc. are kept in a special category. Food stuffs like bakery goods, ready-made items like lai, bhuja, chura, sweets, confectionary are likewise placed in a separate group. Special goods like radios, medicines, newspapers and perfumes form a separate category. Services of all types, like barber, cabbler, tailor etc. have been combined together, Gold, silver, hardware, cement form a other good's category.

Following this, a broad generalizaiton of all the four districts of the division has been attempted. The functional diversity and the preference for various functional groups also vary in different districts of magadh Division.

The durable goods surpass the rest of the items in the region as a whole though they are numerically more important in Gaya district. Next come service components in which again Gaya district outweighs other districts. However, services form less that a quarter of all functions and mostly include rural services such as mochi, lohar, way-side barber, umbrella repairer, tool sharpener, cycle repairers etc. Vegetables and fruits come next. They are rather omnipresent and may be grouped with ubiquitous items. Shops selling food stuffs like home made sweets, lai, bhooja, bakery items etc. are predominant. Special goods like medicines, jewellery, radio sets etc. are found in larger markets only. Goods like tobacco, gur, salt, ghee, caps. leather ropes. jute etc. are sold separately in some markets.

4.7 BEHAVIOURAL ASPECTS

The project in hand contemplates the efficacious role that the rural markets can play in the overall development process. It is through the study of the periodic marketing system that the space-time relationship of rural areas exhibited in the periodic marketing system can be examined thoroughly. It is because the periodic marketing system provide a deep insight into the organization and use of rural space, the latter being the principal component of socio-economic development programmes. The behavioural aspects of the market-place participants add a dynamic dimension to the study of temporal aspects. These may be well illustrated through the study of consumer/trader behaviour.

4.8 AN OVER VIEW

Consumer behaviour varies in spatial, soico-cultural and economic contexts. In traditional and backward societies a consumer is bound by dictates of customs. traditions and rituals. Location theorists Losch,[1] Isard[2] and Christaller[3], however, believe in optimal human behaviour. They presume that consumers procure goods and services from the nearest sources. It there are deviations from this norms, such deviations are the result of optimization of consumer behaviour. similarly, Ullman[4] observes that movement is always to the nearest market opportunity. Reilly[5] on the other hand believes that under normal conditions two cities draw retail trade from a smaller intermediate city or town in direct proportion to some power of population of these two large cities and in an inverse proportion to some power of the distance of each of the cities from the smaller intermediate city. Shrivastava[6], Shrivastava and Nath[7] have examined and emphasised the role of extra-economic and social factors in the orientation of consumer behaviour pattern. Murdie[8] and Shrivastava[9] have proved the importance of cultural factors in consumer behaviour.

Prediction and examination of human behaviour through well established laws is not undesirable so long as they are flexible enough to accommodate empirical findings. Human beings are free to travel and trade where ever they please. To test human behaviour against laws is to non-optimal behaviour guided by imperfect knowledge, social and traditional constraints with optimal behaviour, supported by perfect knowledge and free choice. The question is, does the individual always maximise his space utility under economic constraints, or are there other constraints too? Is it always that the consumer rates his opportunities with distance of cost in mind?[10] The behavioural acts of human beings should be reshaped so that they become more useful interpretative tools.[11]

4.9 THEORETICAL DIMENSIONS

Consumer behaviour is the sum total of the activities that a consumer performs by visiting market places guided therein by his intellectual ability and economic status. Christaller has predicted four groups of factors influencing consumer movement. These are (i) the importance of a central place, (ii) The purchasing power of the consumer, (iii) Subjective economic distance and (iv) The value quality and quantity of goods to be purchased. For goods of higher value and better quality, longer travels to larger centres may be undertaken. Here nothing has been said about the role of locational factors of markets. The location of a market may be different to various social groups depending on the location of their native villages in reference to a market, their capacity to meet the travel cost and the level of their knowledge about the existence of a market. The individual perception of elements of time and distance varies from culture to culture.[12] The diversity of level of education, information, network, personal ability, mode of transport and communication etc. between regions is obvious. Thus the models of economic location theorists need modifications.

The movement of market-place participants is influenced by the distance and direction of the market place form their point of origin and by the nature of the transport network available.[13] This shows that their movement are either distance-biased or direction biased. The direction bias is revealed when a consumer, instead of being influenced by distance in his decision making process, is influenced by the presence of another market place which is more attractive. May be it provides a greater variety of goods at cheaper prices and also has entertainment facilities, etc. He may not choose the nearest market then. Directon-biased movements are of two types, (i) convergent and (ii) divergent. The convergent movement takes place due to the attractive force of a markets centre. Some markets may produce repulsive effects due to high prices of goods, higher cost of journey or inconvenient mode of available transport. These give rise to divergent movement. In direction-bias movement takes place in a particular direction only. For example if in a certain area the consumers are biased toward market X then their movement would be direction biased. On the other hand if in an area the consumers are not biased in favour or against any market, they will choose the nearest market centre. In this case their movement would be distance biased. The two types of movements may also occur thythmically with the opening and closing of a market day. Central places are points of attraction because they provide goods and services, job opportunities, etc. to their dependent population. Villages are places of residence. From rural to urban area convergent movement may thus be expected.

Next comes the transport network. Consumer always prefer the easiest access to a market, similarly, the role of the information network is also important. If consumers are aware of the existence of a market, of the prices and quality of goods, their availability, etc. They orient their market visitation patterns accordingly.

The role of economic constraints is supposed to be operative on consumers universally. Brinkmann[14] observes that human subjectivity may modify economic constraints. In practice consumers make multipurpose trips they are also unware of the availability of goods and prices in surrounidng markets. This is particularly true of the Magadh Division. Even if they know, their means of transport do not allow them to move as they like. Further, if they know and have means of movement they may not be able to take advantage of the opportunity because of their conservation or backwardness. The consumers lose sight of economic rationality as well. Such preferences have been emphasised by Huff[15] as well. The role of social obligation, religious factors and psychological leanings can also not be overlooked.

4.10 BEHAVIOUR OF CONSUMER

There are three main components of consumer behaviour. They are: (i) the range of good, (ii) consumer frequency, and (iii) consumer space preferences. The range of a good means the distance consuemrs are willing to travel for a particular goods, foodstuffs and high quality goods vary. The availability of such goods has also been discussed.

4.11 CONSUMER FREQUENCY

By consumer frequency is meant the number of consumers coming to a market centre from a particular distance class. While choosing a particular centre for particular goods or service he may be guided, as discussed earlier, by his social norms, traditional relations with some markets, information about prices of goods and his own willingness.[16]

For the analysis of consumer frequency the average walking distance of a consumer to a market in the Magadh Division has been taken 5 km. The avearage walking distance means that a rural consumer will be able to cover the to and fro distance on foot in a day without any inconvenience. His reach may be enhanced by the availability of means of transport. The 5 km. limit has been arrived at by averaging the distance travelled by consumers to village market centres on foot. With the help of questionnairs mentioned earlier, consumer/traders were asked their place of origin relative to the market where they are interviewed. Such distance were converted in distance classes and were tabulated. The frequency of all consumers/traders visiting a market was worked out (Table No. 4.1) with the help of such date frequency diagrams have been drawn.

Fig. 4.1 represents consumer frequency trend of some selected sampled markets. All market participants coming to a market on the market day (consumer and trader) have been taken into consideration together. It may be observed that there is a general decrease in the number of market place participants with increasing distance.

This is obvious in case of Targir, Khemda, Kinjar, Amawan and Sherghati market centres. Table no. 4.1 clearly indicates the percentage of visitors in different market centres in various distance classes. Only Sherghati has the no. of visitors in all distance classes it is because Sherghati is a rurban centre and a big market. The maximum % of visitors is of below 1 Km. in Sherghati i.e. 41.29% and minimum is of visitors between 8-9 Km. in Kinjar market (Fig. No. 4.1).

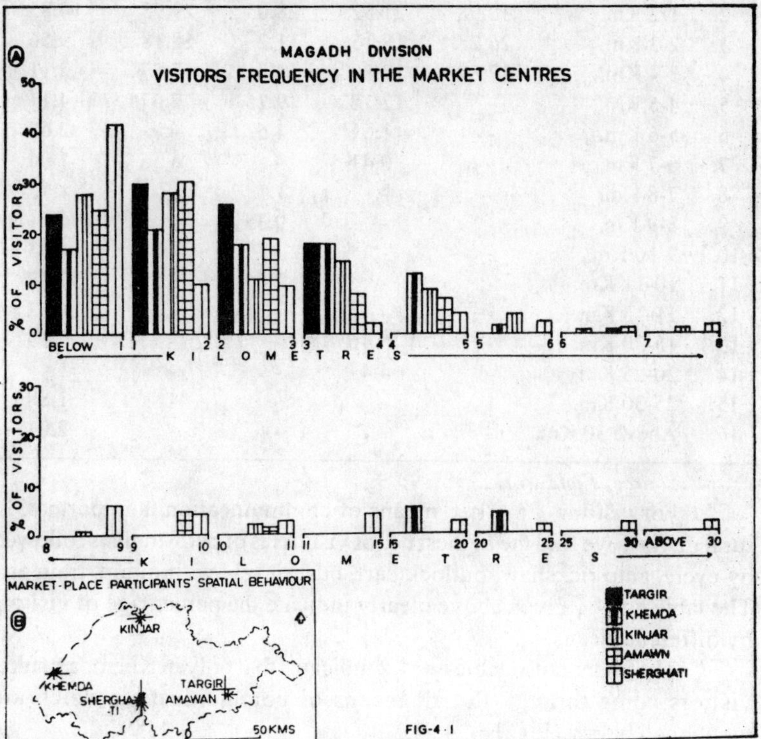
A
MAGADH DIVISION
VISITORS FREQUENCY IN THE MARKET CENTRES
% OF VISITORS
BELOW 1
K I L O M E T R E S
% OF VISITORS
ABOVE 30
K I L O M E T R E S
B
MARKET-PLACE PARTICIPANTS' SPATIAL BEHAVIOUR
KINJAR
KHEMDA
SHERGHA-TI
TARGIR
AMAWAN
50KMS
TARGIR
KHEMDA
KINJAR
AMAWN
SHERGHATI
FIG-4·1

Fig. 4.1

Table No. 4.1

Visiting Frequency in the Market Centres

Sl. No.	Distance class in Km.	% of Visitors in the Market Centres				
		Targir	Khemda	Kinjar	Amawan	Sherghati
1.	Below 1 Km.	24.76	17.47	28.6	24.59	41.29
2.	1-2 Km.	30.98	21.52	28.05	29.95	10.85
3.	2-3 Km.	26.28	18.15	11.2	18.18	9.56
4.	3-4 Km.	17.82	18.80	14.8	7.57	2.11
5.	4-5 Km.	-	12.18	9.25	7.07	4.11
6.	5-6 Km.	-	1.61	4.6	-	2.68
7.	6-7 Km.	-	0.41	-	6.56	1.06
8.	7-8 Km.	-	-	1.1	-	1.9
9.	8-9 Km.	-	-	0.35	-	6.91
10.	9-10 Km.	-	-	-	4.54	4.33
11.	10-11 Km.	-	-	2.05	1.51	2.47
12.	11-15 Km.	-	-	-	-	4.32
13.	15-20 Km.	-	5.46	-	-	2.59
14.	20-25 Km.	-	4.43	-	-	1.44
15.	25-30 Km.	-	-	-	-	1.88
16.	Above 30 Km.	-	-	-	-	2.01

Source: Field work, 1989-90.

For visiting a market, means of communication is importnat. In rural markets we find the highest no. of visitors is of pedistratians followed by cycle, auto rickshaw, bullock cart, bus, rickshaw, tumtum, train etc. The table no. 4.1 given above clearly indicate the percentage of visitors by different means.

The under noted table no. 4.2 indicates that only in Khemda market visitors come through the all means of communication which are mentioned below (Fig. No. 4.2).

Table No. 4.2: Means of Communication

Sl. No.	Market Centres	% of visitors by different means					
		Pedistrian	Cycle	Auto-Rickshaw	Bullock cort	Bus	Others Rail, Rickshaw, Tumtum etc.
1.	Targir	76.00	34.00	-	-	-	-
2.	Khemda	52.84	19.51	5.69	1.62	13.00	7.12
3.	Kinjar	64.58	21.87	3.12	-	10.41	-
4.	Amawan	79.72	13.51	1.35	5.40	-	-
5.	Sherghati	86.38	1.47	-	-	10.29	1.87

Source: Field work, 1989-90.

Table No. 4.3 clearly shows the percentage of visitors of different occupation in the market centre. We find that the percentage of visitors types vary in all markets. The highest percentage of visitors is of business and farming class i.e. 33.66 in Amawan daily market and the lowest percentage is of service class, i.e. 0.62 in Sherghati bi-weekly market.

In Targir weekly market the maximum percentage (33.48) is of farming class followed by business and farming class (22.22%), farming and labour class (17.77%), business and labour class (10.57%), labour class (7.86%), business class (5.33%) and farming, labour and business class (2.23%).

Khemda bi-weekly market has the maximum percentage of business class (30.18%) followed by farming class (22.64%), labour class (18.86%), business and farming class (11.32%), farming and labour class (9.43%), service class (7.57%).

In Kinjar tri-weekly market the maximum percentage of visitors is of farming class (31.31%) followed by business class (24.24%), business and farming class (18.18%), labour class (10.10%), service class and farming and labour class (6.06%), service and farming class and others class (2.02% each).

In Amawan daily market the maximum percentage of visitors is of business and farming class (33.66%) followed by farming and labour class (20%), farming class (16%), labour class (10.66%), business class (6.66%), service and farming class (2.66%), others class (1.03%).

In Sherghati bi-weekly market the maximum percentage of visitors is of business and farming class (52.20%) followed by business class (26.41%), farming class (5.66%), labour class (4.40%), farming, labour and business class (3.17%), business and labour class and others class (2.51% each), farming and labour class (1.88%), service class (0.62%) *Fig. No. 4.3.*

During the field survey we also collected data of annual income of the visitors in some sample market centres and we got an interesting aspect for visitors income which is given in this table.

The under noted table no. 4.4 shows that Kinjar and Amawan markets have the visitors of all income groups where Targir, Khemda and Sherghati markets have the visitors of all income groups except first two income groups i.e. below Rs. 1200/- and Rs. 1,201/- to Rs. 2,000/-. In the whole table the highest percentage is of group 7 (Rs. 7001/- to Rs. 10,000/-) i.e. 28.33% in Amawan daily market, where as the lowest percentage of visitors is of group 1 (below Rs. 1,200/0) i.e. 0.21% which is also of Amawan daily market. Other income group nos. of Amawan

Table No. 4.3

Classification of Visitors According to Occupation

Sl. No.	Name of Market Centre	% of visitors of different occupations									
		Service	Farming	Business	Labour	Service & Farming	Business & Farming	Business & Labour	Farming & Labour	Farming Labour & Business	Others Farming (student, purohit etc.)
1.	Targir	-	33.48	5.33	7.86	-	22.22	10.57	17.77	2.23	-
2.	Khemda	7.57	22.64	30.18	18.86	-	11.32	-	9.43	-	-
3.	Kinjar	6.06	31.31	24.24	10.10	2.02	18.18	-	6.06	-	2.02
4.	Amawan	5.33	16.00	6.66	10.66	2.66	33.66	4.00	20.00	-	1.03
5.	Sherghati	0.62	5.66	26.41	4.40	-	52.20	2.51	1.88	3.17	2.51

Source: Field work, 1989-90.

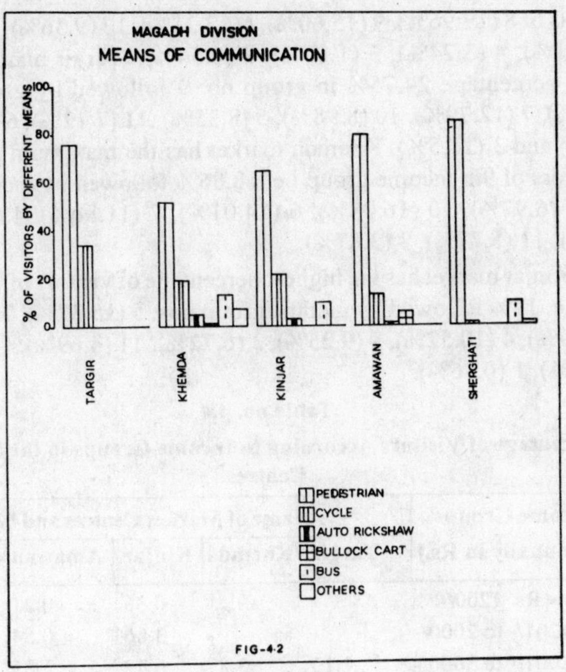
MAGADH DIVISION
MEANS OF COMMUNICATION
% OF VISITORS BY DIFFERENT MEANS
100
80
60
40
20
0
TARGIR
KHEMDA
KINJAR
AMAWAN
SHERGHATI
PEDESTRIAN
CYCLE
AUTO RICKSHAW
BULLOCK CART
BUS
OTHERS
FIG-4·2

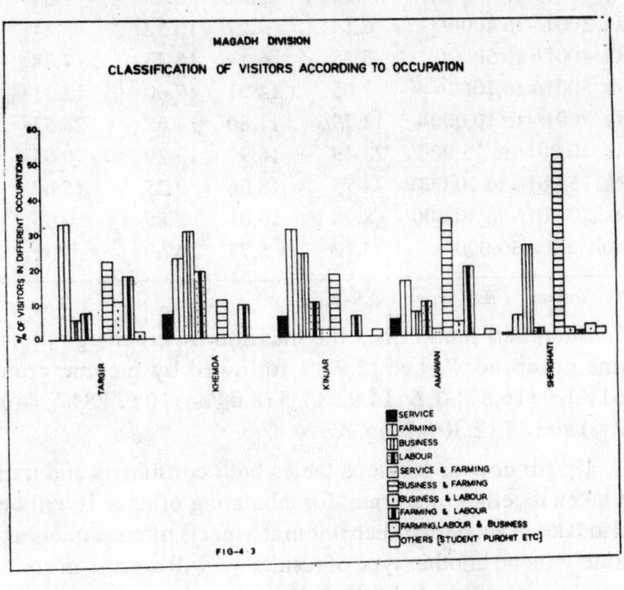
MAGADH DIVISION
CLASSIFICATION OF VISITORS ACCORDING TO OCCUPATION
% OF VISITORS IN DIFFERENT OCCUPATIONS
60
50
40
30
20
10
0
TARGIR
KHEMDA
KINJAR
AMAWAN
SHERGHATI
SERVICE
FARMING
BUSINESS
LABOUR
SERVICE & FARMING
BUSINESS & FARMING
BUSINESS & LABOUR
FARMING & LABOUR
FARMING, LABOUR & BUSINESS
OTHERS [STUDENT PUROHIT ETC]
FIG-4·3

Fig. 4.3

market is of 8 (19.96%), 9 (15.60%), 6(12.31%), 10 (9.36%), 5 (4.78%), 11 (3.31%), 4 (3.24%), 3 (1.85%), 2 (0.54%),. Targir market has the highest percentage 24.75% in group no. 9 followed by group nos. 8 (23.49%), 7 (12.79%), 10 (8.98%), 5 (8.35%), 11 (7.12%), 6 (7.05%), 4 (6.14%) and 3 (1.15%). Khemda market has the maximum percentage of visitors of 9th income group i.e. 18.06% followed by income group nos. 8 (16.97%), 10 (16.08%), 6 (14.01%), 7 (11.80%), 4 (7.27%), 5 (6.14%), 11 (5.77%), 3 (3.87%).

Kinjar market has the highest percentage of visitors of 6th income group i.e. 17% followed by income group nos. 5 (15.37%), 7 (14.63%), 8 (13.29%), 4 (10.52%), 9 (9.25%), 3 (6.72%), 11 (4.69%), 10 (3.89%), 2 (3.66%), 1 (0.36%).

Table no. 4.4

Percentage of Visitors According to Income Groups in the Market Centres

Sl. No.	Income Group (Annually in Rs.)	Name of Market Centres and % of Visitors				
		Targir	Khemda	Kinjar	Amawan	Sharghati
1.	Below Rs. 1200/-	-	-	0.36	0.21	-
2.	Rs. 1201/- to 2000/-	-	-	3.66	0.54	-
3.	Rs. 2001/- to 3000/-	1.15	3.87	6.72	1.85	3.82
4.	Rs. 3001/- to 4000/-	6.14	7.27	10.52	3.24	6.12
5.	Rs. 4001/- to 5000/-	8.35	6.14	15.73	4.78	8.04
6.	Rs. 5001/- to 7000/-	7.05	14.01	17.00	12.31	14.92
7.	Rs. 7001/- to 10,000/-	12.79	11.80	14.63	28.33	22.97
8.	Rs. 10,001/-to 15,000/-	23.49	16.97	13.29	19.96	17.61
9.	Rs. 15,001/- to 20,000/-	24.75	18.06	9.25	15.60	16.87
10.	Rs. 20,001/- to 30,000/-	8.98	16.08	3.89	9.36	7.28
11.	Above Rs. 30,000/-	7.12	5.77	4.69	3.31	2.30

Source: Field work 1989-90.

Sherghati market has the maximum percentage of visitors of income group no. 7, i.e. 22.97% followed by income group nos. 8 (17.61%), 9 (16.87%), 6 (14.92%), 5 (8.04%), 10 (7.28%), 4 (6.12%), 3 (3.82%) and 11 (2.30%) *Fig. No. 4.4.*

Up till now in previous tables both consumers and traders have been taken together in account for tabulating of data. It will be better if we also take in account of behavioural aspects of consumers and traders separately for an another type of results we will discuss in coming pages separately consumers and traders behaviour in certain sample markets.

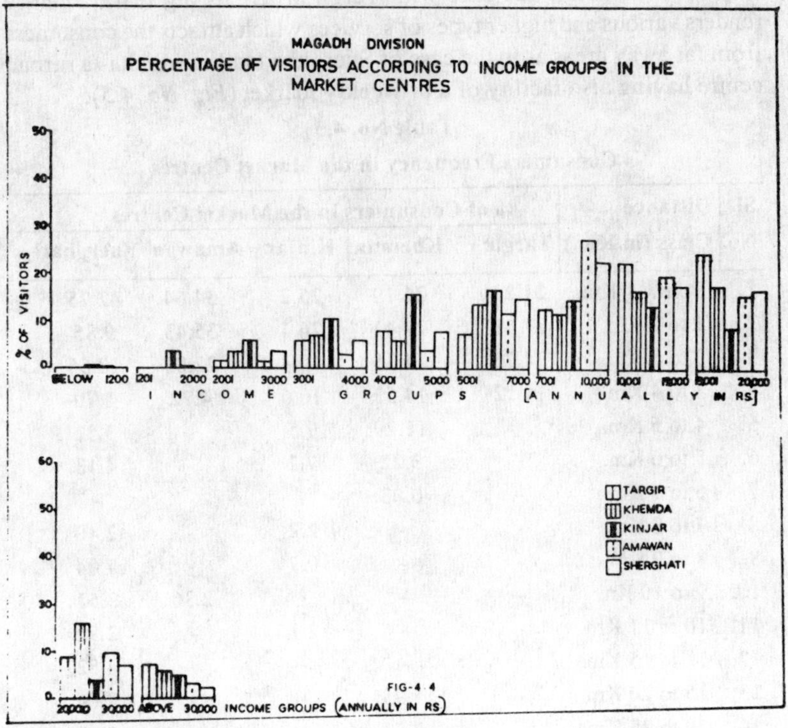
MAGADH DIVISION
PERCENTAGE OF VISITORS ACCORDING TO INCOME GROUPS IN THE MARKET CENTRES
% OF VISITORS
50
40
30
20
10
0
BELOW 1200
1201 2000
2001 3000
3001 4000
4001 5000
5001 7000
7001 10,000
10,001 15,000
15001 20,000
INCOME GROUPS [ANNUALLY IN RS]
60
50
40
30
20
10
0
20,000 30,000
ABOVE 30,000
INCOME GROUPS (ANNUALLY IN RS)
TARGIR
KHEMDA
KINJAR
AMAWAN
SHERGHATI
FIG-4.4

Fig. 4.4

At first we will discuss the behavioural aspect of consumers. Distance is an important factor for consumers frequency at market centres.

Table no. 4.5 clearly indicates that the consumers mostly prefer to travel less to reach a market centre. With the size of market centres area of influence is decreases or increases. Small market centre renders less and inferior types of services which attracts the surrounding areas consumers which is the case with Targir where as big market centre renders various and higher types of services which attracts the consumers from far away areas as in the case of Sherghati market which is a rurban centre having also facility of a bi-weekly market (*Fig. No. 4.5*).

Table No. 4.5

Consumers Frequency in the Market Centres

Sl. No.	Distance Class (in Km.)	% of Consumers in the Market Centres				
		Targir	Khemda	Kinjar	Amawan	Sherghati
1.	Below 1 Km.	21.23	24.19	25.2	34.64	42.25
2.	1 to 2 Km.	27.61	27.41	26.1	35.43	9.85
3.	2 to 3 Km.	34.75	14.35	10.4	22.83	10.56
4.	3 to 4 Km.	16.12	14.53	16.6	4.72	1.70
5.	4 to 5 Km.	-	11.29	9.5	-	3.52
6.	5 to 6 Km.	-	3.22	7.2	-	4.13
7.	6 to 7 Km.	-	0.83	-	-	-
8.	7 to 8 Km.	-	-	2.2	-	2.40
9.	8 to 9 Km.	-	-	0.7	-	7.04
10.	9 to 10 Km.	-	-	-	2.36	3.51
11.	10 to 11 Km.	-	-	2.1	-	2.92
12.	11 to 15 Km.	-	-	-	-	4.82
13.	15 to 20 Km.	-	1.95	-	-	2.06
14.	20 to 25 Km.	-	2.23	-	-	1.63
15.	25 to 30 Km.	-	-	-	-	2.18
16.	30 to 40 Km.	-	-	-	-	1.40

Source: Field work, 1989-90.

The table no. 4.6 clearly indicates that percentage of consumers according to purchasable goods vary in different markets but in every sampled market the highest percentage of visiting consumers is of vegetables and fruits class. Because this is an item of daily use. Durable goods and ubiquitious goods comes next followed by services class, good stuff class, non-vegetarian food class, agricultural inputs class, special

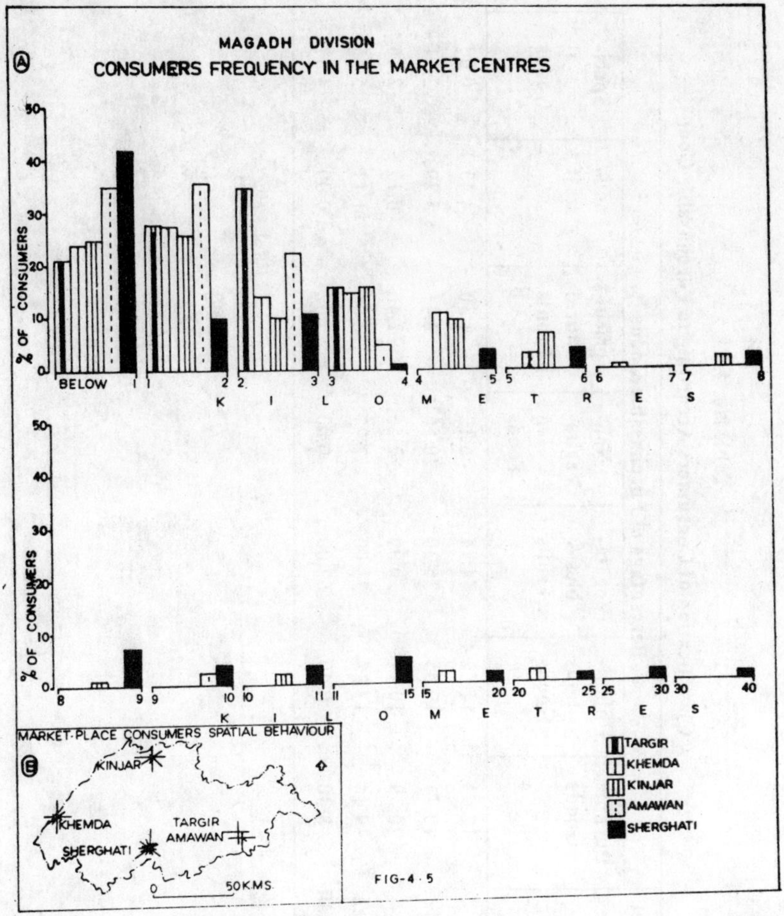
MAGADH DIVISION
(A) CONSUMERS FREQUENCY IN THE MARKET CENTRES
% OF CONSUMERS
BELOW 1
K I L O M E T R E S
MARKET-PLACE CONSUMERS SPATIAL BEHAVIOUR
(B)
KINJAR
KHEMDA
TARGIR
AMAWAN
SHERGHATI
50 KMS.
TARGIR
KHEMDA
KINJAR
AMAWAN
SHERGHATI
FIG-4·5

Fig. 4.5

Table No. 4.6

Classification of Consumers According to Purchasable Goods

Sl. No.	Market Centre	Percentage of Purchasable Goods								
		Durable Goods	Ubiquitious Goods	Vegatables & Fruits	Non-Vegitarian Foods	Agricultural Inputs	Food-stuff	Special Goods	Animals	Services
1.	Targir	12.93	14.52	44.74	6.12	1.30	4.43	0.00	5.61	10.05
2.	Khemda	10.24	17.05	26.30	20.56	2.41	5.29	2.11	0.00	16.02
3.	Kinjar	20.39	10.11	30.09	2.46	2.46	6.17	2.46	2.46	11.00
4.	Amawan	19.44	13.88	25.00	2.77	12.05	11.11	5.55	0.00	9.72
5.	Sherghati	8.30	0.49	62.00	0.00	3.02	0.00	4.07	19.20	1.44

goods class and animals. These percentage reflect the need and choice of consumers for goods in different markets. In Khemda market the second most highest choice is for non vegetarian foods, it is simply because its location on river bank and neighbouring forest areas from which this market gets fishes and mutton (*Fig. No. 4.6*).

Income of consumers is an important aspect of marketing which influence market greatly. The table No. 4.7 given below clearly shows the percentage of consumer according to income groups in the sampled market centres.

Table No. 4.7

Percentage of Consumers According to Income Groups

Sl. No.	Income Group (Annually in Rupees)	Market Centres and % of Consumers				
		Targir	Khemda	Kinjar	Amawan	Sherghati
1.	Below Rs. 1200/-	-	-	0.72	0.04	-
2.	Rs.1201/- to 2000/-	-	-	1.45	0.30	-
3.	Rs. 2001/- to 3000/-	2.13	5.37	3.64	2.13	3.07
4.	Rs. 3001/- to 4000/-	6.60	8.60	5.37	2.56	6.15
5.	Rs. 4001/- to 5000/-	11.51	7.52	19.70	1.70	7.69
6.	Rs. 5001/- to 7000/-	7.64	16.12	6.56	12.82	12.30
7.	Rs. 7001/- to 10,000/-	12.83	12.90	17.51	19.23	18.46
8.	Rs. 10,001/- to 15,000/-	19.91	17.28	16.78	22.22	15.38
9.	Rs. 15,001/- to 20,000/-	17.59	18.27	14.59	21.36	21.53
10.	Rs. 20,001/- to 30,000/-	9.94	10.75	5.83	12.82	10.76
11.	Rs. 30,0001/- and above	11.76	3.22	7.43	4.27	4.61

Targir, Khemda and Sherghati markets have no consumer in first two income groups. Income of consumer vary in different markets according to size and type of markets and prosperity of the surrounding area. In the whole table the lowest and highest percentage is in income groups no. 1 (0.04) and 8 (22.22) of the daily market of Amawan. Other income groups of Amawan according to higher to lower percentage is of income group nos. 9 (21.36%) followed by 7 (19.23%), 6 and 10 (12.82% each), 11 (4.27%), 4 (2.56%), 3 (2.13%), 2 (0.30%).

In Targir weekly market the highest percentage of consumers in income group is of no. 8 (19.91%) followed by nos. 9 (17.59%), 7 (12.83%), 11 (11.76%), 5 (11.51%), 10 (9.94%), 6 (7.64%), 4 (6.60%) and 3 (2.13%).

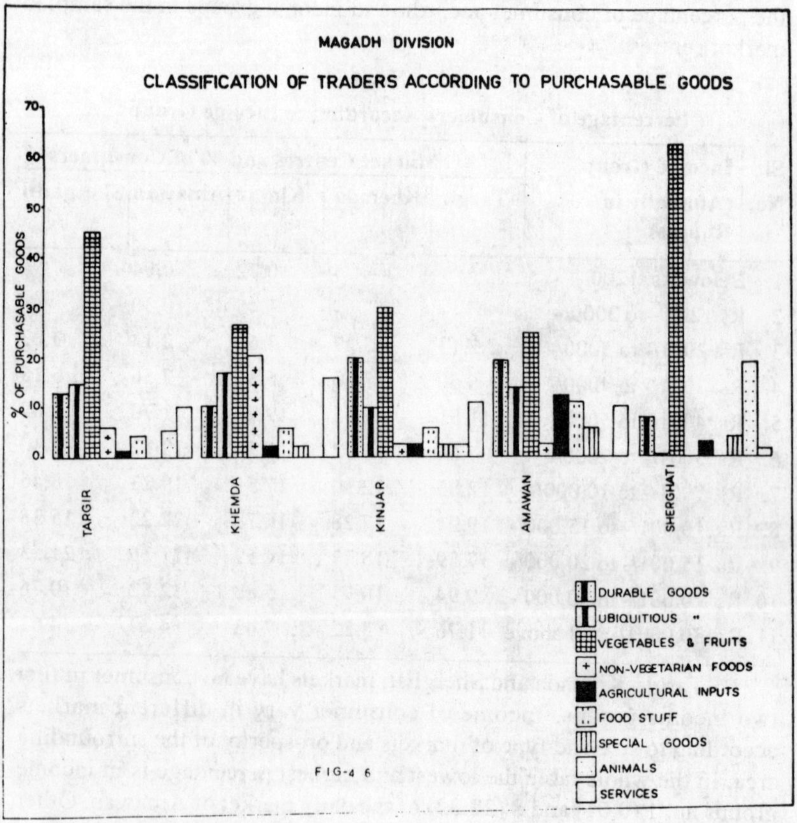
MAGADH DIVISION
CLASSIFICATION OF TRADERS ACCORDING TO PURCHASABLE GOODS
% OF PURCHASABLE GOODS
70
60
50
40
30
20
10
0
TARGIR
KHEMDA
KINJAR
AMAWAN
SHERGHATI
DURABLE GOODS
UBIQUITIOUS "
VEGETABLES & FRUITS
NON-VEGETARIAN FOODS
AGRICULTURAL INPUTS
FOOD STUFF
SPECIAL GOODS
ANIMALS
SERVICES
FIG-4 6

Fig. 4.6

Khemda bi-weekly market has the highest percentage of income group of no. 9 (18.27%) followed by 8 (17.28%), 6 (16.12%), 7 (12.90%), 10 (10.75%), 4 (8.60%), 5 (7.52%), 3 (5.37%), 11 (3.22%).

In Kinjar tri-weekly market the maximum percentage of consumer's income group is of group no. 5 (19.70%) followed by nos. 7 (17.5%), 8 (16.78%), 9 (14.59%), 11 (7.43%), 6 (6.56%), 10 (5.83%), 4 (5.37%), 3 (3.64%), 2 (1.45%) and 1 (0.72%).

Sherghati bi-weekly market has the highest percentage of consumer's income group no. 9 (21.53%) followed by income group nos. 7 (18.46%), 8 (15.38%) 6 (12.30%), 10 (10.76%), 5 (7.69%), 4 (6.15%), 11 (4.61%) and 3 (3.07%). Thus we find in total the maximum percentage of consumers in income group between Rs. 4000/- to Rs. 20,000/- only (*Fig. No. 4.7*).

The pattern of consumer's space preferences varies greatly as compared to the traders. It is because a trader is tied to his market rather permanently. He pays for a place at the market centres and commands goodwill of consumers by his regular presence. A comsumer is free to make his choice of market activity from all available sources. He may change his plan for better price bargain.

A consumer faces less competition than the trader. That is why their visitation patterns differ. A trader is thus tied to the sub-set of a universe of markets in a given region or in a given market cycle. Many markets are thus beyond their practical radius of operation.[17]

The variables related to the participation of market place visitors on special occasions or for special purposes may now be examined. These are related with, as stated earlier, purchases of ceremonial and medical goods, patronage of a town and preference for education. Hats and purely periodic markets either disappear functionally or are weekly responding to one or two of these functions. For example in case of periodic markets like Targir, Amawan etc. the presence of consumers for such goods is exceptional. In general it is thus observed that the number of market-place participants drop greatly in respect of these functions. This may be due to two reasons: (i) all markets do not provide each of the four functions, and (ii) all participants do not avail themselves of all of these functions always. For example medical facilities are either seldom used or, if available, may command a small area.

In respect of ceremonial purchases the restrictive effect of distance is ignored to a great extent. For example in Sherghati market for ceremonial goods a large number of participants came from outside the

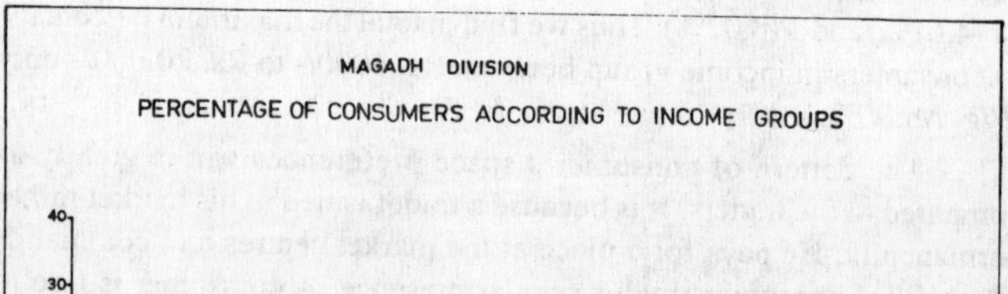
MAGADH DIVISION
PERCENTAGE OF CONSUMERS ACCORDING TO INCOME GROUPS
% OF CONSUMERS
40
30
20
10
0
BELOW 1200
1201 2000
2001 3000
3001 4000
4001 5000
5001 7000
7001 10000
10001 15000
INCOME GROUPS [ANNUALLY IN RS]
15001 20000
20001 30000
ABOVE 30001
INCOME GROUPS [ANNUALLY IN RS]
TARGIR
KHEMDA
KINJAR
AMAWAN
SHERGHATI
FIG-4.7

Fig. 4.7

effective range (5 Km.) of the market. More-over, the spatial range of the market has also increased, which means that participants of other small markets patronize this centre ignoring the deterrent of distance. Similar is the case with Targir in case of ceremonial goods. For medical purposes people are prepared to ignore distance. for example market centres like Sherghati, Kinjar, Khemda, etc. command a much larger area in terms of sale of medicines than the trading area normally commanded by them. Attraction and facilities of a town surpasses all considerations of distance and time. This attraction is evidenced in case of towns like Gaya, Aurangabad, Nawada and Jehnabad etc. Peasants from the approachable villages prefer to go to such towns ignoring the smaller periodic markets nearby. it is because it facilitates multipurpose trips. The preference for obtaining educational facilities for children, however, is dictated by distance to some extent. Most of the visitors who use these markets for this purpose are confined to the effective range (5 Km.) of the market or even less. For obtaining higher education the distance factor has to be ignored, as is the case with Sherghati and Khemda (Barun) which provides education up to graduate level.

It may thus be concluded that the problem of distance becomes inoperative in more than one instance and leads to non-optimal behaviour. The market-place participant may be biased by the attitudes and values that he holds and which necessitate a non-optimizing behaviour. Christaller is also aware of such deviations from norms., as observed earlier, but only if they facilitate optimisation of behaviour. In this case the motivation for non-optimizing behaviour emanates from the personal values, qualities and attitudes of participants that they acquire from the social group of which they are a part. There are, in addition, long established ties with the trader, credit availability, free accommodation, renewing or strengthening of contract etc. For Example if a peasant has been selling his produce to a local trader since a very long time his personal relations will deter him from exploring new settling avenues like government purchasing centres of agricultural mandis.[18] It is because the peasant may obtain regular credit from the trader for an assured supply of goods by the peasant. He may use this money for purchasing seeds, fertilizers or for meeting social or religious obligations at home. Also, the peasant is entitled for free accommodation at traders shop if he is obliged to stay for a couple of days at the place where he has come to sell his goods. All these facilities are made available for social reasons. Such unwritten social bonds influence consumer's choice of markets.

An analysis of spatial patterns of these preferences further confirms the hypothesis that the problem of distance becomes inoperative in this region. Market preference for general purposes, e.g., purchase of vegetables, fruits, meat, kirana, betel leaves, etc. produce a rather uniform movement with a low degree of nesting of lower order market areas with gradually higher order ones. Examples of a low degree of nesting in such cases is observed around Kinjar town in Jehanabad district. The reasons for a weak nesting may be the by passing of nearest market centre for non economic reason, the repulsion of any market centre of a particular good etc. Preferences for special reasons either produce some dominant market areas or vary small ones. Examples of such consumer behaviour may be noted in the north western part of the study area. Observation of some randomly selected empirical studies further confirms the findings cited above.

4.12 TRADERS ROLE AND THEIR FREQUENCY IN MARKETS

A study of the traders is also an important aspect of marketing. During survey study of traders frequency at market centres with distance class, classification of salable goods in the market centres and percentage of traders according to various income groups. Data have been collected for above mentioned purposes in some sampled markets.

The table no. 4.8 clearly shows that only in Sherghati market traders of all distance class come. Here also, like the consumers, maximum percentages of traders who reached Sherghati are of upto 5 Km. area. Like the consumers it is also applicable in the case of traders also that no.. of traders decreases as the distance increases.

Table No. 4.8

Traders Frequency in Market Centres

Sl. No.	Distance-Class (in Km.)	% of Traders in Market Centres				
		Targir	Khemda	Kinjar	Amawan	Sherghati
1.	Below 1 Km.	28.29	10.75	32.00	7.69	40.34
2.	1 to 2	34.36	15.63	30.00	12.30	11.85
3.	2 to 3	17.82	21.95	12.00	10.76	8.56
4.	3 to 4	19.52	23.07	13.00	13.84	2.52
5.	4 to 5	-	13.09	9.00	21.53	4.70
6.	5 to 6	-	-	2.00	-	1.23
7.	6 to 7	-	-	-	20.00	2.13

Sl. No.	Distance-Class (in Km.)	% of Traders in Market Centres				
		Targir	Khemda	Kinjar	Amawan	Sherghati
8.	7 to 8	-	-	-	-	1.40
9.	8 to 9	-	-	-	-	6.79
10.	9 to 10	-	-	-	9.23	5.15
11.	10 to 11	-	-	2.00	4.61	2.02
12.	11 to 15	-	-	-	-	3.82
13.	15 to 20	-	8.97	-	-	3.12
14.	20 to 25	-	6.63	-	-	1.25
15.	25 to 30	-	-	-	-	1.59
16.	Above 30 km.	-	-	-	-	2.63

Source: Field work, 1989-90.

The following is a detail description of traders frequency in different distance classes in some sampled markets. The traders frequency in the whole table is maximum (40.34%) and minimum (1.23%) in Sherghati market in the distance class of below 1 Km and 5 to 6 Km respectively. Other distance classes of traders who visit Sherghati is 1 to 2 Km (11.85%) followed by 2 to 3 Km. (8.56%), 8 to 9 Km (6.79%), 9 to 10 Km (5.15%), 4 to 5 Km. (4.70%), 11 to 15 Km (3.82%), 15 to 20 Km (3.13%), above 30 Km (2.63%), 3 to 4 Km (2.52%), 6 to 7 Km (2.13%), 10 to 11 Km (2.02%), 25 to 30 Km (1.59%), 7 to 8 Km (1.40%), 20 to 25 Km (1.25%). The following is a detail description of traders frequency in different distance classes in some sample markets.

In Targir weekly market out of 16 distance classes traders come only of first four distance class 0 to 4 Km. The maximum percentage of traders frequency is from 1 to 2 Km (34.36%) followed by below 1 Km (28.29%), 3 to 4 Km (19.52%), 2 to 3 Km (17.82%).

In Khemda bi-weekly market out of 16 distance classes traders come of only 7 classes (1 to 5 and 13, 14). The highest percentage is of 3 to 4 Km (23.07%) followed by 2 to 3 Km (21.95%), 1 to 2 Km (15.63%), 4 to 5 Km (13.09%), below 1 Km (10.75%), 15 to 20 Km (8.97%), 20 to 25 Km (6.63%).

Kinjar tri-weekly market's traders frequency is represented in only 7 distance classes (1 to 6 and 11) out of 16 distance classes. The maximum percentage is of below 1 Km (32.00%) followed by 1 to 2 Km (30.00%), 3 to 4 Km (13.00%), 2 to 3 Km (12.00%), 4 to 5 Km (9.00%), 5 to 6 Km and 10 to 11 Km (2.00% each).

Table No. 4.9

Classification of Traders According to Salable Goods

Sl. No.	Name of Market Centre	Percentage of Salable Goods								
		Durable Goods	Ubiquitious Goods	Vegetables & Fruits	Non-vegetarian Food	Agricultural Inputs	Food Stuff	Spl. Goods	Animals	Service
1.	Targir	19.44	7.40	38.88	5.55	1.85	6.03	-	13.48	7.40
2.	Khemda	12.79	4.90	31.66	18,97	3.12	9.85	2.31	-	15.03
3.	Kinjar	20.00	5.5	45.45	7.27	3.60	5.5	1.81	1.81	9.06
4.	Amawan	9.72	4.16	41.66	2.77	8.11	18.88	1.38	-	16.66
5.	Sherghati	14.80	0.80	60.40	-	1.20	-	1.60	20.00	0.40

Source: Field work, 1989-90.

Amawan daily market centre represent traders frequency only in 8 distance classes (1 to 5, 7, 10 and 11) out of 16 distance classes. The highest percentage is of 4 to 5 Km (21.53%) followed by 6 to 7 Km (20.00%), 2 to 3 Km (10.76%), 9 to 10 Km (9.23%) and 10 to 11 Km (4.61%) *Fig. No. 4.8.*

The maximum percentage of traders who are coming to these markets are of within a circle of 5 Km and they are vegetables sellers, pot makers, food stuff sellers etc. But the traders who are coming out of this circle or reaching from far away places are of special goods, durable goods and other goods etc.

Traders of perishable goods like vegetables etc. prefer to sell their produce in near by local markets without investing much on transportation etc. simply to gain maximum possible profit of their produce. In case of traders coming from a long distance or above 5, 10, 20 or 30 Km. are of special goods, durable goods, other goods which are not available locally in those rural markets but has demand for these goods there. For examples cloth, utensils, footwear, readymade garments, stationery items, alcoholic liquores, medicines etc. Hence traders of these items do prefer to sale their items or produce in rural markets simply to gain much profit of their goods, as compare to urban markets they get more prices of their goods in rural markets and they remain gainful after deducting all costs of transportation and fare etc. At the same time consumers get goods of their need in their rural markets through these traders and if rural consumers go to obtain it from urban markets they find that the goods have cost much after adding the transportation cost and fare etc. in comparison to same goods available in their rural markets. Apart from this strain of journey is an additional aspect. So by this way both consumers and traders of rural markets prefer to buy and sale in rural markets.

An attempt has also been made to classify the traders of some sampled markets according to salable goods.

Table no. 4.9 clearly indicates that in the all above mentioned markets the maximum percentage of traders is of vegetables and fruits followed by durable goods, ubiquitous goods etc. This is according to products available in the area and needs of the consumers of the area. In the whole table the maximum and minimum percentage is of vegetables (60.40) and services (0.40) which is of Sherghati bi-weekly market centre (*Fig. No. 4.9*).

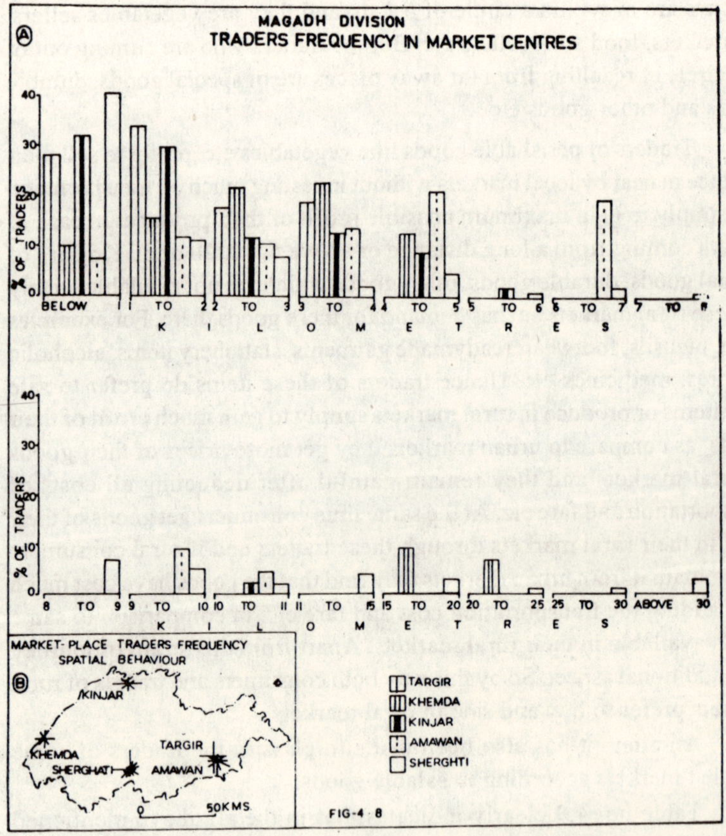

MAGADH DIVISION
TRADERS FREQUENCY IN MARKET CENTRES
A
% OF TRADERS
40
30
20
10
0
BELOW 1
1 TO 2
2 TO 3
3 TO 4
4 TO 5
5 TO 6
6 TO 7
7 TO 8
K I L O M E T R E S
8 TO 9
9 TO 10
10 TO 11
11 TO 15
15 TO 20
20 TO 25
25 TO 30
ABOVE 30
MARKET-PLACE TRADERS FREQUENCY
SPATIAL BEHAVIOUR
B
KINJAR
KHEMDA
SHERGHATI
TARGIR
AMAWAN
0
50KMS.
TARGIR
KHEMDA
KINJAR
AMAWAN
SHERGHTI
FIG-4·8

Fig. 4.8

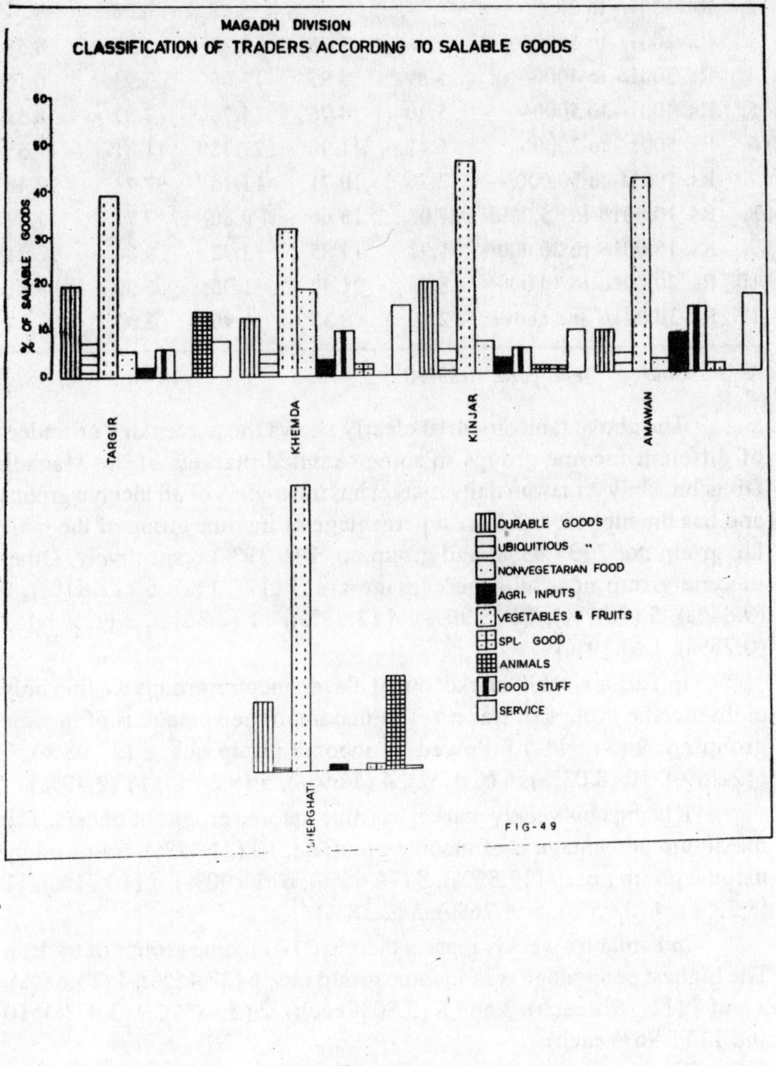
MAGADH DIVISION
CLASSIFICATION OF TRADERS ACCORDING TO SALABLE GOODS
% OF SALABLE GOODS
0
10
20
30
40
50
60
TARGIR
KHEMDA
KINJAR
AMAWAN
SHERGHATI
DURABLE GOODS
UBIQUITIOUS "
NONVEGETARIAN FOOD
AGRI. INPUTS
VEGETABLES & FRUITS
SPL. GOOD
ANIMALS
FOOD STUFF
SERVICE
FIG-49

Fig. 4.9

Table No. 4.10

Percentage of Traders According to Income Groups in the Market Centres

Sl. No.	Income Group (Annualy in Rs.)	Name of Market Centres and % of Traders				
		Targir	Khemda	Kinjar	Amawan	Sherghati
1.	Below Rs. 1200/-	-	-	-	0.39	-
2.	Rs. 1201/- to 2000/-	-	-	5.88	0.78	-
3.	Rs. 2001/- to 3000/-	-	2.38	9.80	1.57	4.58
4.	Rs. 3001/- to 4000/-	5.69	5.95	15.68	3.93	6.10
5.	Rs. 4001/- to 5000/-	5.20	4.76	11.76	7.87	8.39
6.	Rs. 5001/- to 7000/-	6.47	11.90	27.45	11.81	17.55
7.	Rs. 7001/- to 10,000/-	12.76	10.71	11.76	37.43	27.48
8.	Rs. 10,001/- to 15,000/-	27.08	16.66	9.80	17.71	19.84
9.	Rs. 15,001/- to 20,000/-	31.91	17.85	3.92	9.84	12.21
10.	Rs. 20,001/- to 30,000/-	8.03	21.42	1.96	5.90	3.81
11.	Rs. 30,001/- and above	2.49	8.33	1.96	2.36	-

Source: Field work, 1989-90.

The above table no. 4.10 clearly shows the percentage of traders of different income groups in some sampled markets of the Magadh Division. Only Amawan daily market has the traders of all income groups and has the highest and lowest percentage of income group of the table i.e. group no. 7 (37.43%) and group no. 1 (0.39%) respectively. Other income group nos. with percentage are 8 (17.71%), 6 (11.81%), 9 (9.84%), 5 (7.87%), 10 (5.90%), 4 (3.93%), 11 (2.36%), 3 (1.57%), 2 (0.78%), 1 (0.39%).

In Targir weekly market out of eleven income groups we find only eight income groups of traders. The maximum percentage is of income group no. 9 (31.91%) followed by income group nos. 8 (27.08%), 7 (12.76%), 10 (8.03%), 6 (6.47%), 4 (5.69%), 5 (5.20%), 11 (2.49%).

Khemda bi-weekly market has nine income groups of traders. The maximum percentage is of income group no. 10 (21.42%), followed by income group nos. 9 (17.85%), 8 (16.66%), 6 (11.90%), 7 (10.71%), 11 (8.33%), 4 (5.95%), 5 (4.76%), 3 (2.38%).

In Kinjar tri-weekly market there are 10 income groups of traders. The highest percentage is of income group nos. 6 (27.45%), 4 (15.68%), 5 and 7 (11.76% each), 3 and 8 (9.80% each), 2 (5.88%), 9 (3.92%), 10 and 11 (1.96% each).

Sherghati bi-weekly market has only eight income groups of traders and the maximum percentage of income group is of no. 7 (27.48%) followed by income group nos. 8 (19.84%), 6 (17.55%), 9 (12.21%), 5 (8.39%), 4 (6.10%), 3 (4.58%) and 10 (3.81%).

In the whole table no. 4.10 we find tum percentage of traders are between group no. 4 to 9 (Rs. 3001 to Rs. 20,000/- only). The traders are mostly local farmers who sale their products in the rural markets such as vegetables, food grains etc. The traders of rural markets are not big businessmen but are actually very small traders. Except outside traders, most of the traders do this job apart from agriculture. We find very small no. of traders whose average income is more than Rs. 2,000/- and above per month (*Fig. 4.10*).

Actually we find mainly four types of traders who visit Sherghati, bi-weekly rural market. They are:

1. Traders who are retailer and bring their goods to sale in the market;
2. Traders who are whole sale traders an they do sale their goods on a large scale in the market.
3. Traders who are retailer but they do not bring with them the goods, but they buy goods in bulk and again they sale the goods in the same market in retail.
4. Traders who buy some thing in retail and sale them in the same market with marginal profit. These are mainly animal traders.

We found that some visitors are purely farmers but they come in this market to sale their cattle. By this way in the market they behave like a traders but by occupation they are purely farmers and after sale of their animals most of them become turned to consumer and they buy goods of their need and interest out of the income which they have got after the sale of their animals.

The total goods supplied in Sherghati bi-weekly market (hat) may be devided into four groupos. These group are of durable goods (27.65%), ubiquitious goods (1.04%), fruits and vegetables (30.85%) and animals (40.42%). So the maximum supply by the whole sale market is of animals. But actually vegetables accounts 60.40% out of the total goods consumed in bi-weekly market of Sherghati. But vegetables are mostly supplied by the traders who cultivate vegetables themselves and sale it in retail or wholesale. So the percentage of vegetables supplied by wholesale to this market is lesser than the percentage of animals supplied by wholesale markets to this market centre.

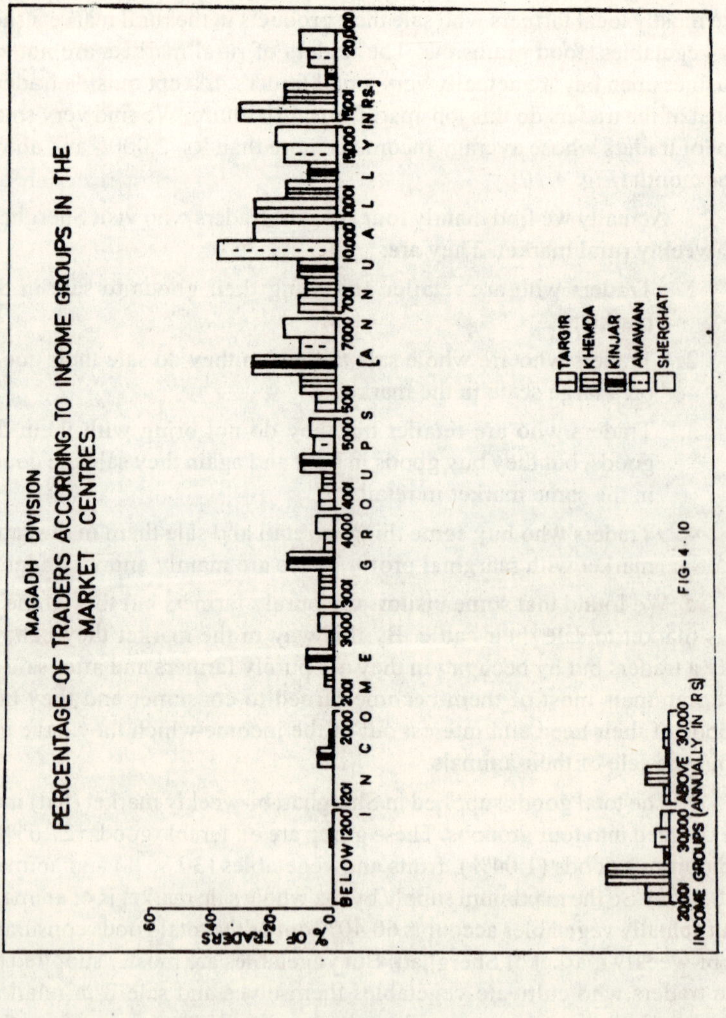
MAGADH DIVISION
PERCENTAGE OF TRADERS ACCORDING TO INCOME GROUPS IN THE MARKET CENTRES
% OF TRADERS
0
20
40
60
BELOW 1200
1201 2000
2001 3000
3001 4000
4001 5000
5001 7000
7001 10,000
10,001 15,000
15,001 20,000
I N C O M E   G R O U P S   (A N N U A L L Y   I N   R S)
20,001 30,000
ABOVE 30,000
INCOME GROUPS (ANNUALLY IN RS)
TARGIR
KHEMDA
KINJAR
AMAWAN
SHERGHATI
FIG-4·10

Fig. 4.10

The wholesale purchasing for Sherghati bi-weekly market centre affect other market centres within a radius of 500 Km. Calcutta is the farest feeder market for Sherghati. Some traders of readymade garments depend for their wholesale purchasing on Calcutta market. Calcutta is south-east to Sherghati and is connected by road and railways. There is a daily bus service for Calcutta. Gaya town is 33 Km. north to Sherghati. Traders who prefer to travel by train, get their train for Calcutta from Gaya which is an important railway junction and station of grand chord section and eastern railway. Calcutta is 458 Km from Gaya. Hence traders cover a distance of 491 Km. to reach Calcutta. The catagory of this type traders is only 2.21% and usually they visit Calcutta monthly or bi-monthly or on before festivals etc. Readymade garments accounts 6.28% of total goods sold in Sherghati market out of this 90.76% is supplied by nearby Gaya town market or by Sherghati market itself and remaining only 9.3% are bought from Calcutta market which is 2.21% of the totala goods which are purchased in whole sale.

Almost all the traders of durable goods, fruits and vegetables depend for their whole sale purchasing on Gaya and Sherghati (within a radious of 10 Km) markets which accounts 58.50%. Traders who buy khaini, bidi etc. in wholesale market are 1.04%, and they mainly depend for it on Sherghati market. Animals traders who are 40.42% of total traders purchase animals in wholesale use to buy cattle even from a distance of 300 Km. For this they visit Hariharchetra (Sonepur) fair about 150 Km north of Sherghati, Brahampur in Bhojpur distt. about 200 Km north west, Varanasi about 230 Km north west, Jamhaur about 100 Km. Rafiganj in Aurangabad distt. about 55 Km north and other native places of the Magadh Division like Bhusanda fair (Gaya), Amas, Mohanpur, Madanpur, Deokund etc. Out of the total animal wholesale, 4.23% traders are those who purchase the animals from Sherghati market and again sale it in Sherghati market on marginal profit. The table no. 4.11 given below indicates the percentage of traders and name of places from where cattle bought for Sherghati cattle market.

Table No. 4.11

Name of Places and Percentage of Traders From where Cattle Bought for Sherghati Market

Sl. No.	Name of Place		% of Traders
1.	Sherghati	-	6.63
2.	Raniganj	-	3.53
3.	Bihta	-	5.26

Sl. No.	Name of Place		% of Traders
4.	Baburi	-	7.89
5.	Jandaur	-	4.60
6.	Madanpur	-	11.05
7.	Shivaganj	-	7.89
8.	Cherki	-	1.97
9.	Rafiganj	-	1.53
10.	Bhusanda (Gaya)	-	3.00
11.	Varanasi (U.P.)	-	8.52
12.	Luca	-	6.26
13.	Brahampur	-	5.02
14.	Hariharchetra	-	15.78
15.	Jamhaur	-	6.89
16.	Deokund	-	3.63
	Total	-	99.45

Source: Field work, 1989-90.

The above table no. 4.11 shows that the maximum percentage (15.78%) of traders who buy animals for Sherghati market from Hariharchetra followed by Madanpur (11.05%), Varanasi, U.P. (8.52%), Baburi and Shivaganj (7.89% each), Jamhaur (6.89%), Sherghati (6.63%), Luca (6.26%), Bihta (5.26%), Brahampur (5.02%), Jandaur (4.60%), Deokund (3.63%), Raniganj (3.53%), Bhusanda Gaya (3%), Cherki (1.97%), and Rafiganj (1.53%) *Fig. no. 4.11*.

Table No. 4.12

List of Wholesale Markets and Percentage of Traders of Sherghati Market Who Visit These Markets for Their Wholesale Purchasing.

Sl. No.	Name of Markets		Percentage of Traders
1.	Gaya		46.61
2.	Calcutta	-	3.62
3.	Dehri-on-Sone		5.69
4.	Aurangabad	-	0.35
5.	Kanpur	-	0.38
6.	Muzaffarpur	-	2.24
7.	Sherghati and neighbouring areas within a radious of 25 Km.	-	38.14
8.	Other markets including Patna, Ranchi, Nagpur, Gwalior, Indore, Japla, Maihar etc.	-	2.97
	Total		100.00

Source : Field work, 1989-90.

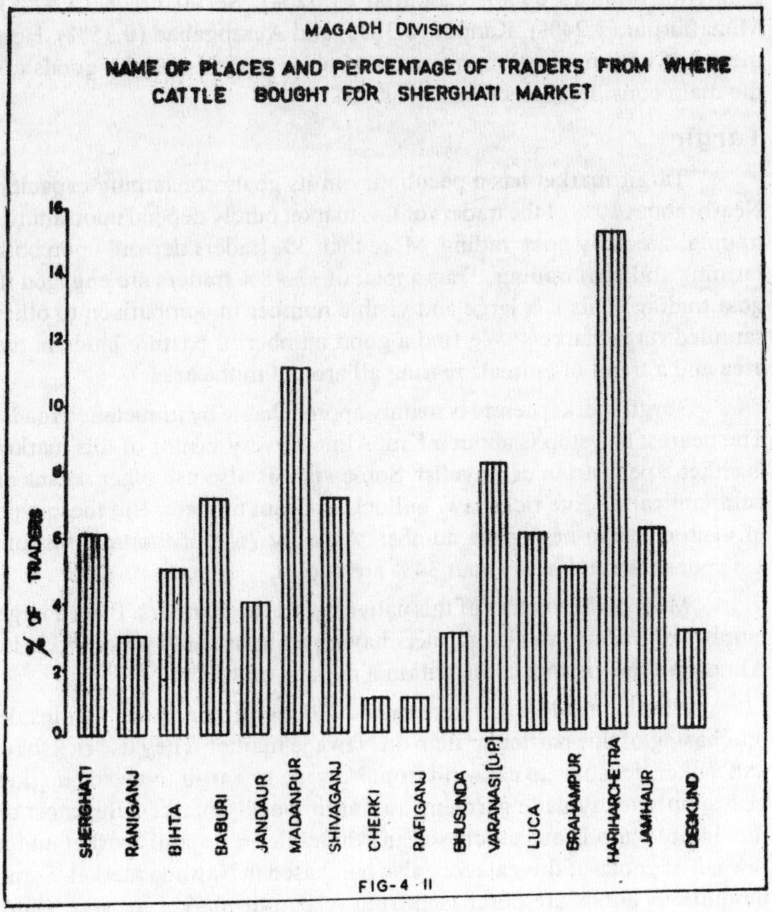
MAGADH DIVISION
NAME OF PLACES AND PERCENTAGE OF TRADERS FROM WHERE CATTLE BOUGHT FOR SHERGHATI MARKET
% OF TRADERS
0
2
4
6
8
10
12
14
16
SHERGHATI
RANIGANJ
BIHTA
BABURI
JANDAUR
MADANPUR
SHIVAGANJ
CHERKI
RAFIGANJ
BHUSUNDA
VARANASI [U.P.]
LUCA
BRAHAMPUR
HARIHARCHETRA
JAMHAUR
DEOKUND
FIG-4·11

Fig. 4.11

The above table no. 4.12 clearly indicates the list of wholesale markets with percentage of traders of Sherghati market who use to visit these markets for their wholesale purchasing. The maximum percentage (46.61%) of traders visit Gaya for their wholesale purchasing followed by Sherghati and neighbouring area within a radious of 25 Km (38.14%), Dehri-on-Sone (5.69%), Calcutta, (3.62%), Serial no. 8 (2.97%), Muzaffarpur (2.24%), Kanpur (0.38%) and Aurangabad (0.35%). Here means of communication, nearness of place and cost of the goods are the main considerations (*Fig. No. 4.12*).

Targir

Targir market has a peculiatiry in its goats consuming capacity. Nearly about 10% of the traders of this market purely depend upon animal trading, specially goat trading. More than 3% traders depend upon both farming and goat trading. Thus a total of 13.48% traders are engaged in goat trading. This is a large and visible number in comparison to other sampled rural markets. We find a good number of pasture lands in the area and a trend of animals rearing all around in the area.

Targir market centre is mainly approachable by unmetalled roads. The nearest bus stop is about 5 Km. Almost every visitor of this market is either a pedestrian or a cyclist. Some visitors also use other means of communication like rickshaw, bullockcart, tum tum etc. But these type of visitors are in negligible number. Actually 76% of the total visitors are pedestrian and near about 34% are cyclist.

Most of the visitors of this native market are farmers. Even a large number of traders are also farmers having a big or small piece of lands. Almost all the visitors come within a radious of 4 Km.

All the traders of kerosine oil depend for their wholesale purchasing of this particular item on Nawada market. They use rickshaw and tanker rickshaw to carry oil from Nawada to Targir. Nawada market also supply readymade garments to Targir weekly market. But most of the durable goods are purchased in wholesale in Rajauli market and a few no. of goods of this category also purchased in Nawada market. Some ubiquitious goods are purchased from Akbarpur market in large scale, such as Betal, Bidi, Khaini etc. Akbarpur market also supply some non-vegetarian foods like eggs and chickens to Targir market.

Khemda

Most of the visitors of this bi-weekly market come within a radious of 5 Km. No. of visitors coming from a distance of 6-7 Km is negligible

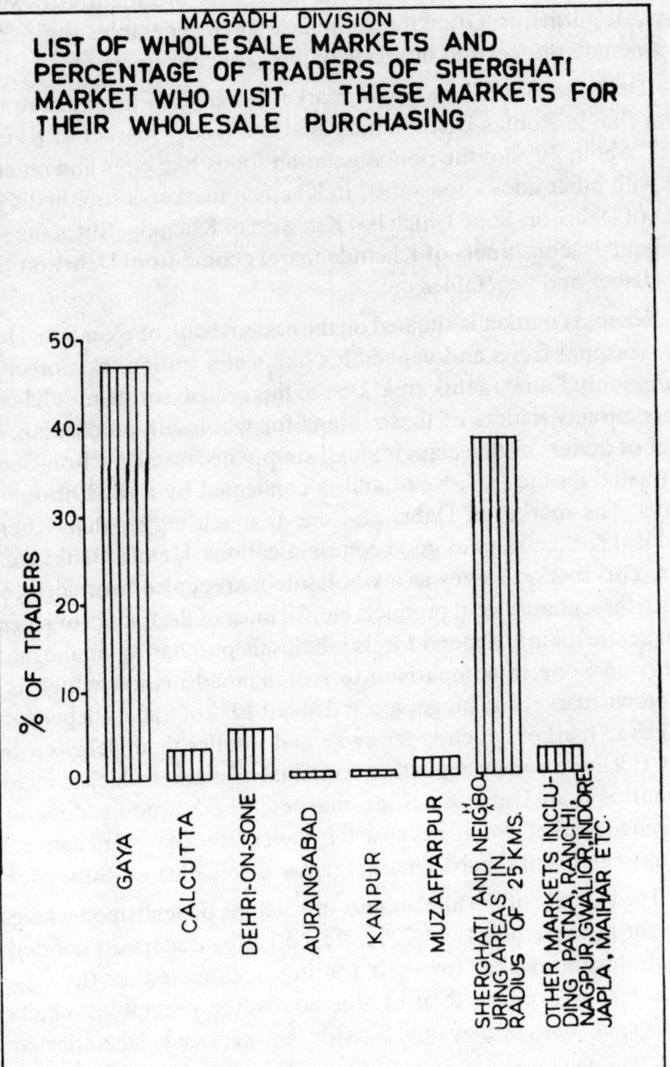

MAGADH DIVISION
LIST OF WHOLESALE MARKETS AND PERCENTAGE OF TRADERS OF SHERGHATI MARKET WHO VISIT THESE MARKETS FOR THEIR WHOLESALE PURCHASING
% OF TRADERS
50
40
30
20
10
0
GAYA
CALCUTTA
DEHRI-ON-SONE
AURANGABAD
KANPUR
MUZAFFARPUR
SHERGHATI AND NEIGBOURING AREAS IN RADIUS OF 25KMS.
OTHER MARKETS INCLUDING PATNA, RANCHI, NAGPUR, GWALIOR, INDORE, JAPLA, MAIHAR ETC.
FIG-4 12

Fig. 4.12

but some visitors come from Aurangabad which is 20 Km from here and Nabinagar which is 23 Km from here and they are mainly traders of readymade garments. Often they purchase some vegetables and fish etc. from Khemda market and in this way they are consumers too.

Dehri-on-Sone is an urban market situated on the western bank of river Son in Rohtas Distt. Which is also a feeder market of Khemda market. About 30% of the non-vegetarian foods like eggs and chickens along with other goods consumed in Khemda market is supplied by the marekt of Dehri-on-Sone which is 4 Km west of Khemda. But at the same time about 3%consumers of Khemda marekt come from Dehri-on-Sone to buy fishes and vegetables etc.

Khemda market is situated on the eastern bank of river Son. Hence fishes, seasonal fruits and vegetables like water millon, cacumber etc. are commonly found in this area. Due to this reason sometimes Khemda markets attracts traders of these things for wholesale purchasing. The number of traders of this class is small simply because Dehri-on-Sone is also situated on the G.T. Road and is connected by a road bridge and railways. The market of Dehri-on-Sone is much bigger than Khemda market and has facilities of good communications, Hotels, Banks etc. for traders. This market serves as a wholesale market also for many goods such as fishes, grains, local products etc. So most of the traders of Khemda market centre mainly depend for its wholesale purchasing on the market of Dehri-on Sone in comparison to Aurangabad market which is the nearest town market and bigger too and about 12% of traders depend upon Aurangabad market which is far away and smaller than Dehri-on-Sone market. But these traders depend on Aurangabad market which is far away and smaller than Dehri-on-Sone market. These traders depend on Aurangabad market simply because it is their native place and convenient for them to visit Aurangabad market rather than Dehri-on-Sone Market.

The exact % of the total traders of Khemda depend upon wholesale market for their trading is 44.73%. Rest 55.27% traders do not depend upon wholesale market for their trading because either they use to cultivate rear or produce their salable goods like vegetables, chickens, fishes, sweets, snaks or they only provide their service to Khemda market.

Khemda is directly connected to its feeder markets through roads as it is situated on the N.H. No. 2, it has also railway connection with Barun which is about 2-3 Km and is directly connected with Punjab to Bengal. Actually Khemda market lies between Grand Trunk Road (N.H.2) and Grand Chord railway section and both run parallel in the area. Usually traders like to visit to wholesalw markets through roads. Out of these

Table No. 4.13

Distance Groups of Feeder Markets

Sl. No.	Name of Market	% of Traders who visit Wholesale Market in Various Distance Groups										
		Below 10 Km	10 to 15 Km	15 to 20 Km	20 to 30 Km	30 to 40 Km	40 to 50 Km	50 to 100 km	100 to 150 Km	150 to 200 Km	200 to 300 Km	300 to 500 Km
1.	Targir	-	58.33	14.58	-	27.08	-	-	-	-	-	-
2.	Khemda	87.95	-	12.05	-	-	-	-	-	-	-	-
3.	Kinjar	12.96	7.40	46.29	-	-	22.22	11.11	-	-	-	-
4.	Amawan	29.41	-	-	70.54	-	-	-	0.05	-	-	-
5.	Sherghati	43.48	-	3.44	3.47	19.54	1.49	5.74	1.49	4.97	4.16	2.21

Source : Field work, 1989-90.

traders 53.62% use buses, 20.29% use autorickshaw, 4.22% use cycle, 2.36% use bullockcart and 15.96% use rickshaw and tum tum etc. for their wholesale purchasing. Only 0.81% of the total wholesale traders use railway for their wholesle purchasing.

Large no. of durable goods consumed in Khemda market is feeded by its wholesale market. Only a few things like hand made fans, some quantity of grains, coir ropes, baskets, hand made toys, bamboo stick etc. are local product. Rest of durable goods are brought in this market by wholesale purchasing. In wholesale purchasing about 22.55% of the total wholesale purchasing of Khemda is durable goods, 12.05% is of ubiquitious goods, 33.72% is of fruits and vegetables, 8.63% non-vegetarian food (mutton, chickens, eggs, fishes), 10.19% is of food stuff (ice cream, biscuits etc.) 6.47% is of special goods (palm juice, medicines, herbs etc.).

Kinjar

This is a tri-weekly market. Traders of this market mostly prefer to visit Jehanabad market for their wholesale purchasing which is 16 Km south-east of Kinjar and is well connected by metalled road and their percentage is 46.29. The other percentage of distance groups of traders who travel for their wholesale purchasing are40-50 Km (22.22%), below 10 Km (12.96), 50-100 Km (11.11%), 10 to 15 Km (7.40%). It has been observed that traders do purchasing upto the state capital Patna and Gaya.

Most of the traders undertake journey by roads (62.79%) followed by railways (30.23%) from the nearest railway station of Jehanabad. Pedestrians (4.65%) from surrounding areas of Kinjar, autorickshaw (2.32%).

The maximum percentage of purchasable goods of wholesale purchasing for Kinjar market is fruits and vegetables (43.90%) followed by durable goods (39.02%), special goods (7.31%), foodstuff (4.87%), non-vegetarian foods and animals (2.43% each).

Traders get perishable goods like vegetables, fruits etc. mostly from surrounding areas and non-perishabel goods from far away places.

Amawan

This is a daily market and is largely feeded by urban markets for its wholesale supply of goods. Most of the traders about 70.54% go to Nawada market for their wholesale purchasing of goods and some go to Rajauli and Akbarpur too. Wholesale purchasing of vegetables etc. are done below 10 Km radious.

About 70.58% traders use buses for their wholesale purchasing who go to Nawada, Rajauli or Akbarpur. About 29.41% of wholesale traders are pedestrian who are mostly vegetables and fruits traders who are of surrounding areas of Amawan market.

The maximum percentage (41.17%) wholesale purchasable goods is of fruits and vegetables followed by food stuff (29.41%), durable goods (20.58%), ubiquitious goods (5.88%) non-vegetarian foods (2.94%).

The Amawan market is well connected by roads and some traders use to go to Patna to buy some goods in wholesale purchsing too.

Discussions of previous pages are given below in the form of tables to show the wholesale trading in some sampled markets.

The under noted table no. 4.13 clearly indicates the percentage of traders who visit different markets for their wholesale purchasing in various distance groups. Only Shergahati has the maximum no. of groups except one. In the whole table maximum percentage (87.95%) is of below 10 Km group for Khemda market and the minimum percentage (0.05%) is of 100 to 150 Km group for Amawan market. We find maximum groups within 20 Km group except one Amawan where 70.54% is of 20 to 30 Km group becasue traders mostly go to Nawada for their wholesale purchasing which is 22 Km (*Fig. No. 4.13*).

Table No. 4.14

Means of Communication for Wholesale Markets

Sl. No.	Name of Market	% of Traders Accrding to Various Means of Communication						
		Rail-ways	Bus	Auto-rickshaw	Cycle	Bull-ock cart	Pedes-trian	Others
1.	Targir	-	87.50	-	8.33	-	4.16	-
2.	Khemda	0.81	53.62	20.29	4.22	2.36	2.00	15.96
3.	Kinjar	30.23	62.79	2.32	-	-	4.65	-
4.	Amawan	-	70.58	-	-	-	29.41	-
5.	Sherghati	2.94	30.88	17.64	-	-	19.11	29.41

Source : Field work, 1989-90.

Table no. 4.14 shows that the maximum traders use buses and travel thorugh roads to reach to their wholesale purchasing in different markets followed by pedestrians, other means like rickshaw, tum tum etc., autorickhsaw, railways, cycle and bullock cart (*Fig. No. 4.14*).

Table no. 4.15 indicates the percentage of different goods purchased in the wholesale markets for some sample markets. This vary

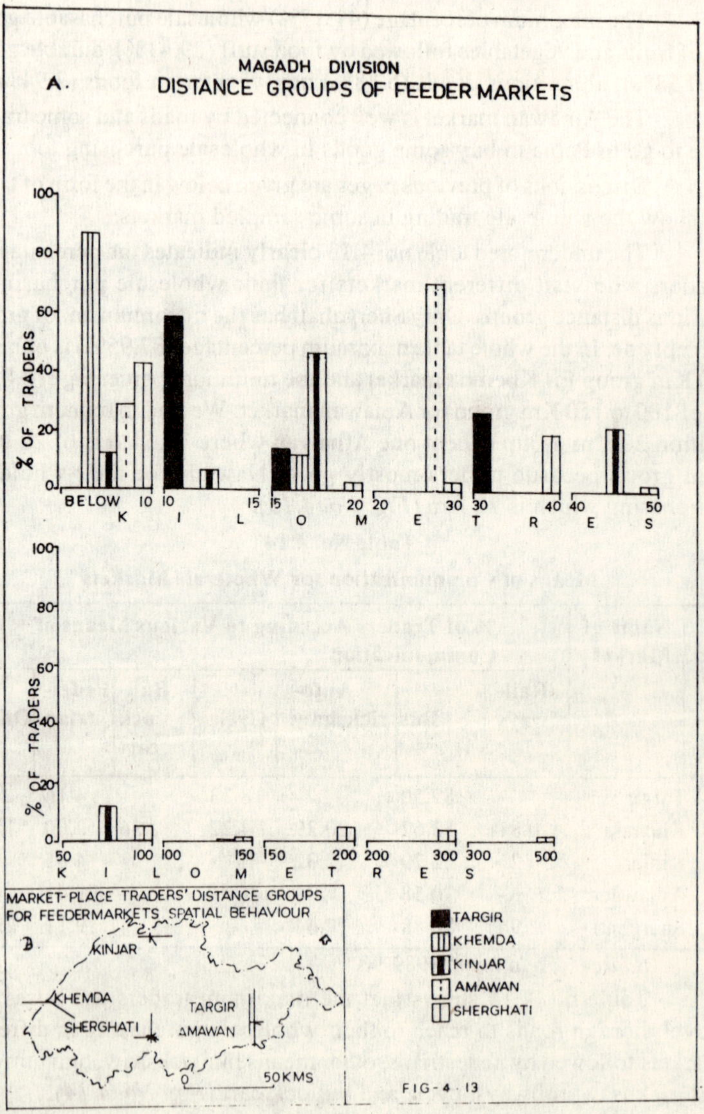
A.
MAGADH DIVISION
DISTANCE GROUPS OF FEEDER MARKETS
% OF TRADERS
BELOW 10
10 15
15 20
20 30
30 40
40 50
K I L O M E T R E S
% OF TRADERS
50 100
100 150
150 200
200 300
300 500
K I L O M E T R E S
MARKET-PLACE TRADERS' DISTANCE GROUPS FOR FEEDERMARKETS SPATIAL BEHAVIOUR
B.
KINJAR
KHEMDA
SHERGHATI
TARGIR
AMAWAN
0 50KMS
TARGIR
KHEMDA
KINJAR
AMAWAN
SHERGHATI
FIG-4.13

Fig. 4.13

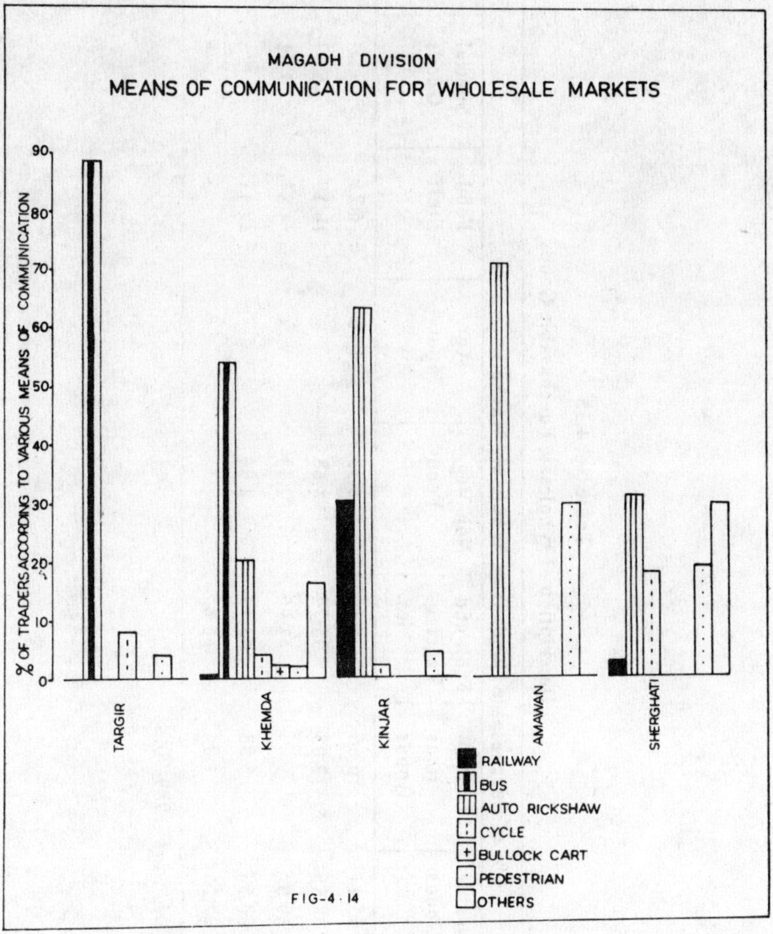

MAGADH DIVISION
MEANS OF COMMUNICATION FOR WHOLESALE MARKETS
% OF TRADERS ACCORDING TO VARIOUS MEANS OF COMMUNICATION
0
10
20
30
40
50
60
70
80
90
TARGIR
KHEMDA
KINJAR
AMAWAN
SHERGHATI
RAILWAY
BUS
AUTO RICKSHAW
CYCLE
BULLOCK CART
PEDESTRIAN
OTHERS
FIG-4·14

Fig. 4.14

Table No. 4.15

Description of Wholesale Puechasable Goods

Sl. No.	Name of Market	% of Purchasable Goods from Wholesale Markets							
		Durable Goods	Ubiqui-tious Goods	Fruit and Vegetag-les.	Non-Veg. Food	Agr. Inputs	Food Stuff	Special Goods	Animals
1.	Targir	35.41	16.66	29.16	8.33	4.16	6.25	-	-
2.	Khemda	28.55	12.05	33.72	8.63	-	10.19	6.47	-
3.	Kinjar	39.02	-	43.90	2.43	-	4.87	7.31	2.43
4.	Amawan	20.58	5.88	41.17	2.94	-	29.41	-	-
5.	Sherghati	27.65	1.04	30.85	-	-	-	-	40.42

Source : Field work, 1989-90.

according to need and interest of buyers but the maximum percentage is for fruits and vegetables, durable goods and ubiquitious goods etc. (*Fig. no. 4.15*).

4.13 REVIEW OF SHERGHATI RURBAN CENTRE

A detailed study of the permanent market of Sherghati has also been carried out during the survey of a rurban centre. Commodities, their wholesale purchasing from different market centres with distance and percentage of shops in the market with percentage of proper goods, means of communication, principal amount invested in the business and percentage of profit earned by each trader have been given in the table no. 4.16. It may be said that a complete economics of Sherghati market has been analysed.

(1) Durable Goods

(i) *Cloths*. About 6.52% of traders are the traders of cloths. Traders investment in this business is between Rs. 20,000/- to Rs. 3,000,00/- and the profit is 20% to 26%. Most of the big wholesale traders whose investment is between Rs. 1,00,000 - Rs. 3,00,000/- visit Indore, Nagpur, Gwalior, Calcutta, Patna and Ranchi for their wholesale purchasing and they account for 21.42%. Majority of the wholesale traders and retailers visit Gaya for their purchasing whose percentage is 77.77% and 5.55% are retail traders who depend on the wholesale traders of Sherghati market. The means of communication is either bus, taxi, truck, train or rickshaw.

(ii) *Readymade Garments*. In Sherghati out of the total traders 5.07% are engaged in the business of readymade garmetns. Traders investment in this business is between Rs. 10,000/- to Rs. 50,000/- and their profit is 15% to 30%. Calcutta is the most favourite market for wholesale purchasing from where 57.14% readymade garments are purchased followed by Gaya 28.57% and rest 14.28% is obtained by the Sherghati market itself.

From Calcutta the traders bring their good either by railways via Gaya or roadways by truck or bus. For Gaya market the means of communication is either bus, taxi or truck. Sherghati local market has the facility of rickshaw as the means of communication.

(iii) *Foot-Wears*. About 2.89% of the total shops of Sherghati market deal in foot-wears. Traders investment in this particular business is between Rs. 2,000/- to Rs. 10,000/- and profit is of 200%. Out

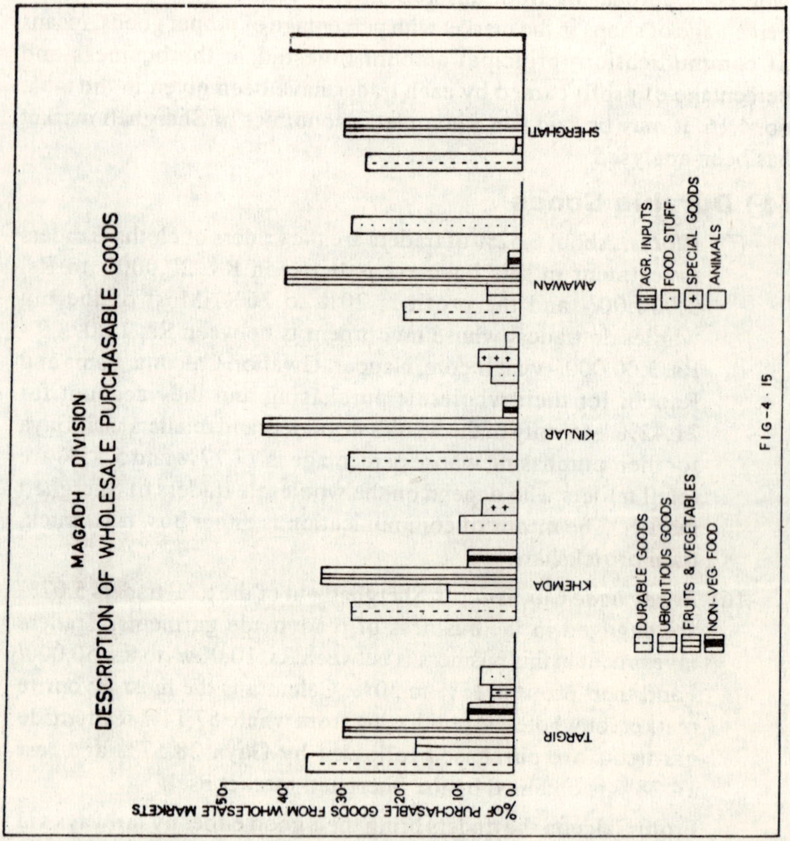
MAGADH DIVISION
DESCRIPTION OF WHOLESALE PURCHASABLE GOODS
%OF PURCHASABLE GOODS FROM WHOLESALE MARKETS
0
10
20
30
40
50
TARGIR
KHEMDA
KINJAR
AMAWAN
SHERGHATI
DURABLE GOODS
UBIQUITIOUS GOODS
FRUITS & VEGETABLES
NON-VEG. FOOD
AGR. INPUTS
FOOD STUFF
SPECIAL GOODS
ANIMALS
FIG-4·15

Fig. 4.15

Table No. 4.16

Rurban Market of Sherghati

Goods and Their Wholesale Purchasing, Principal Amount Invested in its Business and Profit

1	2	3	4	5	6	7	8	9	10	11	12	13
						Wholesale Purchasing of goods from other markets						
Sl. No.	Commodities type	% of shops to the total No. of shops in the market	Name of the goods	% of the shops of proper goods to the total shops in the market	% of shops of the proper goods to the total shops of commodities type in the market	Name of wholesale market of the proper good	Distance of the market from Sherghati in Km.	% of the proper good purchase by the particular market to the total no. of this proper good	% of this proper good purchased by this particular market to the total no. of commodities sold in Sherghati market	Means of communication	Principal amount uaually invested in this proper business by each trader	Usual Profit in % earned by each trader
1.	Durabla goods	47.10	Cloths	6.52	13.84	Gaya	32	77.77	5.08	Roadways	Rs. 20,000 to 3,00,000	20 to 26%
						Indore	1318					
						Nagpur	1286			Roadways		
						Gwalior	867	16.66	1.08	(Truck) or		
						Patna	124			Railways		
						Ranchi	212					
						Sherghati		5.55	0.36	Rickshaw		
			Readymade garments	5.07	10.76	Gaya	32	28.57	1.46	Roadways	Rs. 10,000 to 50,000	15 to 30%
						Calcutta	490	57.14	2.89	Roadways		
						Sherghati		14.28	0.72	Rickshaw		

1	2	3	4	5	6	7	8	9	10	11	12	13
			Manihari	2.53	5.38	Gaya	32	57.14	1.44	Roadways (Bus, taxi)	Rs. 5,000 to 15,000	20 to 25%
						Dheri-on-Sone	70	14.28	0.33	,,		
						Sherghati		28.57	0.76	Rickshaw		
			Timber	1.81	3.84	Gaya	32	80.00	1.35	Roadways (Truck)	Rs. 5,000 to 40,000	45 to 50%
						neighbouring villages and surrounding areas.	within a radious of 25.Km.	20.00	0.46	Rickshaw thela		
						Hunterganj	27	50.00	0.33	Roadways	Rs. 10,000 to 30,000	30 to 45%
			Cori-rope hand made basket, earthern pots etc.	0.77	1.95	Gaya	32	20.00	0.17	,,		
						Surround-ing areas	within a radious of 8 Km.	30.00	0.27	Head load Rickshaw		
2.	Ubiquitious goods	3.62	Betel, Bidi, Tobacco etc.	3.62	100.00	Gaya	32	30.00	1.08	Roadways (Bus)	Rs. 15,000 to 1,50,000	15 to 30%
						Muzaffarpur	341	60.00	2.24	Roadways (Truck)		
						Sherghati		10.00	0.29	Rickshaw		
3.	Vegetables & Fruits	0.72	Vegetable & fruits	0.72	100.00	Gaya	32	20.00	0.14	Roadways (Bus)	Rs. 500 to 1,000	10 to 20%
						Surrounding areas of Sherghati	within a radious 5 Km.	80.00	0.58	Rickshaw		
4.	Non-vegetarian foods	1.81	egg, chicken meat.	1.81	100.00	Gaya	32	40.00	0.73	Roadways	Rs. 1,000 to 3,000	20to 40%
						Sherghati		60.00	1.08	Padestal		

1	2	3	4	5	6	7	8	9	10	11	12	13
5.	Agricultural Inputs	1.44	Seeds, fertilizer, pesticides etc.	1.44	100.00	Gaya	32	100.00	1.44	Roadways	Rs. 10,000 to 30,000	15 tp 27%
6.	Food-stuff	11.95	Shops of cook-ed Baked food	11.95	100.00	Sherghati		100.00	11.95	Rickshaw	Rs. 1,500 to 5,000	30 to 50%
7.	Special goods	7.97	Medicine, Alcholic liquor and herbs used for medical purpose.	7.97	100.00	Gaya	32	77.27	6.16	Roadways (Bus, truck)	Rs. 20,000 to 1,00,000	25 to 30%
						Sherghati		22.73	1.81	Rickshaw & cycle		
8.	Animals		-	-	-	-	-	-	-	-	Rs. 1,000 to 20,000	20 to 60%
9.	Services	8.33	Studio, cobbler, tailor, etc.	8.33	100.00	Sherghati		86.95	7.21	Padestal, cycle, Rickshaw	Rs. 2,000 to 30,000	30 to 100%
						Gaya	32	13.05	1.12	Bus		
10.	Machinary	10.50	All types of Machines, electrical, equipments, electronic goods etc.	10.50	100.00	Gaya	32	62.06	6.52	Roadways Railways	Rs. 5,000 to 1,00,000	20 to 50%
						Calcutta	490	6.89	0.73	Railways		
						Dehri-on-Sone	70	10.34	1.02	Roadways		
						Patna	124	3.44	0.40	”		
						Sherghati		17.27	1.83	Cycle, Rick-shaw		
11.	**Others**	6.52	Gold, Silver and other	1.10	16.66	Gaya	32	66.67	0.73	Bus,Taxi	Rs. 20,000 to 70,000	40 to 50%
						Aurangabad	50	33.33	0.35	Bus, Taxi		
			Hardware	3.26	50.00	Gaya	32	100.00	3.26	Truck	Rs. 10,000 to 50,000	40.45%
			Cement	2.17	33.34	Japala	136	32.41	0.60	Truck	Rs. 25,000 to 70,000	25 to 60%
						Mannihar	564	17.51	0.44	”		
						Gaya	32	33.36	0.73	”		
						Sherghati		16.72	0.37	Rickshaw		

1	2	3	4	5	6	7	8	9	10	11	12	13
			Foot-wears	2.89	6.15	Gaya	32	75.00	2.17	Bus	Rs. 2,000 to 10,000	About 200%
						Kanpur	582	13.00	0.38	Railways		
						Sharghati (leather purchasing for the making of footwears)		12.00	0.34	Padestal		
			Utensils	2.53	5.38	Gaya	32	100.00	2.53	Roadways (Bus or truck)	Rs. 10,000 to 80,000	30%
			General Stores, Book Depot & Stationary	4.34	9.23	Gaya	32	75.00	3.26	Roadways (Bus, truck)	Rs. 3,000 to 50,000	15 to 30%
						Patna	124	8.34	0.36			
						Sherghati		16.66	0.72	Rickshaw		
			Kirana	10.86	23.07	Gaya	32	46.66	5.07	Roadways (Bus, truck)	Rs. 5,000 to 50,000	16 to 20%
						Dehri-on-Sone	70	10.00	1.08	" "		
						Sherghati		43.34	4.71	Rickshaw		
			Food-Grains	9.18	20.76	Gaya	32	22.22	2.17	Roadways (Bus, truck)	Rs. 5,000 to 1,50,000	10 to 35%
						Dehri-on-Sone	70	33.33	3.26			
						Sherghati		25.92	2.53	Rickshaw or Bullock cart		
						neighbouring villages	within a radious of 25 Km.	18.51	1.82	" "		

of the total traders engaged in this business 75% foot wears traders depend upon Gaya for their wholesale purchasing, 13% traders go to Kanpur for leather footwears and 12% traders buy leather and use to make foot-wears themselves. This type of traders generally invest Rs.5,000/- in their business and get an attractive profit. People of rural areas mostly prefer rubbr or P.V.C. foot-wears simply because these are cheap and wearable in all seasons and every where. There are some factories of this type foot-wears manufacturing at Gaya or wholesale agency of this type foot-wears of other outside companies at Gaya.

Traders use bus, taxi or truck for their communication to Gaya and train from here for Kanpur.

There is no shope of international foot-wears maker 'Bata' here. However we see some shops of B.S.C and other companies.

(iv) *Utensils*. This is an important item of any market. In Sherghati market 2.53% are traders of utensils of alluminium, stainless steel, bronze and other metals. Utensils traders invest in this business between Rs. 10,000/- to Rs. 80,000/- and get a profit of about 30%.

There are some factories of alluminium and stainless steel and other metal's utensils in Gaya and has agencies of reputed firms at Gaya. Hence the traders buy utensils from Gaya only in wholesale purchasing. Means of Communication is bus, texi or truck.

(v) *General Stores, Book Depot and Stationery*. In Sherghati market 4.34% shops are of general stores, Book depot or Stationery shops. Most of the general stores sale loose papers, copy, pen, ink etc. Booksellers also sale stationery items. Traders of this business invest between Rs. 3,000/- to Rs. 50,000/- and get a profit between 15% to 30%. Most of the stationery items are sold in Sherghati market. Regarding books we find that book shops only sale text books of Schools and Colleges. We do not get a wide range of books here. However we get book stall at the bus stop and in the market which sale some Hindi novel, magazines and papers. In this business 75% of the traders depend upon Gaya for their wholesale purchasing, 16.66% buy their goods from the local market of Sherghati and rest 8.34% traders go to Patna for wholesale purchasing and are mainly book sellers. From Gaya they go to Patna by train.

(vi) *Kirana*. In Sherghati market 10.86% shops are kirana shops. Kirana shops sale food grains, pulses, spices, salt, oil, vanaspati, flour, soaps, detergent powder, tooth paste and brush and many items of general stores and stationery. Traders of this class invest between Rs. 5000/- to Rs. 50,000/- on this business and get a profit between 16% to 20%.

About 46.66% of traders of kirana shops depend upon Gaya market for their wholesale purchasing, 10% depend upon the market of Dehri-on-Sone and rest 43.34% depend on the local market of Sherghati itself. This 43.34% traders are mostly retailors and some go to Dehri or Gaya for their purchasing but their number is very low. Traders use truck, bus or taxi as means of communication.

(vii) *Food Grains*. Sherghati market has the 9.77% traders of food grains. They are usually retail sellers of food grains who purchases food grains in wholesale. Traders of this business invest between Rs. 5,000/- to Rs. 1,50,000/-. Some traders use to sale kirana items also in their shop along with food grains. The traders get a profit of 10% to 35% but the big wholesale traders earn a profit of 30% to 35%.

About 33.33% of traders buy food grains straight from Dehri-on-Sone mandi across the river Son in Rohtas district. Sherghati and Dehri-on-Sone both are situated on the N.H. No. 2 and distance between them is about 70 Km. Rohtas district is a much fertile district with good lands and irrigation facilities and products a good amount of food grains in the state. So traders get food grains on cheap rates. 25.92% traders depend for their wholesale purchasing on the local market (Gola Bazar) of Sherghati, 22.22% traders prefer Gaya market for their wholesale purchasing and 18.51% of traders depend for their wholesale buy on the villages of surrounding areas of Sherghati. Means of communication are trucks, tractors, bullockcarts and thela.

(viii) *Manihar*. In Sherghati market 2.53% shops are Manihari shops. Manihari shops sale bangles, glass, comb, tikuli sindur, threads, sindur pots or kia and cosmetics items etc. Traders of this particular business invest between Rs. 5,000/- to Rs. 15,000/- and get a profit of 20% to 25%.

For the wholesale purchasing the traders obtain their goods from the following market - 57.14% traders go to Gaya market,

28.57% traders get it in the local market of Sherghati, 14.28% traders depend upon the market of Dehri-on-Sone.

Means of communication is bus, taxi, and rickshaw for local communication.

(ix) *Timber*. In Sherghati 1.81% of shops are timber or furniture shops who bring furniture items from Gaya and their percentage is 80% and rest 20% traders who are carpenters and also make furniture of the wood either they get from surrounding villages and forests or the local market of Sherghati. The traders of this class invest between Rs. 5,000/- to Rs. 40,000/- and get a profit of 45% to 50%. Means of communication is truck, tractor, bullock carts etc.

(x) *Coir-rope, Handmade Baskets, Earthen Pots etc*.: Sherghati market has 0.77% of this class shops. Traders invest in this business between Rs. 10,000/- to Rs. 30,000/- and get a profit of 30% to 45%.

The main supplier of handmade baskets in Sherghati market is Hunterganj which is about 25 Km. from Sherghati and it supply about 50% of goods. Gaya market supply 20% of goods and rest 30% is supplied by local workers or by surrounding villages.

The means of communication are truck, bus, taxi, tractors, rickshaw, thelas, headloads etc.

(2) Ubiquitious Goods

Tobacco, bidi, betel and some drinks form this category. In Sherghati 3.62% shops are the shops of ubiquitious goods. The traders of this business invest between Rs. 15,000/- to Rs. 1,50,000/- and get a profit of 15% to 30%.

The wholesale purchasing of tobacco is done at Muzaffarpur which is about 200 Km. Betels leaves etc. are purchased from Gaya market and some from local market of Sherghati. Tendu leaves for making bidi is obtained from Gaya and the local markets. Usually betel traders invest Rs. 5,000/- to Rs. 30,000/- and the profit is 25% to 30%.

Means of communication is truck, train, bus, taxi and thela.

(3) Vegetables and Fruits

In Sherghati we rarely find permanent shops of vegetables and fruits. Only 0.72% shops of Sherghati market occupy this category.

The traders of this business invest between Rs. 500/- to Rs. 1,000/ and get a profit of 10% to 20%.

Fruits are obtained largely from Gaya market along with some vegetables. Vegetables are supplied mostly by the vegetables cultivators of surrounding areas.

The means of communication is truck, bus, taxi, bullockcart, headloads etc.

(4) Non-Vegetarian Foods

Sherghai market has 1.81% of non-vegetarian shops who sale mutton, chickens, eggs and fishes. Out of these shops 60% sale mostly mutton and fish in little quantity and 40% sale chicknes and eggs. The traders of this business invest between Rs. 1,000/- to Rs. 3,000/- and get a profit of 20% to 40%.

Mutton sellers buy goats from Sherghati weekly animal market and surrounding villages. Some fishes, chickens and eggs are purchased from Gaya market.

Means of communication is truck, bus, taxi, thela etc.

(5) Agricultural Inputs

In Sherghati market 1.44% traders are engaged in the business of agricultural inputs. These shops sale seeds, fertilizers and pesticides etc.

The traders of this class invest between Rs. 10,000/- to Rs. 30,000/- and get a profit of 15% to 27%.

For fertilizers and pesticides they mainly depend on the market of Gaya. For seeds they partially depend on Gaya but local farmers also supply seeds.

The means of communication is truck, bus, taxi, tractors etc.

(6) Food Stuff

These type of shops sale baked and cooked foods in the shape of hotels or restaurants. They provide their consumers cooked food snacks, sweets, hot or cold drink, biscuits etc. One hotel has lodging and fooding facility both. It is bigger and has two storied building.

Usually businessman of this class invest between Rs. 1.500/- to Rs. 5,000/- and get a profit of 30% to 50%.

All the businessmen of this category depend mainly for their raw materials on Sherghati market.

(7) Special Goods

This class include medicines, alcholic liquour and herbs used for medical purposes. In Sherghati 7.97% of traders are engaged in the business of these commodities.

The traders in invest between Rs. 20,000/- to Rs. 1,00,000/- and get a profit of 25% to 30%

For wholesale purchasing 77.27% traders depend on Gaya market and rest 22.73% is an indirect supply and actually 100% is supplied by the Gaya market.

The means of communication is truck, bus, taxi, rickshaw etc.

(8) Animals

Actually there is to specified permanent shop in the Sherghati market for animals selling but it take place in the weekly animal market on Monday at Sherghati. Usually traders of animals invest between Rs. 1,00/- to Rs. 20,000/- and get profit according to time and place which vary between 20% to 60%.

(9) Services

This type of shops are the shops of persons who render their services such as Photo Studio, tailors, cobblers, radio, T.V., saloon, photostat, watch repairers etc. In Sherghati there are 8.33% shops are of this category.

The businessmen of this class invest between Rs. 2,000/- to Rs. 30,000/- and get profit between 30% to 100% according to time and consumers.

The businessmen of this category mainly depend on the market of Gaya and partially on Sherghati market for the goods of their requirement.

The means of communication is bus, taxi, reckshaw etc.

(10) Machinery

This includes machines of all types, electrical equipment, motor parts, spares, electronic goods etc. In Sherghati 10.50% shops form this category.

Traders invest between Rs. 5,000/- to Rs. 1,00,00/- and get a profit between 20% to 50%.

The traders make 62.06% of wholesale purchasing at Gaya followed by Sherghati local market 17.27%, Dehri-on-Sone 10.34% Calcutta 6.89% and Patna 3.44%.

Means of communication is mainly roadways by truck, bus, taxi, rickshaw and railways for Calcutta.

(11) Others

(i) Silver, Gold and Other Valuables

In Sherghati market 6.52% shops are of this class who deal in Silver, gold and other valuables in the shape of ornaments and stones etc.

Businessmen of this class invest Rs. 20,000/- to Rs. 70,000/- on this business and get a profit of 40% to 50%.

Traders depend for their requirements on Gaya (66.67%) and Aurangabad (33.33%) markets.

Means of communication is Bus, taxi etc.

(ii) Hardware

In Sherghati 3.26% shops are of hardware items who sale paints also. Traders invest between Rs. 10,000/- to Rs. 50,000/- in this business and get a profit of 40% to 45%.

Traders of this class mainly depend on the market of Gaya for their wholesale purchaing and means of communication is either truck, bus or taxi.

(iii) Cement

Shergahti market has 2.17% shops of cement and traders invest between Rs. 25,000/- to Rs. 70,000/- and get a profit between 25% to 60%. Traders who buy in wholesale directly form factory of Japla and Manihar earn 60% profit and traders who get it from Gaya or Sherghati market get profit of 25% only.

Means of communication are truck, tractors, bullockarts etc. In the table no. 4.16 apart from the things analysed in preceding pages there are facts also regarding percentage of shops of the proper goods to the total shops of commodities type in the market (column 6), percentage of the proper good purchased by the particular market to the total no. of commodities sold in Sherghati market (column 7-D) etc.

4.14 SPACE PREFERENCES

The behavioural aspects of market place participants may be further amplified through the analysis of their space preference.

Taking consumer space preference at first a general overlapping in observed in the Aurangabad and Jehanabad districts. It is observed that the bigger markets command larger areas then the small markets. For example Daudnagar market in Aurangabad district and Arwal market in

Jehanabad district command larger areas. This shows that the size of market centres and consumers's space preferences are generally correlated. However local exceptions may also be there.

An important aspect is the inter-district participation of consumers outside division. Market lying in Rohtas district such as Dehri-on-Sone and some markets in Patna district drawn consumers from these areas.

A nesting of market area is discerned in the Magadh Division. The market areas of Bisiat, Maksaur, Sonar Majhgawn, Sirdala, Taukatnar, Rajauli, Amawan, Targir, Laun and Parona in Nawada district encompass market areas of small market centres around them. Such examples are also observed in the Jehanabad district in the case of Mau and Dharampur market areas. It may be hypothesised that the nesting pattern of central places is observed in case of market centres which are towns or town areas.

Attention may be drawn to the overlapping nature of space preferences. It is observed in the case of market areas of Haspura, Jakhaura, Ahiyapur, Bihta and Sihrikalan in Aurangabad district. It shows that inter-market compttition still persists and the process of evolution continues. Overlapping of market areas is an evidence of competition among the market centres concerned. This phenomena indicates a zone around the existing market centres in which consumers are in a state of indecision in selecting a market centre in that zone. Alternatively a new market day may also be initiated. The initiation of an additional market day at Amawan is one such example. An earlier statement is thus confirmed.

The case of trader's space preference is altogeher different. Traders travel longer distances. It is true in all the four districts of the Magadh Division. Several sub-sets of trader circuits may be discerned. For example east to west. Targir-Nawada, Amawan-Ranchi, Kinjar-Patna, Sherghati-Calcutta, Khemda-Varanasi etc. The hypothesis of sub-sets of trader circuits within the universe of market centres may thus be established and made open for further verification.

An intra-region thader participation was also observed. Where ever transport allows, traders from beyond the region visit the markets of Magadh Division. In the southern part of the division unbridge rivers and poor transport impede such movement.

Bigger markets draw traders from longer distance and vise-versa. It is obvious from the observation of some small markets.

4.15 ASSESSMENT

The dominant factor which seems to control space preferences is transport. We find that space preference lines are oriented along the major transport axes. It is true to the two national highway (no. 2 and 31) other roads and Grand Chord railway line and Gaya-Patna and Gaya-Kiul railway lines of the Magadh division. The hypothesis that transport routes played a role in the process of evolution of settlement is confirmed.

Some districts of the Magadh division suffers from the disadvantage of overlapping of market area regions. May be that in appropriate market locations on a wrong choice of market days in causing this phenomenon and a rescheduling of markets is called for. In the southern part in Gaya district spatial gaps among areas served by markets are noted. There are potential areas where new market centres may be developed or additional market days organized.

The study of behavioural aspects of rural markets and rurban centre thus reveals that the interplay of many socio-politico cultural factors are still involved in the process of marketing. Consumer behaviour is guided by socio-cultural and economic factors both. Economic rationality is yet to dominate consumer choices.

REFERENCES

1. Losch, A. (1954) : The Economics of Location, Translated by W.H. Woglom and W.F. Stopler, Yale University Press.
2. Isard, W. (1956) : Location and Space Economy, New York.
3. Christaller, W. (1966) : Central Places in Southern Germany, Translated by C.W. Baskin, Printice Hall.
4. Ullman, E.L. (1956) : The Role of Transportation and the Bases for Interaction, in W.L. Thomas (ed)., Man's Role in Changing the face of the Earth, pp. 862-80.
5. Reilly, W.J. (1969) : Methods of the Study of Retail Relationship, Bureau of Business Research, The University of Taxas, Austin, (Reprint of Research Monograph No. 4.)
6. Shrivastava, V.K. (1978) : Theoretical Norms and Interpretations of Market Place Participant's Spatial Behaviour, National Geographer, XIII, pp. 117-24.
7. Shrivastava, V.K. and V. Nath (1981) : Rural Marketing and Social Structure in North India: A Case Study, Proceedings International Conference on Urbanization and Regional change in Developing Countries, Kharagpur.
8. Murdie, R.A. (1965) : Cultural Differences in Consumer Travel, Economic Geography, 41, pp. 211-33.

9. Shrivastava, K.R. (1983) : Periodic Markets and Central Places in Baghelkhand Region of Madhya Pradesh, Ph. D. Thesis accepted by Rani Durgawati Vishwa Vidyalaya, Jabalpur (Unpublished).
10. Shrivastava, V.K. (1978) : Opt. cit.
11. Pred, A. (1978) : Behaviour and Location, Lund Studies in Geography, Series B, Human Geography, No. 27.
12. Shrivastava, K.R. (1983) : Opt. cit.
13. Cox Kevin (1972) : Man, Location and Behaviour, John Willey and Sons, Inc., New York.
14. Brinkmann, T. (1935) : The Economics of the Farm Business, Berkeley, (Translation with Introduction and Notes by E.T. Benedict, Stippler, H.H. and M.R. Benedict).
15. Huff, D.L. (1960) : A Topographical Model of Consumer Space Preferences, Paper and Proceedings of the Regional Science Association, 6, pp. 159-73.
16. Bourne, L.S. (1973) : Comments on Behavioural Approaches in Geography, in John Rees and Peter Newby (eds.), Behavioural Perspectives in Geography, Middlesex Polytechnic, Monographs in Geography, No. 1, London.
17. Good, C.M. (1975) : Periodic Markets and Travelling Traders in Uganda, The Geographical Review, pp. 50-72.
18. Shrivastava, V.K. (1979) : Agricultural Marketing in Uttar Pradesh in Noor Mhod. (ed.), Perspectives in Agricultural Geography, Vol. III, New Delhi.

5

Analysis of Rurban Centres

5.1 NATURE AND DEVELOPMENT OF RURBAN CENTRES

Large rural settlements and small towns compose rurban centres. On such centres, the concentration of service facilities for neighbouring hinterland and business proficiency are of great significance as they serve as levers of regional development. The concept of rurban centres is a new ramification in settlement Geography, where physical landscape is mostly set in a right direction by social behaviour[1] and cultural landscape of the society. Economic prosperity plays an important role in the evolution of rurban centres. Such small town or small city is essentially equivalent to what Brush has included in his three fold classification of hamlets, villages and towns.[2] The study of rurban centres is of academic interest because it represents the lower and of central place continum. Any generalizations, theories, or laws developed for central place should hold good not for large urban places but also for all the hierarchic levels including rurban centres.

Rurban centres[3] have been variously described as 'rurban settlements' by R.L. Singh,[4] 'rurban community' by Galpin,[5] 'urban villages' by Dickinson[6] and 'sub towns' by Smailes.[7] Recent geographic literatures contain some studies of rurban centres.[8] Among the commandable ones are Berry and Garrison's Snohomish, Country, Washington studies,[9] King's comparative study of the Conterbury Provincial District, New-Zealand,[10] and Thomas's study of the functional bases for small Iowa towns.[11]

Monkhouse has used the term 'rurban' similar to that of 'rural-urban fringe' and 'rural-urban continum', but this is misuse of the term 'rurban'. Rurban centre is a small urban centre or larger overgrown village having some importance of secondary and tertiary functions. On the other hand, rural urban fringe is 'a zone of transition around a town in which urban functions, landuse and other activities are intermingled with agricultural-one's. This zone separates the area exclusively devoted to urban uses from that exclusively devoted to agricultural uses.[12]

The rurban centres have distinctive feature of their own. Most of the smaller centres are overgrown villages and still retain their rural character. They show a combination of economic, social and educational functions.[13] Most of the towns have a city region around them, the small towns function as the economic and social capitals of their surrounding essentially agricultural areas. By virtue of its intermediate location and the nature of evolution, the small town has certain advantages and offers unique opportunities in the general scheme of rural-urban and agricultural industrial continum.[14] Hence the study of smaller urban settlement is highly important as they represent the basic connection between the dispersed agricultural population and the agglomerated urban population.[15]

There are several characteristic features which separate rurban centres from the list of rural settlements and urban centres as they are urban islands in the vast sea of rurality.[16] The overwhelming growth of population, laissez faire growth of rural service centres and inadequacy of service facilities in rural areas are highly in need of rurban centres study. The problem of social disorder in rurban centres necessitates the need for planning and at present this should be in the forefront of research in Geography as this provides the levers of regional development and planning.

Rurban centres may be a commercial, administrative, transportational, industrial or religious node, but their locational force has telling effects on the surrounding zone of influence for maintaining the 'ecological balance'. In general within settlements, the aim of balanced development is equally critical. The aim is the combining and common services that are still to be found in provincial cities and 'urban villages'. Such intermediate urban centres for marketing, co-operatives, services and industries serving agriculture must be strengthened. Dispersed and disolate rural settlements need to be brought together. Such a policy offers some hope of lessening the pressure of large scale migrations out of agriculture directly into the biggest cities. This may also provide alternative settlement system designed to achieve more balanced regional development.

Rurban units are characterised by the development of certain significant urban functions. In fact, they are foci of a number of market villages. Such centres often have significant retail and wholesale marketing facilities. Post and telegraph facilities, market, a dispensary, a veterinary hospital, rural professional services, a junior high or high school and community block development offices are other characteristic functional units found in them. Sometimes these centres are trade centres for the neighbouring rural area, or administrative centres due to their being the headquarters of the local administration. On account of their district commercial, cultural and administrative elements, such units are characterized by a greater number and variety of services which are rarely present in a village. Many other functions are attracted to such centres by virtue of their being the seat of local administration.

Many services are found rarely in rural areas, such as cinemas, hospitals, libraries etc. These are today available only in towns, as they are too costly to be operated in open country locations or in very small towns. Some of these services may be located in the country at the margins of a town but this is basically a town location for all practical purposes. Transportation with the help of bus service and the metalled road have greatly lifted the horizones of rural families as far as the accessibility to these services is concerned, yet costs in time and in money are still prohibitive. As a result, most rural families use less of these services than they would, if they lived in a town and belonged to the same income group.

Rurban centres are special types of towns based on services of those involving governmental services of all kinds. Federal and state agencies of various kinds have their offices in rurban centres often in the 'country-seat town'. These include the Block Development offices and the circle offices of the government. The former will have occasion to visit such office as part of his business operations, and to a greater extent the rural family will visit them for various aspects of family living. 'Thus the small towns are quite often seen as the 'bridge' between the urban and rural universe, as the kind of settlement which can offer the best, and none of the worst of both worlds'. Obviously a study of rurban centres would form as much a necessary part of rural settlement Geography, as the study of the larger villages themselves.

The city level centres have distinct advantages over rurban centres in industrial development. But it is difficult, if not impossible to carry out a systematic review of the role of small towns. Although one might conceive of industrialization of the country mainly through large cities, undoubtedly rurban centres, would play an important part in providing the levers of development as well as ancillary services, such as educational and health facilities which are essential for economic growth.

In the hinterland of a rurban centre, the thorough fares of most of the rural settlements have been oriented towards it. This is due to the intimate business and consumer relationship of that market with the surrounding rural settlements. This may be generalized into a law for the location of rural settlements and rurban communities. In this way, the location of a rurban centre guides not only the location of rural settlements but also their transport linkages. This is a new tool with the geographers to study the 'law of rural settlement morphology and rurban centres location'.

5.2 RURBAN CENTRES : A REVIEW OF SOCIAL CHANGES

It is useful to make an inventory of the functions of rurban centres of various types in different locations so that their implications for planned economic development could be reviewed. Two of the functions, actual and potential of the rurban centres are particularly significant. First, rurban centres can act as channels for mobilizing servings and skills which are not available or not easily tapped in large towns. These might be the places, where some portions of income derived from agriculture are invested in industrial establishments such as house hold industry or small and medium scale units. Secondly, rurban centres might also in certain circumstances, be especially suitable as centres of formal education and specialized medical services. Rurban centres may be:

(i) Religious, transportation and administrative towns;

(ii) New industrial or power project towns, such as Barauni and Bokaro Thermal Plant.

(iii) Regional or sub-regional centres of services like school, college, hospital, etc.

(iv) Agricultural market towns or wholesale and retail trade centres, and

(v) Existing small towns in the vicinity of large cities.

These and other types or rurban centres can fullfil specific functions in economic development. Their costs of providing services and maintaining overheads are relatively small. They thus offer several advantages over the larger towns for country uplift. They perform useful functions and have obvious potentialities of growth of community development schemes area at times more effectively carried out in rurban centres than in larger towns. About the social structure of rurban centres we can say that the secondary school age group is the largest component among migrants into rurban centres. On the other hand, the age group of 34 and above show a net migration from rurban centres. Similar trends have been observed in Indonesia and the Philippines,[17] where too, the educational centres draw yound people away from the rural areas.

In such centres the occupational structures are certainly varies. Agriculture is invariably the major source of livelihood in a village but it may be negligible in rurban centres. This difference, however, is not necessarily reflected in the social structure. In the rurban centres of Bihar plain nearly 80% of the people live in areas occupied largely by their own caste or religious groups. The urban character of the settlement has not removed the cultural walls between the groups, instead the urban housing pattern has been modelled up on rural costomes and traditions. The study has revealed that rurban centres do not very much differ from villages in terms of the proportion of joint households and of various types of the kinship units. Moreover, the migrants always move to the quasi rural areas of the town, and thus from strong rural pockets in the urban landscape.

There are several parameters which act as 'carriers and barriers' of rurban centre development, but population migration from rural settlement to rurban centres and the orientation of main thorough fares of rural communities towards the nearest rurban centres are some of the forces which have highly contributed to the growth and development of rurban communities.

The development of rurban in a region has been dependent upon minor points of focus that initially were not associated with retail trade. Cross roads, flour mills, post-offices, railway stations and police stations were there which provided a meeting place for the peasants. Enterprising businessmen took advantages of these facilities to open retail shops at such centres. This, in turn, led to the establishment of grain collecting centres, electric lines, telephones and other similar facilities, and the combination of these elements led to the greater concentration at some of the places, while competition between the growing centres created the hierarchy of rurban communities.

The smallest rurban community is a rural settlement with basic public utility services such as an allopathic doctor, middle school, post-office and a metalled road connection. Rural settlements of this category are closely spaced and may or may not have a retail marketing centre. They do, however, have a weekly or biweekly market known as a hat or bazar.

Rurban centres, generally, provide services like a high school, telegraph office, dispensary, retail market, block development office and a bus stop or a railway station. Such centres are located on the main transport routes between bigger urban centres and are, therefore, interspersed between towns and tiny rural settlements.

Further development of these facilities and the addition of a telephone exchange, bank, cinema, wholesale market, etc. led to the final growth of rurban centres. Rural settlements which have grown into rurban centres are potential towns. A rise in their population coupled with population segregation in land utilization and increase in employment of tertiary services would make them eligible for classification as towns. Evolution and spacing of rurban centres location for a particular period of time and space largely depend on economic property and transport facilities. In the system of rurban centres two sets of variables have deterministic influence on the proper functioning of the centre. The first set of variables includes those having predominance in rural areas and operate through larger village controlling the setellite hamlets. The nearness of smaller villages to larger village or rurban centre attracts a large number of visitors. The higher density of population provides the market for local produce, while a lack of population in sphere of influence always restricts the development of any rurban centre. The second aspect in rural areas is that of topographic condition of the region. Highlands with stony Wabtes prevent the development of rurban centres, riverine productive plains become conducive to their development while lowlands liable to flood abstract the movement of transport vehicles. The third group is that of soil characteristic, economic situation and social and cultural factors each of which have impact upon the development of the centre.

On the urban side three tertiary functions are important for regulating the rurban system. The number of shops, types of shops, utility services and other tertiary services are the main activities of the rurban centre. The other group of factors are nodes of transport. The centre may be located on the roadside, railway side. It may have a riverine location while in some cases three variables may converge at a particular centre and give added impetus to all functions of the rurban system. Still another set of factors is wholesale market control. This regulates the capital investment and is incentive provided to the businessmen. They together determine the market turnover and in return determine the hierarchy of the rurban centre.

When all these factors assemble at one place they give rise to a central place system. Here the decision about the production, distribution and consumption of good is taken through the system of exchange, the process of distribution, the supplies, from producers and the demand of the consumers. Thus a centre is created where the social, economic and cultural functions are performed for the surrounding hinterland. When this centre ranks between the purely urban and the rural sectors, it forms part of the rurban group. Further, development of this system leads to the development of major trade and urban centres as well as subdivisional and district administrative headquarters. Again these three together hope in the development and proper functioning of city level centres reaching ultimately to the regional capital (*Fig. No. 5.1*). This indicates that rurban centre is part and parcel of central place system as envisaged by Christaller and Losch.

5.3 METHOD FOR WEIGHTING AND CLASSIFICATION OF RURBAN CENTRES

For this purpose the Magadh Division has been considered as a region, where the location of large rural settlements and small towns function as the rurban centres. A rurban centre is essentially a local focus of activities and is a marked by commercial, industrial, administrative and cultural institutions. It is, however, difficult to differentiate on functional basis between the large village and the smaller town, and a combined list of criteria has to be developed. The measurement of functional indices, particularly in a developing region much as Magadh Division, must be based on the variety and type of nodel functions other than those available in most of the villages. The nodel functions considered in this study have, therefore, been classified by giving adequate weightage as revealed by the Table No. 5.1.

Centres having at least three nodal functions given in the below table no. 5.1 have been considered rurban centres. Classification of rurban centres on the above basis from the list of villages is easy. But as problem arises in the selection of rurban centres from the list of towns. Both the towns and cities have functions of a higher order as compared to the rural, which creates confusion. Thus for the selection of rurban centres from the list of towns, the following method was employed.

$$RI = Pc \times \frac{tw \times 100}{TW}$$

where RI = Rurban Index

Pc = Total population of the centre

tw = Workers engaged in tertiary occupations in the centre, and

TW = Total number of workers in that centre.

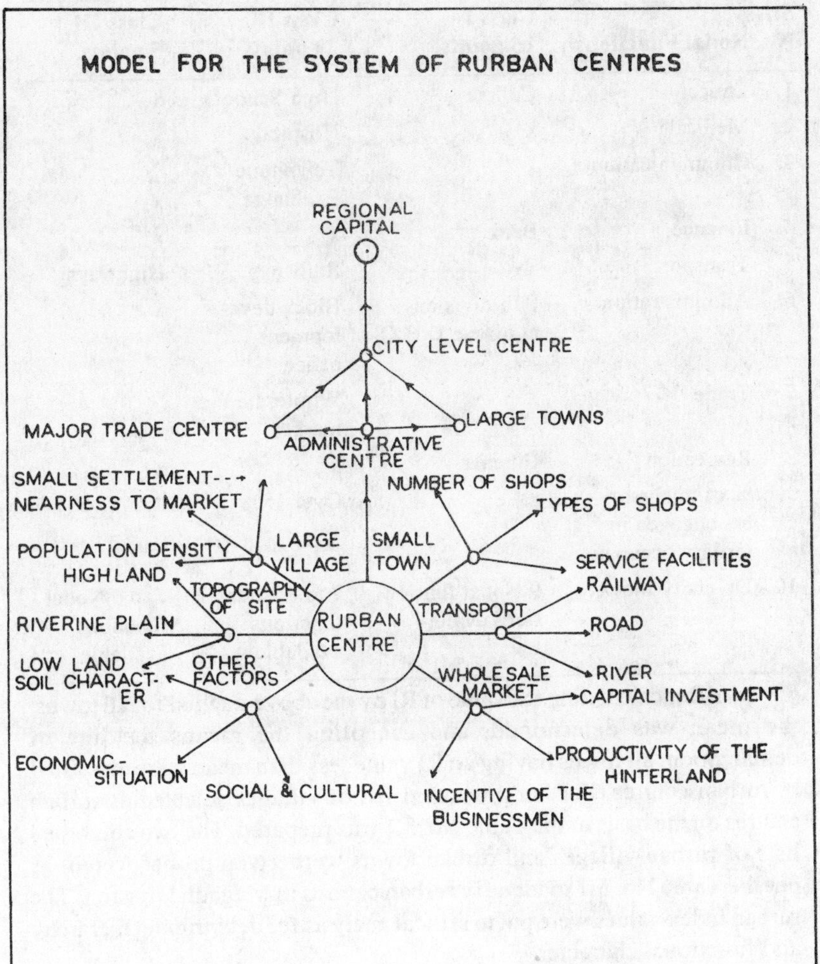
MODEL FOR THE SYSTEM OF RURBAN CENTRES
REGIONAL CAPITAL
CITY LEVEL CENTRE
MAJOR TRADE CENTRE
LARGE TOWNS
ADMINISTRATIVE CENTRE
SMALL SETTLEMENT---
NEARNESS TO MARKET
NUMBER OF SHOPS
TYPES OF SHOPS
POPULATION DENSITY
LARGE VILLAGE
SMALL TOWN
SERVICE FACILITIES
HIGHLAND
TOPOGRAPHY OF SITE
RAILWAY
RIVERINE PLAIN
RURBAN CENTRE
TRANSPORT
ROAD
LOW LAND
SOIL CHARACTER
OTHER FACTORS
WHOLE SALE MARKET
RIVER
CAPITAL INVESTMENT
ECONOMIC-SITUATION
SOCIAL & CULTURAL
INCENTIVE OF THE BUSINESSMEN
PRODUCTIVITY OF THE HINTERLAND
AFTER:- CHRISTALLER & LOSCH
FIG-5·1

Fig. 5.1

Table No. 5.1

Weighting and Classification of Rurban Centres for the Purpose of Obtaining Values of Rurban Index.

Sl. No.	Nodal Functions	Class I 15 points	Class II 20 points	Class III 5 points
1.	Education	Collete	High School	x
2.	Medical	x	Hospital	x
3.	Communication	x	Telephone Exchange	x
4.	Finance	Bank	x	x
5.	Transport	x	Railways	Highways
6.	Administration	Sub-divisional office, D.H.Q.	Block development office	x
7.	Trade	x	Wholesale market	x
8.	Recreation	Cinema	x	x
9.	% of total workers engaged in tertiary occupations	x	Over 15%	25% to 50%
10.	Diversity Index	9 Nodal functions available	7 to 8 Nodal functions available	5 to 6 Nodal functions available

After calculating the value of RI by the above method for all towns, the mean was determined, and accepting the means the line of demarcation, all towns having an RI value less than mean were classified as rurban centres. Further a detailed list of villages selected as rurban centres on the basis of the Table No. 5.1 was prepared. The two combined lists of rurban villages and rurban towns were given proper weight as per the Table No. 5.1 to identify rurban centres in Magadh Division. The rurban index values were put to statical analysis for determining hierarchy and functional character.

5.4 FUNCTIONAL HIERARCHY OF RURBAN CENTRES

One great difficulty in determining the hierarchy of rurban centres in the region under study is lack of relevant data. The services are inadequately distributed, and hardly published material is available. The author has therefore, to depend upon the information contained in census of India 1981, and supplemented by fieldwork.

The R.I. (Rurban Index) values were found to range between 20 and 150, with mean at 52.93 and a standard deviation of 32.46 taking standard deviation as the factor of gradation four groups were recognised. The values were rounded off to the nearest multiple of 5 since the R.I. values increase in steps of 5 only.

These groups are as follows :

Group	R.I. Value	Description	No. of Rurban Centres
I	120 to 150	Above Mean - 2	3
II	90 to 115	Above Mean - 1	2
III	55 to 85	Above Mean -	13
IV	20 to 50	Below Mean -	

Thus out of 18 rurban centres, rest of centres have a value below mean, which may be said to be non-specialised, and, therefore, rural in character. Of the, 3 have a high R.I. value, 2 have a medium value and 13 have a low value. The detailed list is given below and all these 18 centres have been shown in *Fig. No. 5.2* :

R.I. Values of Rurban Centres

Group I : *Centres (R.I. value 150 to 120)*Aurangabad T, Jehanabad T, Nawada T.

Group II : *Centres (R.I. value 115 to 90)*Daudnagar T and Warisaliganj T.

Group III : *(R.I. Value 85 to 55)* Rafiganj T, Bodh-Gaya T, Nabinagar T, Arwal, Hisua T, Wazirganj, Tikari T, Sherghati T, Barun, Obra, Deo, Belaganj and Khizirsarai,

('T' denotes Town)

It is interesting to note that all centres in the first two groups are towns, that is, urban settlements. They are mostly not very large towns, but population is no criterion for determining the R.I. values. In the third group of 13 centres, 6 are towns and the rest are villages. It is these villages which have the highest potentiality of growing into towns, particularly if their population is high. The number of such rurban villages is large in areas where there are fewer towns.

Centres in the first group are district headquartes of administration because they have daily retail market, wholesale market, District Magistrate court for revenue and criminal cases, often a civil court, banks, telephone exchange, colleges cinema and goods transportation facilities which combine to place them in the highest rank. All these centres are

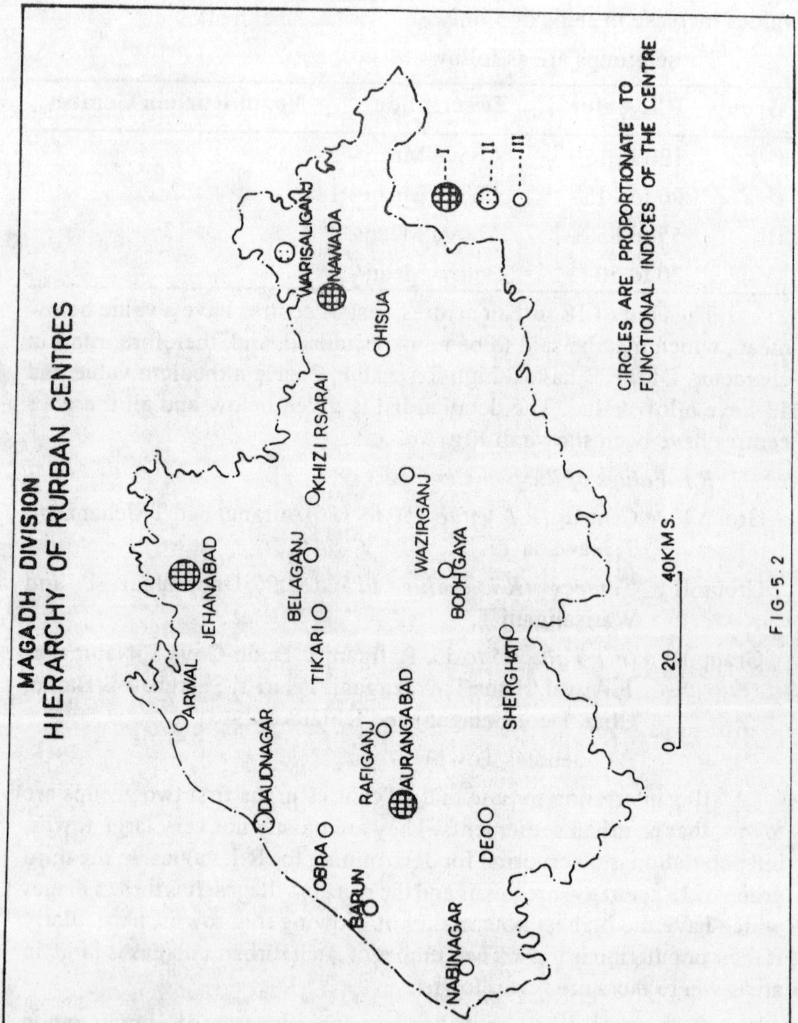
MAGADH DIVISION
HIERARCHY OF RURBAN CENTRES
ARWAL
JEHANABAD
DAUDNAGAR
OBRA
BARUN
NABINAGAR
DEO
RAFIGANJ
AURANGABAD
TIKARI
BELAGANJ
KHIZI RSARAI
WARISALIGANJ
NAWADA
OHISUA
WAZIRGANJ
BODHGAYA
SHERGHATI
I
II
III
CIRCLES ARE PROPORTIONATE TO
FUNCTIONAL INDICES OF THE CENTRE
0
20
40KMS.
FIG-5.2

Fig. 5.2

fullfledged towns with a higher percentage of workers engaged in tertiary functions, as compared to those in primary services. The centres of the highest order having RI values between 150 and 120 provide such basic amenities as education upto college stage, medical facilities, bus or railway transport, telephone exchange, wholesale market etc., but may not always possess, cinema and subdivisional court. Their population ranges from 10,000 to 45,000 and the employment in tertiary services is over 50% of total workers. There is usually a marked tendency for a distinct business core to develop in such centres which is conspicuous by its absence in the lower order centres, that is, in rural villages within the same population group.

The second group includes settlements in which the functional index ranges from 90 to 115. These centres generally have a population of 5,000 to 25,000. They have functions and services of the same type as found in the first group, though of a lower order. The occupational structure of the population also reveals that usually between 35% and 50% of the working force are employed in tertiary services. But the higher order centres of this group are distinguishable by greater nodality and a more pronounced urban character.

The centres of the third group with RI values above mean i.e., 55 to 85, are in number. They include 6 towns and 7 villages. Their population generally ranges from 2,000 to 20,000 and the employment in tertiary services is close to 25% of the total workers. These centres have been greatly benefited by development of transport and communication and thus have acquired the status of regional collecting and marketing centres. They however, lack in the services and functions of an urban centre, They occur in clusters around the larger cities. This effect is well marked in all cases and is discernible as a node in the overall fabric of rural settlements, though the percentage of non-agricultural population is not always high.

The centres below mean number, wherein the agriculture constitutes directly or indirectly the occupation of more than 75% of total workers. The centres of this category are large in size and diversified in nature but are mostly confined to primary activities.

It is distinct from the study that the Block Development Office, wholesale market, hospital and high school occur in close association with each other. These are the primary services available in rurban centres of even the lowest order. Road transport is available together with hospitals and high schools as most of the Block Development Offices today are linked with metalled roads. The correlation between these services ranges from + 0.92 to + 0.98.

The relationship between the distribution of highways and railways and that between railway station and telephone exchange are equally high and are close to 0.80. Services of a higher order such as banks, cinemas and colleges, however, show a low relationship with the services of the lower order. There is a high correlation between the distribution of banks and cinemas and that between cinemas and subdivisional courts. These are located usually in towns rather than in purely rural centres. This is also reflected by the high correlation co-efficient of 0.90 between tertiary workers and the distribution of colleges or subdivisional courts. The tertiary services however, have a very low correlation with the distribution of hospitals and high schools. Banks which have a high relationship with wholesale markets, show a low correlation with the distribution of high schools, hospitals and roads, the correlation coefficient in each of the above cases is less than 0.10.

It is apparent that there is a clear division between rurban centres of low order containing Block Development Office, hospitals, high school and wholesale market and those of the higher order containing subdivisional court, college, bank and high percentage of tertiary workers. The centres of the higher order contain most of the places mentioned in group I above, contain all services of the lower order. The area, therefore, is marked by greater diversity. This is apparent, when we consider that the correlation co-efficient between high school, Block Development Office, wholesale market and roads on the one hand and diversity index on the other hand is less than 0.10. Diversity index is highest where the percentage of tertiary workers is also high. This fully justifies the hierarchy groups suggested earlier.

5.5 SPACING OF RURBAN CENTRES

The spatial distribution of rurban centres depicts several aspects of geographical interest. Each centre possesses its own specific sphere of influence within which it dominates over the surrounding villages. The delimitation of actual configuration of each sphere of influence would entail a detailed study of consumer behaviour in the area which is outside the scope of this chapter. Nevertheless, certain generalization can be made from the pattern obtaining here.

Rurban centres are closely spaced in the Magadh Division. The spacing in kilometres is 27.88. The average population size of the centres is 8,883 (1981). This shows that the number and spacing of rurban centres are directly related to the level of regional development.

The functional magnitude can be defined as a measure of the importance of a settlement in terms of all the nodal functions considered. The usefulness of this quantitative index in the study of service centres rests on its capacity to reveal at a glance the relative significance of the settlements under study in terms of all the nodal functions they perform.

To conclude, there is a distinct class of settlements in the Magadh Division which may be termed rurban settlements 18 rurban settlements have been identified by which 11 are towns and 7 are villages. Broadly speaking, they are divisible into three groups on the basis of statistical analysis. The centres of higher order are marked by specialised services like subdivisional courts, banks and cinemas, while centres of the lower order are marked by Block Development Offices, hospitals, high schools and wholesale markets. The chief distinguishing feature is the high percentage of workers engaged in tertiary services in these centres although broadly speaking the centres of the higher order also have a higher population.

The concept of the rurban centres is useful because it serves to distinguish rural settlements with a bias towards public utility services, commercial services and non-agricultural population structure. Similarly, there are full fledged towns which lack something in their basic urban character and cannot be termed as rural settlement. The geography of rurban rural settlements in the Magadh Division would be incomplete without identifying such hybrid settlements, which have a high potentiality of rurban growth. By definition the rurban centres are partly rural and partly urban and have, therefore, to be viewed as part of the broad settlement geography. In this way rurban centres will work as 'economic and social capitals' for the adjoining villages.

Functions and behavioural characteristics of Sherghati rurban market have also been discussed in detail in chapter no. 4 and morphology in chapter no. 6 of this book.

REFERENCES

1. Mandal, R.B. (1973) : "Rurban Centres in Bihar Plain", Indian Geographical Studies, Research Bulletin, No. 1, pp. 12-23.
2. Brush, J.E. (1953) : "The Hierarchy of Central Places in South Western Wisconsin". Geographical Review, Vol. 43, pp. 380-402.
3. Mandal, R.B. (1978) : "Law of Village Anatomy and Rurban Centres Location on Loschian Landscape". Proceedings of Small Towns, Varanasi.

4. Singh, R.L. and Singh, S.M. (1960) : "Mungra Badshahpur: A Rurban Settlement in the Ganga-Ghaghra Doab West". National Geographical Journal of India, Vol. VI, pp. 199-206.
5. Galpin, C.J. (1915) : The Social Anatomy of Agricultural Community, University of Wisconsin, Agricultural Experiment Station, Research Bulletin No. 34.
6. Diskenson, R.E. (1932) : "The Distribution and Functions of the Smaller Urban Settlements of East Anglia". Geography, Vol. XVII, pp. 20-30.
7. Smailes, A.E. (1944) : "The Urban Hierarchy in England and Wales", Geogrpahy, Vol. XXIX, pp. 41-51.
8. Gloward, A. and Stafford Jr. : The Functional Basis of Small Towns", Economic Geogrpahy, pp. 165-175.
9. Berry, B.J.L and Garrison, W.L. (1958) : "The Functional Bases of the Central Place Hierarchy", Economic Geography, Vol. 34, pp. 145-154.
10. King, L.J. (1962) : "The Functional Role of Small Towns in Canterbury", in Proceedings of 3rd New Zealand Geographical Conference Palmerrston North.
11. Thomas, E.N. (1960) : :Some Comments on the Functional Bases for Small Iowa Towns", Iowa Business Digest, p. 10.
12. Monkhouse, F.J. (1972) : A Dictionary of Geogrpahy, London, Edward Arnold, p. 302.
13. Singh, R.L. and Singh, S.M. : Op. Cit., p. 199.
14. Singh, K.N. : "Small Towns as Rural Development Centres in Uttar Pradesh", in Abstracts of Proceedings of Fifty-fourth session, Indian Science Congress Association, p. 11.
15. Thomas, E.N. : Op. Cit.
16. Davos. Kingsley (1966) : "Urban Research and Significance", in Gibbs, J.P. (Ed.) : Urban Research Method, New Delhi, p. XI.
17. Urban-Rural Differences in Southern Asia (1964) : Report on Regional Seminar, Delhi, 1962, London, p. 3.

6

Micro Geography of Sample Markets

6.1 MORPHOLOGY

The present chapter deals the study of intramarket-place relationships. The layout and arrangement of shops, their main types and the presence of services etc. have been analysed. The object is to test whether the size and functional characteristics of markets discussed in preceding pages are reflected in sample markets too or do they vary in internal layout. A few selected rural markets of all types from all four districts of the division and from all directions and a rurban centre have been analysed for the purpose.

6.2 TARGIR WEEKLY MARKET

Targir weekly market (Location code no. 219*) lies in the Rajauli block of Nawada district which is in the eastern part of the Magadh Division. The situation of this market is about 8 km. west from national highway no. 31 (connects Patna to Ranchi via Nawada). This is connected with N.H. 31 by an unmettaled road. The district town of Nawada is 31 Km. north and block headquarter is 10 Km. north east. The prominent tree of this market area is 'Taar' (Palm) and that's why this market is called Targir. This market was started about thirty years ago. The area of the market is fertile and has a low water level, hence there is a good number of tubewells. Condition of agriculture is good, multicropping and vegetables cultivation is common in the area. Targir village has a area of 253.73 hectares having a population of 1,275 persons with 187 households. The village has primary, middle and high schools and primary health sub centre, post office, well and hand pump water supply and electricity for agricultural purpose. The facility of bus service is available at a distance of 5 Km.

The market is held in the east-south of the village Targir. The market place is connected by ways from all directions. On the northern side of the market one way to the north is for village Pasraila and another way to the west goes to Targir village. On the southern end one road goes to west for Hisua. On the east-south corner of the market one road goes south to village Amawan and to the east a 8 Km. long meandering road connects the market with the national highway no. 31.

The shops of the market are laid out roughly in a checker board and linear patterns. The market is expanded mainly from north to south with the main road in its middle. To the west of this road from north to south are hotel, manihari shop, general store, middle school and its field, lower school, cobbler's shop, cloth shops, grain shop and to the right turn of this line is two goat meat shops, gumti, carpenter and blacksmith shops and a few meters ahead on the southern side of this road is situated Kisan High School, Targir with two stationery shops. To the east of main road from north to south are manihari shop, gumti, bicycle shop, hotel, carpenter, loudspeaker shop, black smith, stationery shop, manihari shop, hotels, grain shop, stationery shop grains shops chicken's shop etc. Between these two lines, on the either sides (footpath) of the main road, the shops are of only green vegetables. In front of soutth end of this road is cloth shop, primary health sub-centre, cycle shop, stationery shop. On the southern corner of this market there is a space for cattle market too which is surrounded by cycle shop, cobbler shop, cycle shop, manihari shop, cycle shop, loudspeaker shop, hotel, general store, cloth shop, hotel, stationary, hotel, manihari, sweet, stationery, hotel, sweet, stationery, and manihari shops. On the south-east corner of the market there is a temple of God Hanuman which dominates the cultural landscape. There are about sixty shops in the market (*Fig. No. 6.1*)

In Targir market the maximum percentage of the goods purchased from wholesale markets is of durable goods (35.41%) followed by fruits and vegetables (29.16%), ubiquitous goods (16.66%), non-vegetarian foods (8.33%), food stuff (6.25%), agricultural Inputs (4.16%). Selling of edible oil, kerosene oil and fuel in single units is worthy of note. It is because the labour class demand these items for cooking their food each day and in a short duration a large number of them come to buy these goods. Targir market held on every Monday (weekly). The market time is between 10.00 A.M. to 6.00 P.M. but the peak hours of the market are between 2.00 P.M. to 5.00 P.M.

6.3 KHEMDA BI-WEEKLY MARKET

Khemda is a bi-weekly market (Location code no. 154*) lies in the Barun, block of Aurangabad district which is on the western border of the Magadh Division. Actually Khemda is the old name of present Barun. The market is situated on the eastern bank of river Son which is 1 Km. South of the national highway no. 2 (Shershah Suri Marg formerly

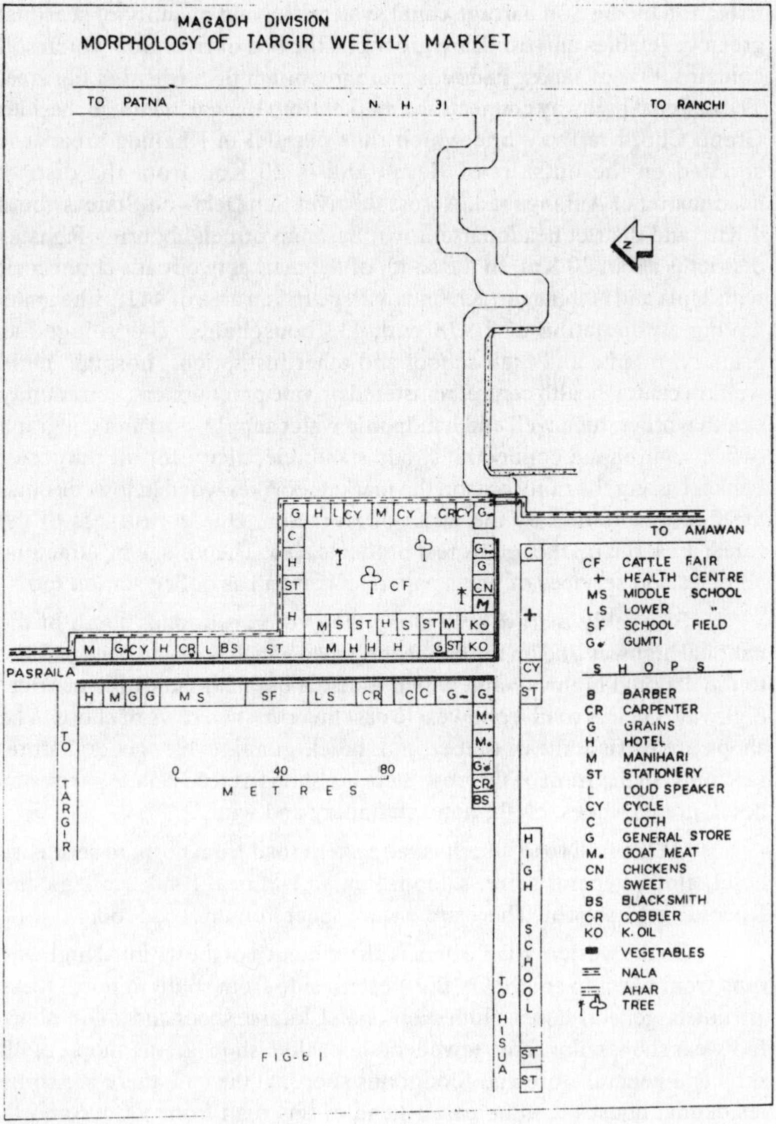
MAGADH DIVISION
MORPHOLOGY OF TARGIR WEEKLY MARKET
TO PATNA
N. H. 31
TO RANCHI
TO AMAWAN
PASRAILA
TO TARGIR
TO HISUA
HIGH SCHOOL
CF
0 40 80
METRES
FIG-6 1
CF CATTLE FAIR
+ HEALTH CENTRE
MS MIDDLE SCHOOL
LS LOWER "
SF SCHOOL FIELD
G. GUMTI
SHOPS
B BARBER
CR CARPENTER
G GRAINS
H HOTEL
M MANIHARI
ST STATIONERY
L LOUD SPEAKER
CY CYCLE
C CLOTH
G GENERAL STORE
M. GOAT MEAT
CN CHICKENS
S SWEET
BS BLACKSMITH
CR COBBLER
KO K. OIL
VEGETABLES
NALA
AHAR
TREE

Fig. 6.1

G.T. Road) and is well connected to it by a metalled road. The location of the market is ideal. The area has fertile lands, which get benefit of irrigation by the Son barrage canal system. A good quantity of seasonal green vegetables and fruits are grown on the bed of river Son which soil contains 90% of sands. Paddy is more important than wheat in the area. The national highway connects the market from Bengal to Punjab, besides Grand Chord railway line which runs parallel in Khemda area. It is situated on the outskirt of Barun and is 20 Km. from the district headquarter of Aurangabad. Across the river Son Dehri-on-Sone is about 4 Km. and district headquarter town Sasaram of neighbouring Rohatas district is about 20 Km. In the south of the market two roads connects it with Japla and Nabinagar. Khemda village has an area of 441.91 heactars having a population of 2,978 with 433 households. The village has primary, middle and high school and other institutions, hospital, child welfare centre, health centre, registered private practitioners, community health worker, tube well and handpump water supply, post and telegraph office with phone connections, bus stand, electricity for all purposes, banks. During the rainy season the market receives wooden logs through the free trnsprtation by the water of river Son. Due to nearness of the forest area, the market get forest products also. The village has tractors, vehicles and services of news papers. Khamda has police station too.

Bi-weekly market held along the two branch roads south of the national highway and on the connecting road which is east to west parallel to the national highway and which is also a branch road of the national highway. On this road from west to east there are two rows of shops. The shops are of fish, meat, timber, gul, hotel, gumti, cycle, general store, sawmills. In the front of this row there are shops of readymade garments. hotel, grains, shoes, cloth, hotel stationery and wine.

On the first road which is the eastern road from north to south has hotel, cloth, general store, saloon, Punjab National Bank, college and Khemda high school. There are vacant spaces on this road too.

On the western road which is also a branch of the national highway runs from north to south. On the western side from south to north there are hotels, general stores, cloth shops, hotel, kirana, shoes and tailors shop, footwear shop, tailor shop, jewellers shop, cloth shop, grains shops, cloth shop and general store and foodgrains shops, at the end, there are some residential houses. On the eastern end of this road from south to north we find hotels, cloth shop, utensil shop, general store, cloth shops, wine shop, readymade garments shop, tailor shops, cloth shop, general stores, stationery and general. Thus we see that there are zones for kirana shops, tailoring shops, hotels, cloth shops and timer shops. The market held between 8.00 a.m. to 6.00 p.m. twice in a week but the peak hours of the market are between 1.00 p.m. to 5.00 p.m. The market is linear in layout. The core is located at the junction of roads near police station. On the either sides of the main road of the market there are continuous shops of vegetables and fruits (*Fig. No. 6.2*)

The maximum percentage of goods purchased for the Khamda market from wholesale markets is of vegetables and fruits (33.72%) followed by durable goods (28.55%), ubiquitous goods (12.05%), food stuff (10.19%), non-vegetetarian foods (8.63%), special goods (6.47%).

6.4 KINJAR TRI-WEEKLY MARKET

Kinjar is a tri-weekly market (location code no. 218*) lies in the Karpi block of Jehanabad district which is on the northern border of the Magadh Division. The market is situated on the eastern side of the Punpun river on the Jehanabad to Patna via Arwal road which is east to west in direction. Jehanabad is 16 Km. east. The area is fertile due to alluvial deposition by Punpun river. This market started about 50-60 years ago. In beginning a few cultivators used to sale their vegetables only. Due to the direct road connection with the state capital Patna this market gets goods from there also. Kinjar village has a total area of 52892 hectares with a papulation of 4,271 persons having 603 househods. Kinjar has primary, middle and high schools, primary health centre, registered private practitioners, well, handpump and river water supply, post and telegraph office, bus service, metalled road and unmetalled road, irrigation by electrified tubewells etc. The village has also services of about 100 copies of newspapers, motor cycles, car, jeep and tractors. Nearest town is Jehanabad which is situated at a distance of 16 Km. east. Electricity is available for all purposes. This market held on Thursday and Saturday of the week. Main staple food of this villages is rice and wheat. Market time is from 8.00 a.m. to 6.00 p.m. but the peak hours are 12.30 p.m. to 4.30 p.m.

The main market of Kinjar is situated on Jehanabad Arwal road from east to west up to river Punpun. On the both sides (foot path) of these roads there are shops of vegetables and fruits sellers. On the northern side of the road from west to east we find shops of general store, cycle, tailor, utenciles, general store, stationery, grains, stationery, general stores and now this road turns to the north which has some shops of fertilizer, medicines, seeds, utencils, general stores. Again on the main road northern side we find shops of stationery, hotel, cloth, flour mills, general stores,

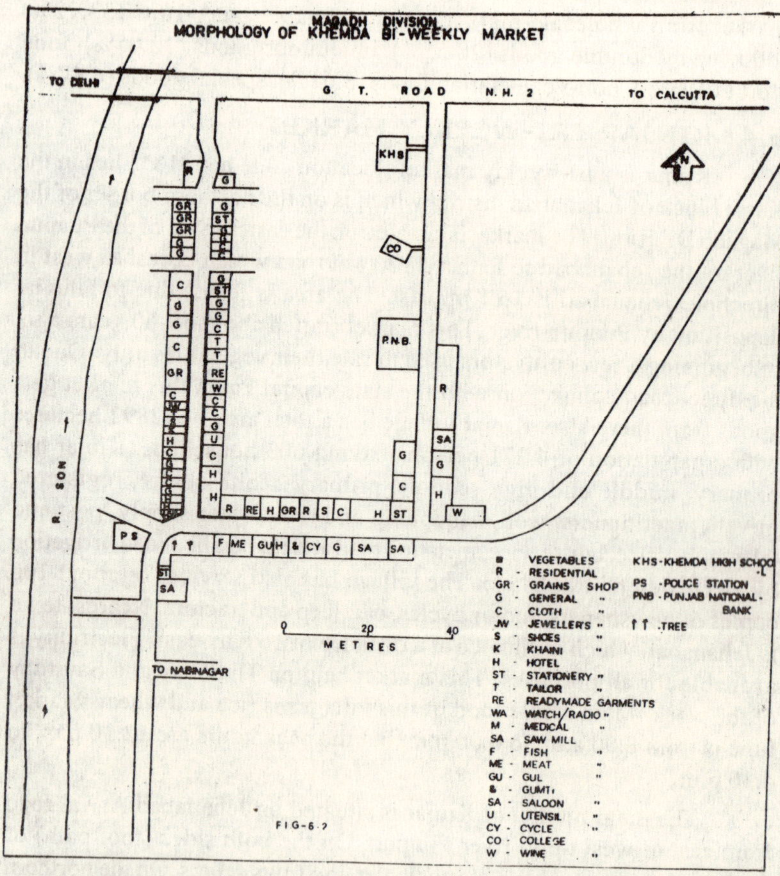
MAGADH DIVISION
MORPHOLOGY OF KHEMDA BI-WEEKLY MARKET
TO DELHI
G. T. ROAD N. H. 2
TO CALCUTTA
KHS
CO
P.N.B.
N
SON
R.
PS
TO NABINAGAR
0 20 40
METRES
FIG-6.2
VEGETABLES
R - RESIDENTIAL
GR - GRAINS SHOP
G - GENERAL "
C - CLOTH "
JW - JEWELLER'S "
S - SHOES "
K - KHAINI "
H - HOTEL
ST - STATIONERY "
T - TAILOR "
RE - READYMADE GARMENTS
WA - WATCH/RADIO "
M - MEDICAL "
SA - SAW MILL
F - FISH "
ME - MEAT "
GU - GUL "
& - GUMTI
SA - SALOON "
U - UTENSIL "
CY - CYCLE "
CO - COLLEGE
W - WINE "
KHS - KHEMDA HIGH SCHOOL
PS - POLICE STATION
PNB - PUNJAB NATIONAL BANK
TREE

Fig. 6.2

hotel, saw mill, grains, tailor, cement, general stores and medical and a few yards ahead of this we find police station of Kinjar and High School of Kinjar.

On the southern side of the main road from west to east we find shops of saloon, hotel, grains, cloth, general stores, hotel, cloth, general stores, utensils, clinic, cloth, watch, hotel, petrol pump, studio, cement, fertilizer, Magadh Gramin Bank, bicycle, coal depot. On the southern part of road over river Punpun we find shops from west to east gumtis, utencils, general stores, washerman, stationery, utencil, general stores, cycle, fertilizer, grains, tailor, cloth, general stores, hotel, stationery, grains, general store, cement and washerman (*Fig. No. 6.3*).

The maximum percentage of goods purchased for Kinjar market from wholesale markets is of fruits and vegetables (43.90%) followed by durable goods (39.02%), special goods (7.31%), food stuff (4.87%), non-vegetarian and animals (2.43% each).

6.5 AMAWAN DAILY MARKET

Amawan is a daily market (Location code no. 192*) lies in the Rajauli Block of Nawada district. This is an old small market situated 4-5 Km. west of the national highway no. 31 which connects Ranchi and Patna via Nawada. The district headquarter Nawada is 22 Km. north-west. The approach road is 6 m. wide on which daily market is held from north to south direction in 500-600 meters long area. The block headquarter Rajauli is about 8 Km. northeast. The area is fertile hence the condition of agriculture is good. Market held daily between 7.00 a.m. to 6.00 p.m. but peak hours are between 3.00 p.m. to 6.00 p.m. The total area of the village is 1,131,49 hectares having a population of 8,133 persons and 1,087 households. Amawan has primary, middle and high schools and other institutions, maternity and child welfare centre, primary health centre, primary health sub centre, dispensary, community health workers, well, tank, handpump, river water supply, post office, bus service, electricity for agriculture purpose. Sources of irrigation are well, tubewell, tank and river. The village has motorcycles and tractors. The main staple food is rice and wheat.

On the southern end of the market to the middle of the market either footpaths have shops of vegetables. On the western side of the road from south to north we find veterinary hospital, health clinic, residential houses, primary schools, cloth shop, timber shop, sanghat, utencial shop, general stores, hotel, utencil, saloons, cloth shop, fruits shop, cloth shop, hotels, meat shops, fruits shops, stationery, general store, cloth shop. A girl's school is also behind this row.

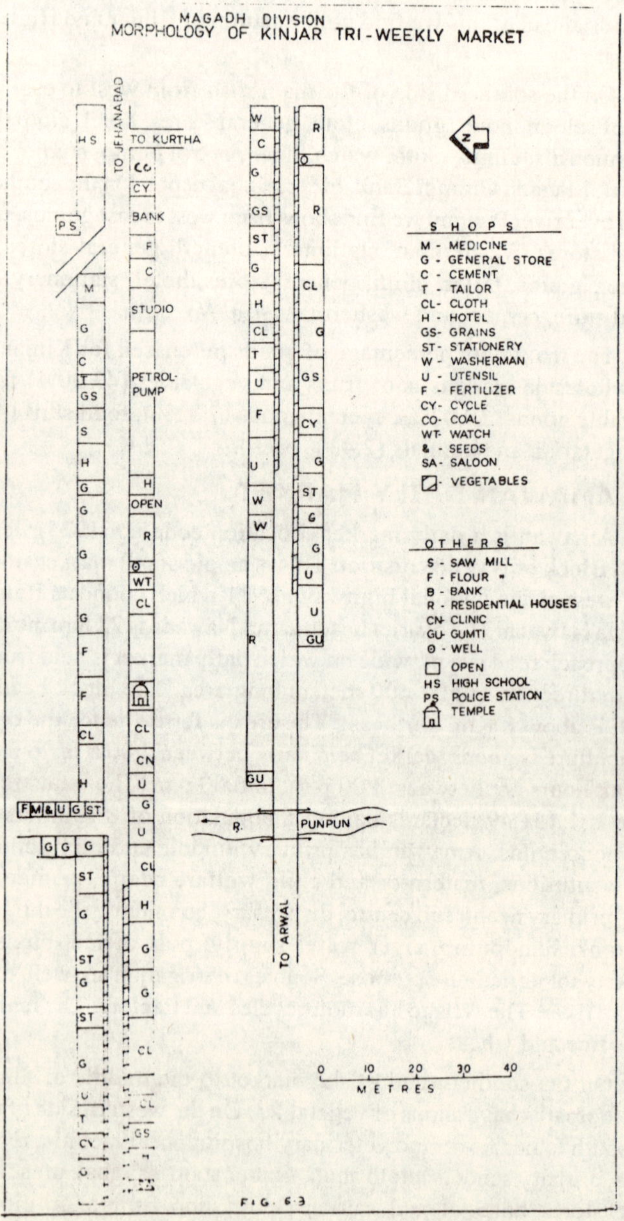
MAGADH DIVISION
MORPHOLOGY OF KINJAR TRI-WEEKLY MARKET
TO JEHANABAD
TO KURTHA
TO ARWAL
PUNPUN R.
SHOPS
M - MEDICINE
G - GENERAL STORE
C - CEMENT
T - TAILOR
CL - CLOTH
H - HOTEL
GS - GRAINS
ST - STATIONERY
W - WASHERMAN
U - UTENSIL
F - FERTILIZER
CY - CYCLE
CO - COAL
WT - WATCH
& - SEEDS
SA - SALOON
VEGETABLES
OTHERS
S - SAW MILL
F - FLOUR "
B - BANK
R - RESIDENTIAL HOUSES
CN - CLINIC
GU - GUMTI
WELL
OPEN
HS HIGH SCHOOL
PS POLICE STATION
TEMPLE
0 10 20 30 40
METRES
FIG. 6.3

Fig. 6.3

On the eastern side of the road from south to north we find high school, middle school, residential houses, general stores, hotels, general store, cloth shops, general stores, hotel, fruits shops, cloth shop, hotel, stationery shop, hotel, stationery shop, and office building. Amawan market may be said to be a linear pattern market (*Fig. No. 6.4*).

The maximum percentage of goods purchased for Amawan market from wholesale market is of vegetables and fruits (41.17%) followed by food stuff (29.41%), durable goods (20.58%), ubi quitous goods (5.88%) and non-vegetarion food (2.94%). The main road of the market has slight turn to the east and then north and then east is seen on the northern end of the road in Awawan market.

6.6 SHERGHATI RURBAN MARKET

Sherghati is a sub-divisional headquarter town (Location code no. 441*) of Gaya district. Administrative sub-division of Sherghati created on 10.7.1983. Actually it is a rurban centre having a permanent market with the facility of bi-weekly market. It lies in the southern part of the Magadh Division. It is situated on the national highway no. 2 Shershah Suri Marg (formerly G.T. Road) which connects it from Calcutta to Delhi and Punjab. Divisional headquarter town of Gaya is 32 Km. north and connected with a metalled road. It is a class III town. State capital Patna is 124 Km. north. Sherghati has an area of 10.79 Sq. Km. having a population of 20,289 persons with 2,933 households and a density of 1,880 persons per sq. km. Scheduled Castes and Scheduled Tribes population is 3,354 persons. Length of metalled and unmetalled roads in Sherghati is 7 Km. and 20 Km. respectively. Civic administration of Sherghati is governed by the Notified Area Committee (NAC). Tap, well and the wells are the main sources of water supply. Electricity is available for all purposes. Sherghati has hospitals, health centre, family planning centre, degree college with arts and science subjects, short-hand type writing institutes etc. Primary, middle and high schools, public library. Three nationalised banks, 22 agricultural credit societies, 2 non-agricultural credit societies. Cloth, fertilizer and medicines are the three most important commodities which are imported into Sherghati and rice, wheat and sweets are the three most important commodities exported by Sherghati. Shoes, soap and sandal are the three most important commodities which are being manufactured in Sherghati. Sherghati is situated on an interfluve of rivers Morhar and Sorhar. Sherghati has a good roadways communication system and it is connected nicely by bus services to Gaya, Patna, Banaras (U.P.) and Calcutta (West Bengal) etc.

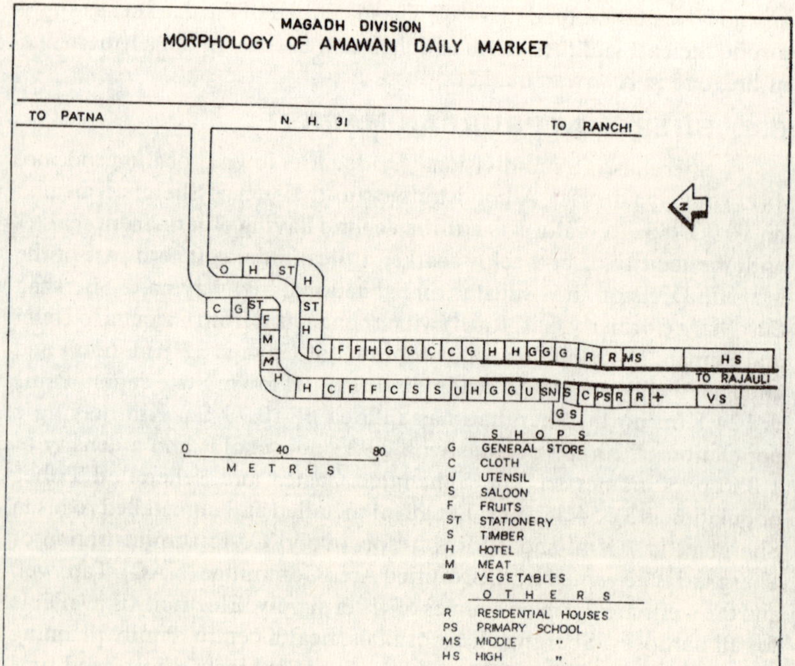

MAGADH DIVISION
MORPHOLOGY OF AMAWAN DAILY MARKET
TO PATNA
N. H. 31
TO RANCHI
TO RAJAULI
0 40 80
M E T R E S
S H O P S
G GENERAL STORE
C CLOTH
U UTENSIL
S SALOON
F FRUITS
ST STATIONERY
S TIMBER
H HOTEL
M MEAT
VEGETABLES
O T H E R S
R RESIDENTIAL HOUSES
PS PRIMARY SCHOOL
MS MIDDLE "
HS HIGH "
+ HEALH CENTRE
VH VETERINARY HOSPITAL
GS GIRLS'SCHOOL
SN SANGAT
O OFFICE
FIG-6.4

Fig. 6.4

The permanent market of Sherghati is spread from Block Office (north) to S.D.O. Office (south). The pattern of market is linear. The road of the market is 4-5 meters wide and has a length of about 2 Km. From block to towards south after a few yards we find the national highway no. 2, crossing. At this crossing we find shops at N.H. too. Here vegetables and fruits shops are good in number. From this point to the south the road has some slight turning at 4 or 5 points. There are about 400 shops of big, medium and small sizes in Sherghati.

In Sherhati market we find shops of kirana, hotels, tailors, radio, cloth, cement, grains, meat and fish, medical, photostat, general stores, cycle and its parts, diesel parts, books, watches, jewellers, motor parts, utencils, hardware, saloon, furniture, tobacco, shoes, vegetables and fruits, readymade garments, musical band, electrical goods, sweet, meat. Besides this we nd biscuit factory, oil mills, saw mills and flour mills (*Fig. No. 6.5*).

6.7 SHERGHATI BI-WEEKLY MARKET

The bi-weekly market held on Monday and Friday at Sherghati. These markets held near the crossing of national highway and in the open space near Jain Market, a cattle market is held weekly on Monday near S.D.O. Office and a chicken and egg market is held near the main market.

The bi-weekly market is held in a linear pattern along the main road from north to south. The road is 4 meters wide. In this market we find mainly shops of vegetables and fruits, clothes, grains, saloon, manihari, electrical goods etc.

In the bi-weekly market of Sherghati-cattle market is held on Monday only. Near the S.D.O. court a wide space of 230 meters by 110 meters is meant for cattle market where buffaloes, oxen, cows and goats are sold.

At another place near main road of the market an open space of 35 meter by 20 meters is meant for chickens and eggs market where chicken, cocks and eggs are sold (*Fig. No. 6.6*).

In both the above mentioned markets animals, chickens and eggs are mostly brought from outside Sherghati.

5.8 RENT PATTERN IN SHERGHATI RURBAN MARKET

In Sherghati market 41.31% traders have their own shops. Traders who pay rent for shops in different rent groups are Re.1/- to Rs. 50/- (1.45%), Rs. 51/- to Rs. 100/- (26.64%) this is the maximum percentage,

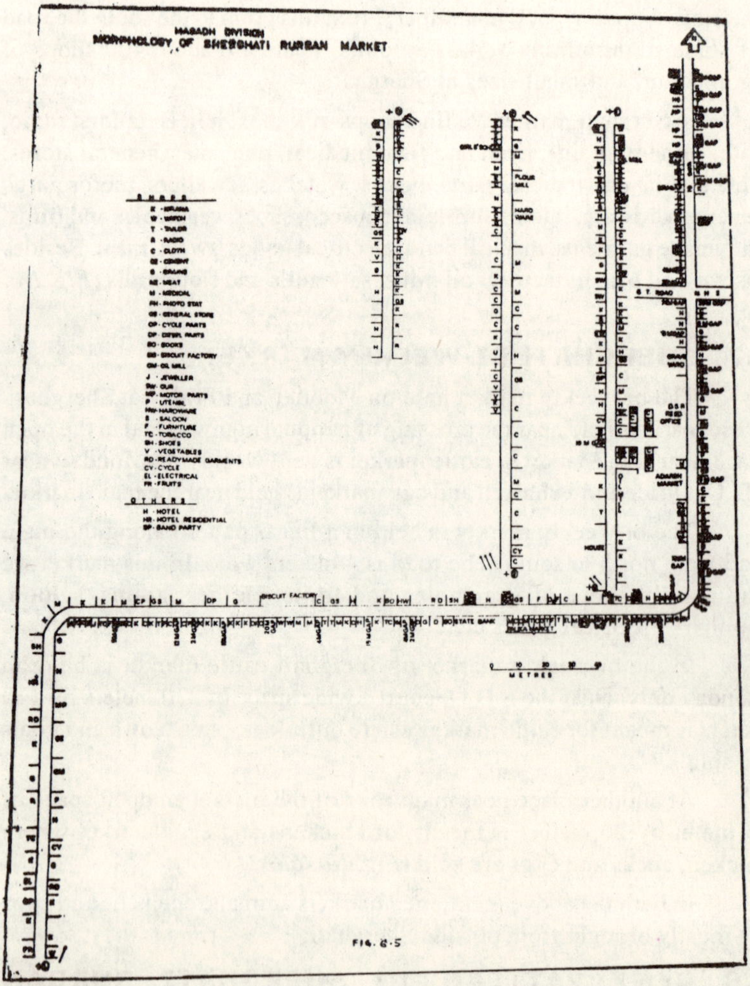
MAGADH DIVISION
MORPHOLOGY OF SHERGHATI RURBAN MARKET
SHOPS
T - TAILOR
R - RADIO
C - CLOTH
M - MEDICAL
PH - PHOTO STAT
GS - GENERAL STORE
CP - CYCLE PARTS
J - JEWELLER
MP - MOTOR PARTS
P - UTENSIL
HW - HARDWARE
S - SALOON
F - FURNITURE
TC - TOBACCO
SH - SHOES
V - VEGETABLES
RD - READYMADE GARMENTS
CY - CYCLE
EL - ELECTRICAL
FR - FRUITS
OTHERS
H - HOTEL
HR - HOTEL RESIDENTIAL
BP - BAND PARTY
FLOUR MILL
HARD WARE
G T ROAD
ADARSH MARKET
BISCUIT FACTORY
STATE BANK
METRES
FIG. 6.5

Fig. 6.5

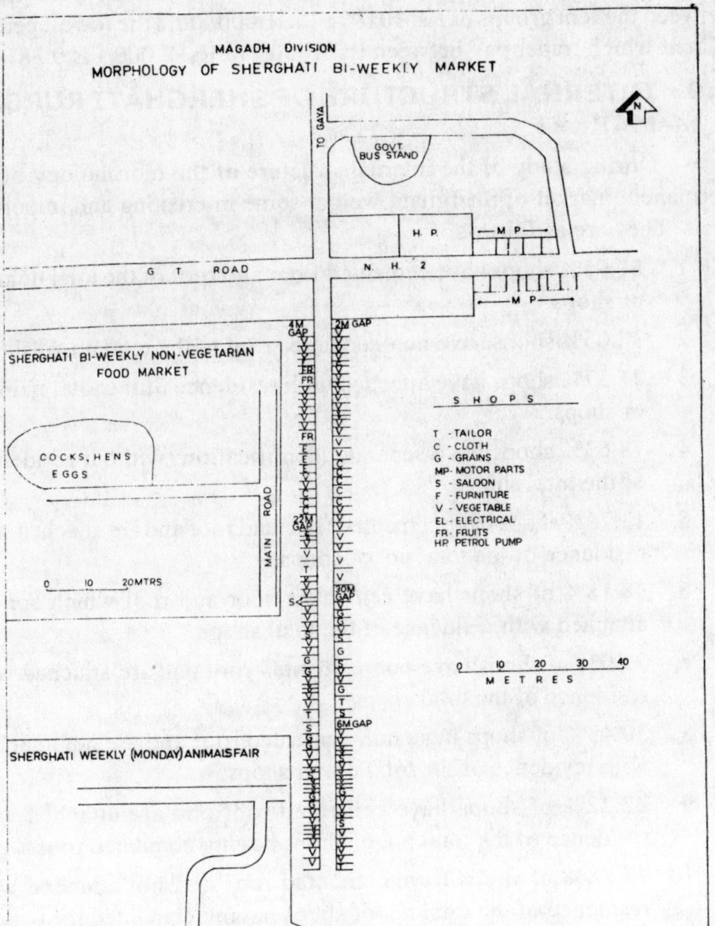
MAGADH DIVISION
MORPHOLOGY OF SHERGHATI BI-WEEKLY MARKET
N
TO GAYA
GOVT. BUS STAND
H. P.
M P
G T ROAD
N. H. 2
M P
4M GAP
2M GAP
SHERGHATI BI-WEEKLY NON-VEGETARIAN FOOD MARKET
COCKS, HENS EGGS
MAIN ROAD
22M GAP
30M GAP
6M GAP
0 10 20MTRS
S H O P S
T - TAILOR
C - CLOTH
G - GRAINS
MP - MOTOR PARTS
S - SALOON
F - FURNITURE
V - VEGETABLE
EL - ELECTRICAL
FR - FRUITS
HP - PETROL PUMP
0 10 20 30 40
M E T R E S
SHERGHATI WEEKLY (MONDAY) ANIMALS FAIR
GO ATS
OXEN
BUFFALOES
COWS
0 20 40
FIG- 6.6

Fig. 6.6

Rs. 101/- to Rs. 150/- (17.77%), Rs. 151/- to 200/- (8.49%), Rs. 201/- to Rs. 250/- (2.31%), Rs. 251/- to Rs. 300/- (1.91%), there is no trader between the rent groups of Rs. 301/- to Rs. 1,000/- and the lowest percent of rent which trader pay between Rs. 1000/- to Rs. 2,000/- is 0.38%.

6.9 INTERNAL STRUCTURE OF SHERGHATI RURBAN MARKET

During study of the internal structure of the morphology of the permanent market of Sherghati, we got some interesting and important facts. They are as follows:

1. 61.95% shops have cemented floor and roof of the total number of shops.
2. 38.05% shops have non-cemented roof of the total no. of shops.
3. 21.37% shops have attached with residence of the total number of shops.
4. 78.63% shops have separate identification (without residence) of the total shops.
5. 13.76% shops have cemented floor and roof and are attached with residence of the total no. of shops.
6. 48.18% of shops have cemented floor and roof which are not attached with residence of the total shops.
7. 7.60% of shops have non-cemented roof and are attached with residence of the total shops.
8. 30.43% of shops have non-cemented roof and are not attached with residence of the total no. of shops.
9. 22.22% of shops have cemented roof and are attached with residence of the total no. of shops having cemented roof.
10. 77.78% of shops have cemented roof and not attached with residence of the total no. of shops having cemented roof.
11. 20% of shops have no cemented roof and attached with residence of the total no. of shops having non-cemented roof.
12. 80% of shops have non-cemented roof and not attached with residence of the total no. of shops having non cemented roof.
13. 41.34% are own (non-rented) shops of the total no. of shops.
14. 58.69% are rented shops of the total no. of shops.
15. 17.39% of own shops have cemented roof of the total no. of shops.

16. 28.07% of own shops have cemented roof of the total no. of shops having cemented roof.
17. 21.37% of own shops have non cemented roof of the total no. of shops.
18. 56.19% of own shops have non-cemented roof of the total no. of shops having non-cemented roof.
19. 43.81% of rented shops have non-cemented roof of the total shops having non-cemented roof.
20. 71.93% of rented shops have cemented roof and floor of the total no. of shops having cemented roof and floor.

In a permanent market or shop 'floor and 'roof' are two important aspects of marketing. That's why a detail study had been carried out on these aspects in Sherghati market. Govt. of India has also decided to conduct such type of survey of households during coming census of 1991.

There are two types of building used for shops in Sherghati market:

i. Shops having cemented roofs and cemented floors, we can call it 'Pacca Shops' and
ii. Shops having non-cemented roofs (like tiles or tin etc.), we can call it 'Kachha shops'.

The shopkeepers usually pay Rs. 50/- to Rs. 100/- per month as the rent for their 'Kachha' shops according to their location and size. The rent of 'Pacca' shops are usually between Rs. 100/- to Rs. 300/- per month according to their location and size. But some shopkeepers pay Rs. 20/- or Rs. 30/- only per month for their 'Kachha shops' also which accounts 1.45% of the total shops, Exceptionally some renters pay to Rs. 1800/- per month for 'Pacca' building used for the purpose of a nursing home. 61.95% of the total shops are 'Pacca' and they pay between Rs. 150/- to Rs. 300/- per month as rent of their shops.

According to trading manner there are three types of shops in Sherghati market:

1. The shops which deals in wholesale, we may call them wholesale shops.
2. The shops which deals in retail, we may call it retail shops.
3. The shops which deals in wholesale and retail both. We may call them wholesale-cum-retail shops.

Retail shops are in a majority with 76.14% of the total shops followed by wholesale-cum-retail shops 18.70% and wholesale shops 5.76%.

At Sherghati 93.84% of the total traders are totally dependent upon business, 0.74% traders depend upon both service and business. Most of them are either retired personnels or are non govt. employees, 0.96% traders are either buisnessman, farmer or serviceman. 3.98% of the total traders are both farmer and businessman but they are very small farmers having a piece of land which is less than 5 acres. 0.48% of the total traders are students whose occupation of business is a part-time job, obviously their number is negligible.

In Sherghati we got various groups of length of the business establishements. The maximum percentage is of ancestral shops 35.42% followed by five to ten years shops - 20.29%, more than two years and less than five years old shops -18.08%, more than ten years and less than twenty years old - 11.43%, one to two years old shops - 11.07% less than one year old shops - 2.58% and twenty to thirty years old shops - 1.10%.

Traders are satisfied by the progress of their business and all traders feel that their business is growing well. But surprisingly only 8.33% of the total traders like trading as first preference for their children. 91.66% of the total traders prefer govt. services for their children. Out of these traders 51.08% prefer service as their first and business as second choice but 40.58% of service liking traders are determined to opt service as profession for their children.

The maximum percentage of goods purchased for Sherghati weekly and bi-weekly market from wholesale markets is of animals 40.42% followed by fruits and vegetables 30.85%, durable goods 27.65% and ubiquitous goods 1.4%.

6.10 ASSESSMENT

Following the description of market-morphology of centres discussed above, some generalizations may be deduced.

The market morphology of the centres in the Magadh Division in general consists of clear two parts. These two parts consist of durable and perishable goods. Durable goods mainly constitute cloth, hosiery, kirana and foodgrains, whereas perishable goods constitute vegetable and fruit shops.

Generally it is seen that perishable goods shops are located adjacent to village settlement. It is due to village folk coming for vegetables only find such shops easily accessible. Durable goods are almost always away from village residences. Customers seeking these goods are expected to endeavour more than for other goods. The frequency of visits for perishable goods would be more than for durable goods.

Craftsman like pot-makers, carpenters, blakcsmiths and bamboo goods makers are always, located towards the periphery and occupy separate locations away from each other. The nature of their work or goods is such that they demand separation. For example a pot-maker needs a large space for spreading his earthen pots. He cannot occupy a central location for two reasons, firstly his goods are not costly enough to pay for the high cost of the central area. Secondly, hectic activity in the centre endangers his goods. Similar reasons work for other craftsman too.

Meat and fish shops are mostly locate themselves on the periphery because of the entire operation from Jhataka[1] or Halal[2] of the animals to the priming of meat is carried out on the spot. The entire operation may be psychologically repulsive to customers. Such shops, therefore, need seclusion but at an easily accessible point.

Among special goods being sold at these markets are wooden ploughs, tobacco, leather ropes, red chilli etc.

6.11 THE ZONAL ARRANGEMENT OF SHOPS

The above mentioned characteristics may be examined in a model developed earlier.[3] It is based on quality differences of goods and their spatial drawing power. Durable goods like cloth and hosiery are found to be the most nucleated goods and comprises a kind of a resource area of high quality. This is a specialised functional area which derives its threshold from a small number of customers who are prepared to pay more. Adjacent to it is identified an area which is similar to the preceding one in so far as the quality image of goods and their threshold values are concerned. This area consists of food grains and kirana shops. The low quality shops selling ubiquitous goods become scattered in between high quality shops. Services represent a sectoral arrangement. Vegetables and fruit shops occupy the most easily accessible area.

The conclusion may be drawn that it is not necessary that high quality goods draw a large number of customers and vise versa. A tendency of clustering is associated with nuclear goods, scattering is associated with ubiquitous goods and a sectoral arrangement goes with services.

Regarding the constructions of the shops we find both 'Pucca' and 'Kaccha' and some traders have residential facility with their shops too. Shops are own (non-rental) or rented which rents vary between Rs. 20/- only to Rs. 1,800/- per month according to their site, size and built.

In the last it is interesting to note that the traders inspite of their business profession, do not prefer to put their children remain in business, rather they have a craze for services specially for government jobs.

REFERENCES

* Location code numbers are Village Thana no. which have been taken from District Census Handbooks, 1981.

1. Jhatka means slaughtering of animals with one stroke.
2. Halal means slowly slaughtering an animal till it bleads to death.
3. Srivastava, V.K. and K.R. Srivastava (1984) : Geographical Personality of a Rural Market of the Indian Tarai, The Indian Journal of Marketing Geography II, I.G.U. Special Number, pp. 82-87.

7

Marketing and Rural Development

7.1 SUBJECT OF RESEARCH

An assessment of the role of periodic markets in rural development planning is a key area of research. For obvious reasons a growing awareness towards integrated area development has been marked among social scientists and policy planners both (Johnson, 1970;[1] NCAER 1972;[2] Bromley 1975[3] and U. Ram, 1982[4]). The results of development planning through industrialization have led to an exodus of the work force from villages to cities. The migration of manpower from villages creates acute shortages of labour in rural areas. Moreover, the migrant's major share of income is spent in meeting their day-to-day needs at the place of work. The parent villages receive a negligible proportion of their income which hardly compensates for the loss of manpower. If such a situation prevails it is bound to lead to a state of imbalance in the life style of the nation and disturb the delicate economic equilibrium. The much wanted need of the hour is to prepare a viable, integrated rural area development plan which could check the exodus of rural population and develop villages in such a way that urban amenities, facilities and employment opportunities are created in rural areas. Also, planning for development ought to be assimilative with the socio-cultural base of the rural masses and gradually transform the behavioural attitude of the peasants so that the changing scientific and technological infrastructure is voluntarilly adopted by them.

The Indian Science Congress Association also took up Integrated Rural Development as its focal theme in its Waltarie Session, 1976.

7.2 THE NEED FOR A POLICY OF RURAL DEVELOPMENT

For centuries it has been said that 'India is a rich country inhabited by the poor'. How was it so? India is a country of villages and its real soul lives in her villages with 77% of its total population. It is a fact that the largest number of the poorest are still living in rural India and they represent some of the poorest rural population of the world. So far as our national income is concerned we do not figure anywhere near the first hundred of the world. But why[5]? So far the area is concerned it is the seventh largest country and the second most populous country of the world.

The economy of India is a mixed type, but agriculture's share is more larger in comparison to industry. Hence economic development of rural India including this area of study depends greatly on the performance of agricultural productivity. India has one of the richest fertile plains of the world having favourable climate conditions. Historically, India's agricultural tract was most prosperous. But it lost its pre-eminence due to a variety of reasons such as exploitation of the peasantary under the system of Zamindari, Talukdari and subinfeudation, growing pressure of population on land and fragmentation of holdings, inadequate means of communication, absence of good market system, droughts, floods, pests and diseases, neglect of irrigation, draingage and water management programmes and consequently difficulty in adoption of modern technology in agriculture at large scale.[6] These constraints and continuing backwardness of the Magadh Division of Bihar calls for a policy of Rural Development. This pioneer fringe still possesses potential for the development of agriculture and agro-industries. The farmers need incentives in the form of opportunities of inter-market and inter regional exchange of their produce. The establishment of vertical trade will augment their income and inputs in agriculture will consequently rise leading to greater production. The development cycle will then begin.

Rural markets act as levers of development. They serve as assembly points for various commodities produced in the surrounding area and large proportions of assembled goods are transshiped to distant places from such assembly points. Their location in space and time and their functional status needs to be adjusted according to the need of the area in which they operate.

Regulation of markets and goods can also lead to more efficient trade. This region lacks regulated markets. There are only eight regulated agricultural mandis. Their number must be increased to provide for a uniform spatial coverage. Their successful functioning should not be determined by the quantum of trade transactions alone. It should be assessed in the context of the availability of saleable produce in an area and its disposal by the mandi centres. Market news in such areas is scant.[7] By creating an awareness among the rural masses about the existence and functioning of larger centres of production and trade, a better articulation of goods and services can be generated from the grass root level. Ways and means of increasing the informational resources of the farmers should be devised. This task can not be performed by a central agency alone. Regulated market societies can devise such ways and means.

Simply, the numerical multiplication of markets will not solve the problem. Their locational viability in the context of intra-regional and inter-regional socio-economic condition should be given priority in planning a locational strategy.

It may thus be note that the overall development of this region call for the generation of an efficient marketing system. A cohesion of spatial, functional and institutional characteristics pari passu the techno-economic considerations are necessary for developing an efficient marketing system. This can not be achieved informally. For this policy implications will have to be defined and debated before being implemented. Markets are generative entities. They are procreative in essence. A Planning priority for their development will certainly induce rural development. These are the constraints in rural development not only in Magadh Division of Bihar but in the most parts of our country. Hence, considering these constraints a policy of rural development is a need of the hours.

Taking into account the importance of rural markets for a peasant society, is so far as the creation and development of economic, social and cultural institutions are concerned, the following strategies may be suggested for integrating the rural economy leading to development.[8]

i. Market Days Synchronization

The primary task in outlining a policy programme for market based rural development is to plan an integrated system of periodic markets. Periodicity is a persistent phenomenon of the markets of this region. Even in daily markets, there is still a weekly or bi-weekly pulsation of market activity. These days should be synchronized to give a wide spread of market days over the week. Also the market days neighbouring centres should be well separated to avoid competition and facilitate mobile trader's movement. Probably, potential market sites could be developed on a less preferred market days in a market cycle so that the trader cycles become stable.

ii. Establishing New Market Centres

New market centres may be established to improve the village market ratio and to fill in the gaps. The criteria for establishing new markets should be based on empirical evidences of consumer preferences along with the accessibility, centrality, transport facility and site suitability of the market centres.

iii. Market Regulation

The synchronization of market days and the obvious need to initiate new markets can be realised only through market regulation. The existing market system bears marks of the days of Zamindari when markets were destroyed by feuds. This has created anomalies in the spatio-temporal relations among the markets. Market regulation should be effectively enforced to set a pattern of action in designating areas and goods for an appropriate number of markets in the region. This would further help in establishing standards of market practising, enhancing the reach of farmers, utilizing potential market sites and in controlling real marketing, ultimately leading to rural development.

iv. Improving Information Networks

If the farmer could be made aware of the price levels, availability of goods and other amenities like mandi system, government purchasing centres, articulation of goods and services for the benefit of the farmers can be achieved. This can be realized if primary services like post office, telegraph offices are rationally distributed, newspaper circulation is regularised in rural areas and television and radio coverage is improved. An important role can be played by cinema and charcha mandals. Besides farmers training and functional literary programme (FTEL) can give hard core farm information to peasants, particularly to the rural youth. Rural broadcasting programme, such as initiated in Allahabad in 1935, can also play a great role through organizing Radio Rural Forums.[9]

v. Other Locational Strategies

Market are institutions serving as nuclei of human congregation at a certain place and time with the motive of exchange. Their existence and scale of operation influences the utilization of resources, induces productivity, creates employment opportunities and activates the nonfarm sector. While a strongly developed market system influences economic growth the overall development of the region may not be possible without the establishment of complementary institutions. These institutions are schools, colleges, libraries, hospitals, clinics, places of entertainment, local self government and other administrative offices, community centres and so on. Growing markets should be allocated such facilities in roder of their hierarchical importance and anomalies, if any, should be eliminated in a planned manner. Such a locational strategy will greatly improve the drawing power of the markets and will gradually encourgae transformation of periodic markets to daily markets where a wide range of goods and services will always be available. Ignoring the existing market system in locational planning of facilities may give rise to maladjustment between an established market which may never be over matched and a superimposed administrative centre which never gains in importance as it should. A long view of the growth prospects of markets should also be a basic criterian in allocation of services and facilities.[10] Also a rational allocation of facilities like godowns, cold storages,[11] post offices, hospitals etc., will be helpful in checking rural flow of people.

Until markets become stabilized, mobile services organised by the government and other public agencies can make use of the periodic congregation of people in introducing innovations. Public policies aiming at social welfare like population control, raising the standard of living of people, and economising resources can also make good use of the occasion.[12] Such periodic services can shuttle between periodic markets in cycles from a permanent base which may either ba a daily market in that cycle or a central place close to that cycle.

It may thus be seen that an efficient periodic marketing system can accelerate the pace of rural development.

7.3 DEVELOPMENT POLICY AND STRATEGIES

Regarding the constraints mentioned earlier. policy meameasures needed to overcome them to usher in a process of accelerated rural development in this area, which may be applicable in the whole state of Bihar and also in the other parts of our country. Hence, there is need for strategies in the shape of developmental measures for rural areas of this region.[13] They are the following:

Land Policy

Encouragement should be given to farmers to form small groups or Association to deal with common problems. Leasing of holdings by small and marginal farmers and there should be fixation of a "floor" limit for operational holdings. Funds should be specially allocated by the Planning Commission to the State for this purpose.

Ground Water

Exploitation of ground-water resources should be given top priority compact areas in 'white' and 'gray' blocks should be covered by a battery of tube-wells and pump sets, either electric or diesel. This will serve a dual purpose - (i) provide protective irrigation in kharif and productive irrigation in rabi and (ii) drain out excess water during kharif.

Construction of dugwells should be taken up in areas, where there is scope. A failed well compensation scheme for shallow tubewells or dugewells should be introduced by NABARD in consultation with Govt. of India and State Govt. There should be a sound policy for running and maintenance of various of tube-wells.

Surface Irrigation

Release of water and closure of canals should be timed according to the requirements of crops. Lining of canals should be taken up. Lakes and irrigation tanks should be managed and maintained properly. Also new tanks should be constructed wherever there is potential.

Crop Planning

In areas where rainfall fluctuations are heavy, rice should be mixed with or substituted by low duty crops. With a view to economising on water, wheat should be given preference over summer (boro) rice.

Rice is grown in rainfed conditions in large area. Some of them are quite unsuitable for rice cultivation. In such areas, it is more profitable to grow pulses, oilseeds or millets.

In irrigated areas, a 3-4 crops system with at least one short duration Legume should be taken by rotation. Area under H.Y.V. rice, wheat and maize should be increased. Cultivation of companion crops particularly in rabi season should also be encouraged.

In the case of small and marginal farmers, a significant improvement in their incomes cannot be brought about merely by growing ordinary varieties of staple crops. In small farms with assured irrigation and having access to motorable roads to marketing centres, farmers should be encouraged to raise on a part of their holdings high value crops such as vegetables, flowers, fruits or H.Y.V. of staple crops. The area devoted to high value crops can be increased step by step. This will improve the economy of farming operations.

Along with cultivation of high value crops, marginal and small farmers should be encouraged to take up ancillary activities such as animal husbandry, fisheries, poultry etc.

For improving efficiency of labour, use of modern but less expansive form machinery and implements should be encouraged.

Inputs Supply

Proper supply of the inputs items is a must for a good agricultural product. The State so faced with shortage of H.Y.V. or improved varieties of seeds. Hence, seed multiplication programmes should be encouraged.

Seed storage and distribution points should be set up preferably at panchayat level.

Fertilizers should be easily available to the farmers. To suit requirements of marginal and small farmers as also to reduce chances of adulteration when sold loose, supply of sealed packets of 10 Kg. or 20 Kg. should be arranged. In predominantly vegetable growing areas, packets of 5 Kgs. should be made available. Distribution network needs to be strengthened.

Bio-fertilizers like blue green algae (BGA) are useful to supplement nitrogen content of the soil. Government should therefore take up a scheme for producing BGA culture for distribution to farmers for multiplication and use by them.

Pesticides

The surveillance unit located in Patna to keep vigilance over the incidence and spread of pests and diseases, need strengthening. Further, such units should be located at all divisional levels with quick transport facilities. Improved facilities should be provided for hiring sprayers. The District Agricultural Officer should also act as the vigilance officer and should periodically check the stocks maintained by private dealers to prevent adulteration. Further State Government should ensure that prices charged are according to stipulations.

Credit

The programme for achieving higher productivity and output calls for a marked increase in the volume of both production and investment credit, with a large share going to the weaker section and the backward areas. The bulk of the farmers in this region are small and marginal farmers. Their resources are meagre. On their own they cannot afford to take up the needed on farm investments and go in for yield-augmenting inputs like H.Y.V. seeds and fertilizers. Their credit entitlement is limited. They are more liable to default in the even of a crop failure or price slump than others.

There is, therefore, a need for such credit policies and programmes as would enable the small and marginal farmers to make step by step progress towards scientific and intensive use of their limited land resources by a greater input of both labour and capital. Most of the costraints they face cannot be overcome unless their capital resources are augmented, step by step, on a case by case basis.

Crop Insurance

There is a need for introduction of crop insurance in case of the failure of crops. Premium should kept low to induce farmers to avail of the facility. General Insurance Corporation in consultation with the State Government should work out the details of the scheme.

There should be vast agricultural research, extension and training programme through agriculture universities, institutes and audiovisual aids to benefit the farmers.

Marketing Facility

A good market system, where farmers can easily sale their products on a genuine price is a must for their all round development. So at first the number of primary and secondary markets should be increased. Regulated markets should be extended to cover all assembling, wholesale and terminal markets. For this a time bound programme should drawn up. All rural markets, assembling, wholesale and terminal need to be brought under the purview of the Agricultural Produce Markets Acts. The State Govt. should prepare comprehensive plans for development of regulated markets. Effective market committees in all regulated markets with due representation of both traders and producers, including small farmers should be organised. Government should notify all important crops, livestock and forest produce that can be traded in these markets. Adequate facilities for sale/auction, grading, weighing, storage and market information etc. should be provided. Regular appointment of market functionaries should be made and their control should be vested with market committees. Efforts should also be made to reduce the number of supervisory level, one level of supervision should be sufficient. Apex type organization for perishable and non-perishable commodities should be created separately.

There should be a good storage facility for perishable and non-perishable commodities at the farm, processing centres and at wholesale and retail market centres. If this facility is increased the farmers can avoid a loss.

Transport

Transport infrastructure is unsatisfactory. The road network is inadequate outside urban limits. It is also unsatisfactory in interior areas. The network of roads needs to be strengthened considerably so that all villages can be brought within easy access of market centres and nearby urban areas. High priority needs to be given for maintenance of rural roads.

Management and Organizational Reforms

The administrative departments and agencies involved in management of various programmes should be reoriented and geared to achieve the developmental objectives in a corodinated and efficient manner. It is also important to ensure proper sequencing of actions by the concerned departments. The key word in this context should be innovative management, instead of conventional administration.

If the above mentioned measures are taken, it is bound to achieve an all round development of agriculture, which will ultimately pave the way for rural development in this region or in the most parts of rural India.

Apart from above mentioned measures, attention on the following eight items should also be given for rural development as in 1981 of 658,140,676 the majority to the extent of 501,592,169 live in villages and in Bihar out of total population of 69,823,154 the no. of rural population is 61,124,141. (i) Education, (ii) Drinking water supply, (iii) Rural Electrification, (iv) Housing, (v) Nutrition, (vi) Health facilities, (vii) Roads, (viii) Unemployment.

More than four decades of planning in India has definitely given our experts sufficient experience and intution to feel the pulse of national economy in general and rural India in particular. More industrialisation may not effect the millions unless the fruits of planning reach the majority of population. The new Indian Government looks at the whole development strategy with a fresh angle.

Education

Next to irrigation, agro-industry, health and agriculture the most burning problem that faces five hundred million Indian villagers is education.

Unfortunately our planners are not assigning top priority to rural education. That is the real crux of the mass unemployment throughout India. That is a also the reason for heavy load on cities job is a double edged dagger. There should be a universal free elementary education for the age group 6-14 with special emphasis on girls, and simultaneously involvement of students and voluntary agencies for the removal of adult illiteracy. Article 45 of the Indian constitution also promises free and compulsory education for all children in the age group of 6-14 years. According to government programme by 1990 all the 16.3 crore children estimated in the age group 6-14 will have to be enrolled in elementary schools, either in the formal or non-formal system of education.

Knowledge is power. One of the aims of the free India is to eridicate illiteracy.

It is not an ordinary challenge. In fact, this is perhaps the most difficult task before the country, the magnitude of the problem can be judged from the fact that even in the beginning of the century (1901) the percentage of overall literacy was only 5.35 out of which females represented only 0.60. From the miserable plight of size out of a thousand literate females, today in 1981 we have reached a stage where we find 248 in a thousand against 460 males and 360 of total literates.[14]

Perhaps female literacy is more important than male literacy. It is mother who moulds the family. Unless she gets the light of knowledge, the society stands no where. It is all the more necessary to have women's literacy to make the family welfare schemes a success.

Unfortunately we have failed to impart real education to our young generation. Dignity of labour at least one item which is delected from modern westernised education.

Providing higher education, after the secondary stage, to the rural youth and inculcating in them a spirit of service to the community and sympathy for the rural way of life, besides training them for careers in the rural development programmes of the central and state governments is a need of the hour.

There is also a great scope for spreading adult literacy in rural India. This is a task which can be better implemented by voluntary agencies in the rural area. The community development personnel can also take up the task. The best institution to take up this gigantic challange is of course the village school centre. There may be centres of literacy for workers in our factories also.

Our whole approach to the problem of rural India is basically wrong. To educate these millions we do not need huge buildings. Nowadays, the first thing that is done in the name of spreading education is building big mansion like constructions. Real education is the main victim. It is just like building big temples at enormous cost. A devotee needs no huge temple. Similarly, spreading of real knowledge does not need big constructions. We need huts, good, free atmosphere. Tagore built a huge university at Santiniketan in a peaceful rural environment, silently and patiently. So did Hakim Ajmal Khan in Delhi.

For rural millions we need consultancy institutions. Vocational training institutes will play more important roles in village India in solving multiple inter connected problems. Agricultural education is important for rural area.

To eridicate the evils of communalism, castisim, dowry, untouchability, terrorism, over population etc. from the rural society, imparting true education is must for each and all.

Drinking Water Supply

In our country which is a land of rivers not only land is thirsty, men are more thirsty, all water is not drinkable. It is a very long standing problem. Wells, tube wells, ponds have become more or less out dated but they have been set aside before alternative arrangements could be placed. There are about 2 lakh villages which are facing this problem in this country.

In a civilized society, like ours, the effort should be made to cover all the identified problem villages with at least one source of safe portable water available throughout the year. The needs of the scheduled castes and scheduled tribes population in the rural area should also be given due priority. Water is life and clean drinkable water is a must for good health.

Electrification

In the present modern age electricity is essential for all round progress and for this maximum generation of power, improvement of the functioning of electricity authorities are important.

Still a good number of villages have not availed the facility of electricity. But for electrification of all villages and to raise the standard of living in rural areas a Rural Electrification Corporation was set up in 1969. An outley of Rs. 1173 crores has been provided to disburse for rural electrification schemes in states by this Corporation during the sixth five year plan (1980-85). About 3.5 lakhs villages have been electrified in the country as against 5.76 lakhs villages. In Bihar 19,000 villages have been electrified by the end of sixth five year plan.

Housing

Rural housing is one of the most important problems of national development. Unfortunately, not much attention was paid to it, the magnitude of the problem is obvious from the fact that out of 5.79 lakh human settlements, eighty percent live in 5.76 lakh villages. The remaining 20 per cent live in 3.119 urban settlements. Rural housing poses a complex problem. It is a state problem.

The number of eligible rural landless families needing housing assistance is extimated around 15 millions in Bihar this number is 2,400 thousand out of 35 thousand families have been alloted house sites. Government has done a good job in this direction but much has to be done for the rural housing since housing is one of the basic needs of man.

Emphasis should be given on the need to reduce substantially the number of absolutely shelterless people and to provide conditions for others to improve their housing environment.

Nutrition

Nutritious diet is essential for a good healthy human body. In India a large number of population is still below poverty line and they do not get even two times full meal. In the present situation talking of nutritious diet seems to be a joke. But this can not be left unsolved as it is connected with the national health which makes a country strengthful.

Hence, there should be more programmes of welfare for women and children and nutrition programmes for pregnat women, nursing mothers and children. Merely programmes will do nothing but more important is its honest implementation.

Health

Between education and health perhaps education commands greater attention. But both are equally important. It is well said that 'health is wealth'. People of rural India suffer from many diseases, they lack proper sanitation and medical facilities and live in inhygenic condition. Our national health and average of life is much less in comparison to the other countries of Europe and America. A number of surveys on health facilities in rural India reveal that we are still lagging much behind the target.

Government programmes have been launched in the direction, but unfortunately, the achievements during the plan periods fell short of the target.

Hence there should be efforts to (i) control and eridicate the major communicable diseases - which causes a good number of lives every year, (ii) provision of curative, preventive and promotional health services, (iii) augmentation of training programmes of medical and para-medical personnel, (iv) strengthening the primary health centre complex for undertaking preventive and curvative health services in rural areas, (v) development of referral services by providing specialist's attention to common diseases in rural areas, (vi) Doctor and free medicines for each village.

Roads

Rural roads are the arteries and veins of the whole country. On their proper functioning depends the mobility of the whole economy. We have not yet realised that. The slow progress in this sphere shows that clearly.

Construction of rural roads is, by and large, a responsibility of the state government. Special emphasis is being laid on the development of rural roads. They are necessary for the growth of the rural economy and for increase in agricultural production. Priority is to be given to roads leading to market towns and centres. There are more than 2,000 villages in Bihar alone that have to be connected by all weather roads.

Rural roads are necessary also to give the over crowded cities a breathing gap. Quite a considerable section of city people may live in better spacious accommodation in the country side with linking roads motorable and comfortable to move to and fro.

Even from the point of view of environmental relief from pollution it is essential for mutual benefit to connect villages with towns and save both from stagnation and suffocation.

Unemployment

The most burning problem in rural India, is the solution of unemployment. The problem is of greater magnitude than it appears from outside. The 'educated' youth are shifting to towns never to return to villages. The uneducated block to factories and pose fresh problems both to Government and to themselves.

Employment is essential to human happiness. It is not only an economic problem. It is the biggest social tension and the major most political responsibility. Idleness and indolence are the causes of misery. Above anything else it is a human problem.

The gap between the 'haves' and 'have nots' is indeed alarming. India in general and Central Bihar in particular is facing a disturbing situation in the villages which may cause an explosion if the growing disparity among the rural people is not tackled effectively. The problem has to be tackled on a wide front effectively and imaginatively.

There are some remedies to this problem (i) The first solution lies in the redistribution of land among the landless, (ii) The bulk of farmers who fall under the category of under employment can get subsidiary jobs by keeping themselves busy in agroindustries. There is scope for further development of agro based industries in rural India with local resources,

(iii) The development of hanidcrafts, handlooms, small and village industries with advancement of their technology, (iv) Unemployed people in the villages can try to get themselves occupied through their own scheme. This can be done through the active participation of the nationalised banks and the co-operative societies in rural India, (v) Crash programme undertaken two decades ago to fight rural unemployment. It is the programme of the community development projects. The programme to provide employment to 1,000 persons in each districts of the country. It was quite useful. The works undertaken under it was rural roads, minor irrigation, afforestation reclamation and conservation. Through such constructive works in villages - e.g. road buildings, canal digging, irrigation, school buildings etc., the unemployed persons in rural India may be absorbed to some extent to do something for themselves and their community, (vi) Our unemployed to educated village boys may take up, on their own, new projects to educate the illiterate village people including farmers.

REFERENCES

1. Johnson, E.A.J. (1970) : The Organization of Space in Developing Countries, Cambridge.
2. NCAER (National Council of Applied Economic Research), 1972 : Market Towns and Spatial Development, New Delhi.
3. Bromley, R.J. (1975) : Periodic Markets and Rural Development Policy, Cambria, pp. 155-64.
4. Ram, Udhaw (1982) : Periodic Markets and Rural Development in Lower Ganga-Ghagra Doab, Ph. D. Thesis (Unpublished), University of Gorakhpur.
5. Bhattacharya, Dr. V.R. (1982) : New Face of Rural India, pp. vii. Metropolitian, New Delhi (1982).
6. Sinha, Ashok Kumar (1989) : Some Aspects of Agricultural Productivity in South West Alluvial Plains Zone of Bihar. p. 2. A Paper Presented in National Seminar on Rural Development in India at M.U. Bodh-Gaya in Dec. 1989.
7. Zemanian, A.H. (1986) : Multi level Marketing Networks in Less Developed Countries, Applied Mathematics and Computation, 18, pp. 185-210.
8. Shrivatava, V.K. (1977) : Periodic Markets and Rural Development in Bahraich District : A Case Study, National Geographer, XII, pp. 47-55.
9. Reddy, G.Y. (1982) : Role of Communication in Rural Development for Eradication of Rural Poverty, Indian Journal of Regional Science. XIV. pp. 104-109.

10. Taylor, D.R.F. (1974) : The Role of Small Urban Place in Development : The Case of Kanya, in E.E.I. Shakhs and R. Obudho, (ed.), Urbanization, National Development and Regional Planning, New York.
11. Shrivastava, V.K. (1987) : Storage of Foodgrains in Eastern Utter Pradesh : Present Status and Future Planing, The Geographer, XXXIV, pp. 78-87.
12. Shrivastava, V.K. (1985) : Marketing and Rural Development in K.N. Singh and D.N. Singh (eds.) Rural Development in India, Problems, Strategies and Approaches, National Geographical Society of India, Varanasi, pp. 183-88.
13. Sinha, Ashok Kumar (1989) : Opt. Cit. pp. 13-19.
14. Census of India (1981).

8

Summary and Conclusion

The making of Magadh Division traces its background from its unknown past to the current century. Gaya, one of the oldest city of the world, unrolls its progress and decay. The profile of the project denotes eight chapters. Each chapter consists of documents of physico-cultural landscape of rural markets and rurban centres of Magadh Division.

Magadh Division has swelled with human population to evolve rural markets where variety of commodities agglomerate during day and disappear as the sun sets. Rural centres scatter over dissected scarps in its southern sector. Outliers of Chota Nagpur highlands drive away rural centres to concentrate in the fertile Magadh plain to appear as congested to disperse rural segments. Rural centres are the storehouses of commodities ranging from salt to grains, vegetables etc. Weekly, bi-weekly, tri-weekly and daily markets act as migratory hub of exchanges of various goods. Monsoon climate, rich alluvial soil and improved irrigation surcharge Magadh Division to grow a variety of agricultural crops which rush to rural markets and rurban centres.

Land produces variety of crops to describe rural market system and define rurban centres of Magadh Division.

Evolution and growth of rural market centres portray spatio temporal characteristics. Magadh Division contains 216 rural markets and a rural market serves 31.75 villages of this Division Threadbare analysis of periodic markets throw light of their percentage in different districts of Magadh Division. Periodicity by days, market frequency by days and chi-squared test throw a comparative light of rural markets.

The concept of market cycles is related to time whereas marketing is related to space. Complete and incomplete market cycles create gaps where weekly markets are less frequent.

The evolving rural settlements seem to function as central place where disparity dots but as time runs to record optimum conditions, markets of similar type becomes equally spaced. Modifications of various ways operate to reflect relation betweensettlement and consumers.

Evolution and spacing of rural central places are tied up with economic prosperity and transport facilities.

The pivot of market is function whereas participants revolve round it. Shelter for review depends upon data, sampling, questionnarie and field limitations.

Consumers play a dominant role in shaping rural markets and changing behaviour. *Consumer behaviour* has three components: (i) the range of good, (ii) consumer frequency and (iii) consumer space preference. Consumer do not mind travel for a particular goods, foodstuffs and high quality goods. Role of traders is linked with marketing. Traders frequent movement in market and their varying income groups vary in different market centres of Targir, Khemda, Kinjar, Amawan and Sherghati.

Sherghati Rurban Centre catalogues durable goods, readymade garmetns, footwears, utensils, general stores, book depot and stationery, kirana, food grains, manihari, timber, coir rope, baskets etc. ubiquitous goods, vegetable and fruits, non-vegetarian foods, agricultural inputs, food stuff, special goods, animals, services, machinery, precious minerals, hardware and cement. Each has been discussed to note their significance.

Rurban Centres act as significant component of the study. *Large rural settlements and small towns compose rurban centres*. Their attributes, development and functions draw their profiles. Functional classification of rurban centres as administrative, power project, sub-regional, agricultural market and small towns within campus of large cities reveal specific function.

Critical study has been made of micro-geography of sample markets of Targir, Khemda, Kinjar, Amawan and Sherghati ot outline their morphology, functions and facilities.

Internal structure of the morphology of permanent market has been traced. Various facts have been explained by *calculated percentage*. The market morphology of the centres in the Magadh Division consists of two parts - (i) durable and (ii) perishable goods. Shops need zonal arrangement.

Marketing and Rural Development are considered as interlink without which their projected profiles fail to trace similarity of evolution and development. The zone of research has to be carefully traversed to fathom traders performance. Rural markets no doubt, *function as levers of growth*. To portray rural markets in their poly-phase, it is essential to balance markets, traders, goods movement and complexities.

Marketing is the biggest problem ever faced by advancing rural industrial sector. Rural industrial sector is unorganised and has little strength to withstand the stiff competition it faces from the organised large and medium industries. Lack of standardisation in the products and lack of proper advertisement, education and persuation are marketing difficult problems. Lack of adequate market outlets dampens the enthusiasm of rural artisans who need help in terms of product designs, consumer preference, latest product styles and designs.

A creation of an effective marketing infrastructure is needed to produce products of rural industries. The level of technology in rural and small scale industries is low and the products are not standardised. *A Central Marketing Organisation* is to be evolved to supply specific designs and models.

Rural industries produce a variety of commodities which have to be sold at fair prices. The marketing efforts of the existing village enterprises lack proper organisation, product standardisation, due publicity and accessibility to market. The stupendous task of marketing requires multidimensional approach.

If agriculture functions as the heart of Magadh Divisional economy, rural industries will act as its lungs to balance production of commodities and their sale on fair price in markets.

Appendix - I

MAGADH DIVISION
IMPORTANT STATISTICS

Sources : District Cenus HandBooks, 1981

			BIHAR STATE	AURANGABAD DISTRICT	GAYA IN-CLUDING JEHANABAD DISTRICTS	NAWADA DISTRICT	MAGADH DIVISION	% OF BIHAR
1			2	3	4	5	6	7
POPULATION	TOTAL	Persons	69,914,734	1,237,072	3,134,175	1,099,177	5,470.424	7.82
		Males	35,930,560	632,537	1,597,238	549,120	2,778,895	7.73
		Females	33,984,174	604,535	1,536,937	550,057	2,691,529	7.91
	RURAL	Persons	61,195,744	1,151,185	2,794,171	1,026,116	4,971,472	8.12
		Males	31,170,556	587,066	1,415,928	510,996	2,513,990	8.06
		Females	30,025,188	564,119	1,378,243	515,120	2,457,485	8.18
	URBAN	Persons	8,718,990	85,887	340,004	73,061	498,952	5.72
		Males	4,760,004	45,471	181,310	38,124	264,905	5.56
		Females	3,958,986	40,416	158,694	34,937	234,047	5.91

1		2	3	4	5	6	7
DECENNIAL POPULATION GROWTH		+24.06	+21.75	+23.03	+23.00		
RATE 1971-81							
AREA (Sq. Kms.)		173,877	3,305	6.545	2,494	12,344	7.09
DENSITY OF POPULATION (Per Sq. Km)		402	374	479	441	443.44	
SEX RATIO (Number of Females per 1000 Males)		946	956	962	1,002	968.56	
LITERACY RATE	Persons	26.20	28.49	30.07	26.53	29%	
	Males	38.11	42.50	44.33	40.31	43.11%	
	Females	13.62	13.83	15.25	12.77	14.42%	
PERCENTAGE OF URBAN POPULATION TO TOTAL POPULATION		12.47	6.94	10.85	6.65		
PERCENTAGE TO TOTAL POPULATION							
(i) Main Workers	Persons	29.68	27.72	30.81	31.00		
	Males	49.20	46.26	47.74	48.35		
	Females	9.06	8.33	13.21	13.67		
(ii) Marginal Workers	Persons	2.67	2.42	1.82	1.80		
	Males	0.98	0.97	0.68	0.68		
	Females	4.44	3.94	3.01	2.92		

1		2	3	4	5	6	7
(iii) Non-Workers	Persons	67.65	69.86	67.37	67.20		
	Males	49.82	52.77	51.58	50.97		
	Females	86.50	87.73	83.78	83.41		
BREAKUP OF MAIN WORKERS							
	Primary Population	16405738 (79.20%)				1363376 (82.70%)	
	Secondary Population	622988 (3.00%)				54614 (3.3%)	
	Tertiary Population	3683489 (17.80%)				230361 (14.00%)	
PERCENTAGE AMONG MAIN WORKERS							
(i) Cultivators	Persons	43.57	46.26	43.04	49.40		
	Males	46.71	50.50	47.95	55.50		
	Females	25.54	21.63	24.59	27.85		
(ii) Agricultural Labourers	Persons	35.50	35.93	38.84	36.22		
	Males	30.65	30.06	30.78	27.44		
	Females	63.33	70.04	69.11	67.22		
(iii) Household Industry	Persons	2.38	3.51	2.55	2.46		
	Males	2.32	3.54	2.74	2.64		
	Females	2.76	3.34	1.84	1.82		

1		2	3	4	5	6	7
(iv) Other Workers	Persons	18.55	14.30	15.57	11.92		
	Males	20.32	15.90	18.53	14.42		
	Females	8.37	4.99	4.46	3.11		
PERCENTAGE OF SCHEDULED CASTES POPULATON TO TOTAL POPULATION	Persons	14.51	22.88	25.54	24.52		
	Males	14.36	22.89	25.34	24.45		
	Females	14.67	22.86	25.76	24.58		
PERCENTAGE OF SCH-EDULED TRIBES POPULATION TO TOTAL POPULATION	Persons	8.13	0.03	0.04	0.11		
	Males	8.11	0.03	0.04	0.11		
	Females	8.52	0.03	0.04	0.11		
NUMBER OF OCCUPIED PRESIDENTIAL HOUSES		9,891,123	155,948	402,073	138,110	696,131	
NUMBER OF VILLAGES	Total	79,208	1,884	3,873	1,099	6,856	
	Inhabited	67,546	1,749	3,513	967	6,229	
	Uninhabited	10,302	116	519	124	759	
	Constituents of Towns	1,360	19	41	8	68	
NUMBER OF TOWNS		220	5	5	3	13	
NUMBER OF RURAL MARKETS	Weekly		17	54+7=	61	21	99
	Bi-weekly		20	23+24=	47	02	99
	Tri-weekly		01	0+05=	05	00	06
	Daily		00	0+07=	07	05	12
				(G) J			Total–216

N.B. - G. = GAYA. J. = JEHANABAD.

Appendix - II

MAGADH DIVISION
TYPES OF RURAL MARKET CENTRES
WEEKLY MARKETS

Sl. No.	Name of the Village or Place	Day of Market/Hat	Name of Development Block and Distt.
1	2	3	4
1.	Chakand	Wednesday	Gaya Town Block, Gaya
2.	Khap	Saturday	Bodh-Gaya, Gaya
3.	Kharanti	Saturday	-do-
4.	Harli Kalan	Tuesday	-do-
5.	Ghogharia	Friday	-do-
6.	Khajawati	Saturday	-do-
7.	Bom Bazar, Cherki	Saturday	Sherghati Block, Gaya
8.	Parri	Wednesday	-do-
9.	Karmauni	Wednesday	-do-
10.	Amarut	Wednesday	-do-
11.	Ghoraghat	Wednesday	-do-
12.	Tanarwa	Thursday	Amas Block, Gaya
13.	Kothi	Saturday	Imamganj Block, Gaya
14.	Pakri Guria	Friday	-do-
15.	Raniganj	Sunday	-do-
16.	Goti Bandh	Tuesday	Dumaria Block, Gaya
17.	Dumaria	Thursday	-do-
18.	Narayanpur	Tuesday	-do-
19.	Majhauli	Thursday	-do-
20.	Narayanpur	-do-	
21.	Arsikalan	Sunday	Gurua Block, Gaya
22.	Baswan	Sunday	Pariya Block, Gaya

1	2	3	4
23.	Amawan	Thursday	Tikari Block, Gaya
24.	Bela	Thursday	Belaganj Block, Gaya
25.	Bihta	Sundya	Khizirsarai Block, Gaya
26.	Khider Saray	Wednesday	-do-
27.	Sadipur	Wednesday	-do-
28.	Taunsa	Thursday	Atri Block, Gaya
29.	Upthu	Monday	-do-
30.	Titua	Tuesday	-do-
31.	Sahora	Tuesday	-do-
32.	Reula	Sunday	-do-
33.	Tankuppa	Monday	Wazirganj Block, Gaya
34.	Sultanpur	Tuesday	-do-
35.	Tarawan	Saturday	-do-
36.	Jagarnathpur	Wednesday	Fatehpur Block, Gaya
37.	Lodhwe	Friday	-do-
38.	Fatehpur	Monday	-do-
39.	Dumri Chatti	Thursday	-do-
40.	Gamhri	Tuesday	-do-
41.	Kathautiya Kewal	Saturday	-do-
42.	Dharhara	Monday	Mohanpur Block, Gaya
43.	Dangra	Thursday	-do-
44.	Bongea	Sunday	-do-
45.	Lakhipur	Sunday	-do-
46.	Itwan	Friday	Mohanpur Block, Gaya
47.	Amatari	Friday	-do-
48.	Sarwan Khas	Tuesday	Barachatti Block, Gaya
49.	Bhelwa	Thursday	-do-
50.	Bhadeya	Sunday	-do-
51.	Dhanganin	Monday	-do-
52.	Gajragarh	Saturday	-do-
53.	Sabalpur	Wednesday	-do-

1	2	3	4
54.	Barwadih	Wednesday	-do-
55.	Tehta	Saturday	Makhdumpur Block, Jehanabad
56.	Ibrahimpur	Wednesday	Kurtha Block, Jehanabad
57.	Manikpur	Tuesday	-do-
58.	Fauladpur	Sunday	-do-
59.	Bara	Sunday	Kako Block, Jehanabad
60.	Kako	Sunday	-do-
61.	Sikariya	Sunday	-do-
62.	Nawada	Friday	Nawada Block, Nawada
63.	Bhadauni	Friday	-do-
64.	Sandohra	Monday	-do-
65.	Quadirganj	Thursday	-do-
66.	Koiri Bigha	Saturday	Akbarpur Block, Nawada
67.	Bhat Bigha	Saturday	-do-
68.	Akbarpur	Saturday	-do-
69.	Bandarkol	Saturday	-do-
70.	Kahuara	Tuesday	Hisua Block, Nawada
71.	Pararia	Tuesday	-do-
72.	Bhatta	Wednesday	Gobindpur Block, Nawada
73.	Takuatanr	Friday	Rajauli Block, Nawada
74.	Rajauli	Tuesday	-do-
75.	Targir	Monday	-do-
76.	Bisiait	Monday	Sirdala Block, Nawada
77.	Meksaru	Friday	-do-
78.	Paroria	Sunday	-do-
79.	Laun	Sunday	-do-
80.	Sonrah Majhganwa	Wednesday	-do-
81.	Rupai	Friday	-do-
82.	Chamotha	Sunday	-do-
83.	Kapasia	Tuesday	Aurangabad Block, Aurangabad

1	2	3	4
84.	Anjanian	Tuesday	-do-
85.	Ketaki	Thursday	-do-
86.	Pipra Bagahi	Thursday	Kutumba Block, Aurangabad
87.	Sanra	Friday	-do-
88.	Naur	Sunday	Nabinagar Block, Aurangabad
89.	Jogiya	Sunday	Barun Block, Aurangabad
90.	Amauna	Sunday	Daudnagar Block, Aurangabad
91.	Tarar	Sunday	-do-
92.	Ahiyapur	Wednesday	Haspura Block, Aurangabad
93.	Bihta	Tuesday	-do-
94.	Goh	Tuesday	Goh Block, Aurangabad
95.	Dewakund	Monday	-do-
96.	Pauthu	Wednesday	Rafiganj Block, Aurangabad
97.	Karama Masud	Sunday	-do-
98.	Arthua	Monday	-do-
99.	Madanpur	Sunday	Madanpur Block, Aurangabad

The individual no. of the above mentioned market centres in the Districts of (i) Gaya - 54, (ii) Jehanabad - 7, (iii) Nawada -21, (iv) Aurangabad - 17 = 99.

BI-WEEKLY MARKETS

1	2	3	4
1.	Barwan	Monday & Friday	Sherghati Block, Gaya
2.	Nawada	Monday & Friday	-do-
3.	Sherghati	Mondya & Friday	-do-
4.	Roshanganj	Sunday & Wed.	Amas Block, Gaya
5.	Barki Sawo	Tuesday & Sat.	-do-
6.	Amas	Monday & Thurs.	-do-
7.	Imamganj	Monday & Friday	Imamganj Block, Gaya
8.	Bharaundha	Sunday & Wed.	Gurua Block, Gaya
9.	Gurua	Thursday & Sat.	-do-
10.	Konchi	Monday & Friday	Pariya Block, Gaya.

1	2	3	4
11.	Barorah	Sunday & Thurs.	-do-
12.	Mathurapur	Sunday & Wed.	-do-
13.	Ajmatganj	Sunday & Wed.	Pariya Block, Gaya
14.	Anti	Sund. and Thurs.	Konch Block, Gaya
15.	Mau	Sund. & Thurs.	Tikari Block, Gaya
16.	Kapea	Mond. and Fri.	-do-
17.	Manikpur Baliari	Tues. & Saturday	-do-
18.	Alipur	Tues. & Sat.	-do-
19.	Mathya	Tues. & Sat.	-do-
20.	Pai Bigha	Wed. & Sat.	Belaganj Block, Gaya.
21.	Bahorma	Wed. & Sat.	Atri Block, Gaya
22.	Jethian	Sund. & Thurs.	-do-
23.	Babhandih Wazirganj	Sund. & Thurs.	Wazirganj Block, Gaya
24.	Kenwri	Wed. & Sat.	Jehanabad Block, Jehanabad
25.	Tali	Tues. & Fri.	-do-
26.	Bhewar	Sund. & Thurs.	-do-
27.	Matipur	Monday & Fri.	Kurtha Block, Jehanabad
28.	Khemkaran Saray	Sunday & Wed.	-do-
29.	Dharampur	Tues. & Wed.	-do-
30.	Khatangi	Wed. & Sat.	-do-
31.	Sarya	Sund. & Thurs.	-do-
32.	Shahar Telpa	Mond. & Thurs.	Karpi Block, Jehanabad
33.	Belkharakhas	Tues. & Fri.	-do-
34.	Mali	Tues. & Fri.	-do-
35.	Sonbarsa	Mond. & Fri.	Arwal Block, Jehanabad
36.	Wasilpur	Wed. & Saturday	Arwal Block, Jehanabad
37.	Bhadasi	Mond. & Tues.	-do-
38.	Kaler	Tues. & Friday	-do-
39.	Teri	Monday & Thurs.	-do-
40.	Pinjora	Mond. & Thurs.	Kako Block, Jehanabad
41.	Bishunpur Okri	Mond. & Thurs.	Ghosi Block, Jehanabad

1	2	3	4
42.	Jaitipur Kurwa	Mond. & Thurs.	-do-
43.	Bandhuganj	Tues. & Fri.	-do-
44.	Ghosi	Mond. & Fri.	-do-
45.	Shaho Bigha	Wed. & Saturday	-do-
46.	Dhuriari	Wednesday & Sat.	-do-
47.	Surajpur	Tues. & Fri.	-do-
48.	Nardiganj	Mond. & Fri.	Hisua Block, Nawada
49.	Sirdala	Mond. & Thurs.	Sirdala Block, Nawada
50.	Pawai	Wed. & Sat.	Deo Block, Nawada
51.	Deo	Mond. & Fri.	-do-
52.	Israur	Tues. & Sat.	-do-
53.	Pachokhar	Wed. & Sat.	-do-
54.	Baluganj Brandi	Sund. & Thurs.	-do-
55.	Kutumba Kapchanpur	Sund. & Thurs.	Kutumba Block, Aurangabad
56.	Deoriya	Sund. & Wed.	-do-
57.	Simra Telpura	Mond. & Fri.	-do-
58.	Amba	Sund. & Tues.	-do-
59.	Basidiha Gopal	Mond. & Thurs.	-do-
60.	Maharajganj	Monday & Friday	Kutumba Block, Aurangabad
61.	Dumri	Wed. & Sat.	-do-
62.	Akorha	Mond. & Fri.	Nabinagar Block, Aurangabad
63.	Mahuawan	Tuesday & Sat.	-do-
64.	Salaia	Tues. & Sat.	-do-
65.	Barem	Mond. & Fri.	-do-
66.	Tanarwa	Mond. & Thurs.	-do-
67.	Tendua	Sund. & Wed.	-do-
68.	Bariyawan	Tues. & Sat.	-do-
69.	Thumba	Wed. & Sat.	-do-
70.	Bairia	Sund. & Thurs.	-do-
71.	Barki Regania	Wed. & Sat	-do-

1	2	3	4
72.	Charan Kalan	Mond. & Thurs.	-do-
73.	Mali	Mond. & Fri.	-do-
74.	Simra Kalan	Sund. & Thurs.	Barun Block, Aurangabad
75.	Bhalua	Sund. & Thurs.	-do-
76.	Mahtha	Sund. & Thurs.	-do-
77.	Mitraj	Sund. & Thurs.	-do-
78.	Khemda	Sund. & Thurs.	-do-
79.	Siris	Sund. & Wed.	-do-
80.	Khanda	Sund. & Thurs.	-do-
81.	Obra	Fri. & Thurs.	Obra Block, Aurangabad
82.	Kara	Sund. & Wed.	-do-
83.	Bharup	Wed. & Sat.	-do-
84.	Khudwan	Tues. & Wed.	-do-
85.	Hanspura	Monday & Thursday	Haspura Block, Aurangabad
86.	Sihri Kalan	Mond. & Fri.	-do-
87.	Jakhaura	Wed. & Sat.	-do-
88.	Deohra	Sund. & Wednesday	Goh Block, Aurangabad
89.	Upahra	Sund. & Wed.	-do-
90.	Majathi	Sund. & Thurs.	-do-
91.	Bhetaniyan	Sund. & Thrus.	Rafiganj Block, Aurangabad
92.	Barahi	Sund. & Thrus.	-do-
93.	Bhadwa	Wed. & Sat.	-do-
94.	Thakurar	Sunday & Friday	-do-
95.	Kasman	Mond. & Thurs.	-do-
96.	Khiriawan	Thes. & Sat.	Madanpur Block, Aurangabad
97.	Warkhas	Mond. & Tues.	-do-
98.	Teldiha	Tues. & Sat.	-do-
99.	Nima Anjan	Sund. & Wed.	-do-

The individual no. of the above mentioned market centres in the Districts of : (i) Gaya - 23, (ii) Jehanabad - 24, (iii) Nawada - 02, (iv) Aurangabad - 50 = 99.

TRI-WEEKLY MARKETS

1	2	3	4
1.	Karpi	Mond., Wed. & Sat.	Karpi Block, Jehanabad
2.	Kinjar	Tues., Thurs. & Sat.	-do-
3.	Welidad	Sund., Tues. & Fri.	Arwal Block, Jehanabad
4.	Parasi	Mond., Thurs. & Sat.	-do-
5.	Usri	Tues., Thurs. & Sat.	-do-
6.	Dharhara	Sund., Tues. & Fri.	Rafiganj Block, Aurangabad

The individual no. of the above mentioned market centres in the Districts of : (i) Gaya - Nil, (ii) Jehanabad - 05, (iii) Nawada - Nil, (iv) Aurangabad - 01 = 6.

DAILY MARKETS

Sl. No.	Name of the Village or Place	Name of Dev. Block and District
1.	Makhdumpur	Makhdumpur Block, Jehanabad
2.	Markarpur	-do-
3.	Bishunganj	-do-
4.	Sipah	Arwal Block, Jehanabad
5.	Badrabad	-do-
6.	Mehdiyabad	-do-
7.	Ouazi Sarai	Kako Block, Jehanabad
8.	Narhat	Narhat Block, Nawada
9.	Chakwae	Warisalignaj Block, Nawada
10.	Pakri Barwan	Pakri Barwan Block, Nawada
11.	Kawakol	Kawakole Block, Nawada
12.	Amawan	Rajauli Block, Nawada

The individual no. of the abvoe mentioned market centres in the Districtss of (i) Gaya - Nil, (ii) Jehanabad - 07, (iii) Nawada - 05, (iv) Aurangabad - Nil = 12

FAIRS

Sl. No.	Name of the Village or Place	Name of Dev. Block and District
1.	Deo Mela	Deo Block, Aurangabad (Twice in a year)
2.	Budhagare Fair	Manpur Block, Gaya (Twice in a year)

The individual no. of the above mentioned fair in the Districts of : (i) Gaya - 02, (ii) Jehanabad - Nil, (iii) Nawada - Nil, (iv) Aurangabad - 02 = 4.

Appendix - III

MAGADH DIVISION
LIST OF VARIABLES WITH GROUPS OF SHOPS

1. *Durable Goods* : Books, Stationery, Building material, Cloth, Crockery, Cycle shop, Hosiery, Dry fruits, Electirc appliances, Furniture (Steel/ Wooden/Cane), Footwear, General goods, Readymade garmetns, Kirana, Manihari, Ghee/oil, Soap, Toys, Sports goods, Utensils, Food grains, Pot maker, Broom, Bamboo stick, Rain coat, Bamboo basket and Fans, Handmade fans, Coir rope, Cap, Cotton, Timber.
2. *Ubiquitous Goods* : Betel leaves, Tobacco, Bidi, Kerosine Oil, Pan shop, Earthen pots, Salt, Cold drink, Confectionery, Bangles.
3. *Vegetables and Fruits* : Green vegegables and fruits.
4. *Non-vegetarian Foods* : Meet, Egg, Chicken and Fish.
5. *Agricultural Inputs* : Agricultural equipments, Wooden plough, Fertilizer, Seeds, Pesticides.
6. *Food Stuff* : Baked food, Bakery, Food stuff, Sweets, Tea shops, Snacks, Ice cream, Restaurant, Lai, Bhuja, Chura.
7. *Special Goods* : Alcholic liquour, Medical shop, Herbs used for medicines, Newspapers, Palm juice (Tari.), Radios, Perfumes, Printing press, Leather rope, Patsan (Jute), Animal feed.
8. *Animals* : Cow, Ox, Buffalo, Sheep, Goat.
9. *Services* : Auto shop, Bank, Cobbler, Barber, Binding, Black-smith, Cinema, Cycle repair shop, Dentist, Doctor (Allopathic, Homoeopathic, Auyurvedic), Drama materials, Dry cleaner, Eye specialist, Flour mills, Fuel shop, Hotel, Carpenter, Lawyer, Optician, Photo framers, Pot maker, Glodsmith, Oil mills, Restaurant,

	Rest house/Dak Bunglow, Watch repairer, Photostate copier, Photographers.
10. *Machinery Items* :	Motor parts, Sewing Machine, Watch, Radio and loose parts, T.V., Two-in-one radio tape recorder, Record player, Cassettes, Records, Electronic and Electrical goods.
11. *Other Goods* :	Gold, Silver, Hardware, Cement.

Glossary

Sl. No.	Hindi Word		Meaning in English
1.	Ahar	-	Small water reservoir having U shaped or rectangular embankment.
2.	Aghani	-	Winter rice.
3.	Anchal	-	Circle for administrative purpose
4.	Bazar	-	Market.
5.	Bhadai	-	A type of crop of early rainy season.
6.	Bhuja	-	Made of baked grains.
7.	Bidi	-	A cheap smoke made of tobacco and kendu leaves.
8.	Boro	-	Spring rice.
9.	Charcha Mandal	-	Group discussion
10.	Chura	-	Flattend rice.
11.	Garma	-	Summer rice.
12.	Ghee	-	Obtained from butter.
13.	Gur	-	Sweet cake made of sugarcane juice.
14.	Halal	-	Slowly slaughtering an animal till it bleeds to death.
15.	Hat	-	Rural periodic market.
16.	Hathia Nakshatra	-	A period of useful heavy rains of about 15 days (Septermber/October).
17.	Janeu	-	Secred thread ceremony celebrated by Hindus.
18.	Jhatka	-	Salughtering of animals with one stroks.
19.	Kachha	-	Made of mud.
20.	Kewal	-	Clayey soil.
21.	Khaini	-	Dry tobacco leaf.
22.	Kharif	-	A type of crop of rainy season.
23.	Kia	-	Pot to keep sindur.
24.	Lai	-	A type of sweet.

Sl. No.	Hindi Word		Meaning in English
25.	Lohar	-	Blacksmith.
26.	Mandi	-	Held at a place where business transacted daily on a large scale.
27.	Manihari	-	Rural cosmetic shop.
28.	Mochi	-	Cobbler
29.	Mundan	-	Head shaving ceremony of the Hindus for the first time after birth.
30.	Pacca	-	Cemented.
31.	Patwa	-	Weaver.
32.	Pinda	-	Rice balls or flour cakes
33.	Pind Dan	-	Offering oblation .to manes or deceased persons.
34.	Pyne	-	Artificial water channel for irrigation purpose.
35.	Rabi	-	A type of crops sown in autumn (Sept. Oct.).
36.	Samiti	-	Committee.
37.	Sindur	-	Vermilion applied by married Hindu women on their head.
38.	Talukdari	-	Contract to collect land revenue.
39.	Tikuli	-	Colourful chips of various shapes and sizes applied by Indian women on their forehead.
40.	Tumtum	-	Horse cart for passengers.
41.	Zamindar	-	Land Lord
42.	Zamindari	-	Land Lordship.

Bibliography

Adalemo, I.A. (1976) : Competition Among Temporally Separated Markets, in Gormens, E., (Ed.), Manizer Geographisches Studien, 10, pp. 27-30.

Ahmad, E. (1952) : Rural Settlement Types in the Uttar Pradesh (United Provinces of Agra and Oudh), Annals of the Association of American Geographers, XIII, pp. 233-46.

Agricultural Research Institute: 'Soil Survey Report', Technical report No. 10, Sabour (Bihar).

Alao, N.A. (1968) : Periodic Markets in Western Nigeria : Theory and Empirical Evidence, North-Western University, Department of Geography, Research Papers No. 42, pp. 2-3.

Berry, B.J.L. (1967) : Geography of Market Centres and Retail Distribution, Englewood Cliffs, New Jersey.

————. (1969) : Policy Implications of an Urban Location Model for the Kanpur Region in Desai, P.B., (ed.), Regional Perspective on Industrial and Urban Growth, Bombay, pp. 205-19.

Berry, B.J.L. and Garrison, W.L. (1958) : Recent Development of Central Place Theory, Papers and proceedings of the Regional Science Association, 4, pp. 107-20.

Bhatt, L.S. Kundu, A. et al., (1976) : Micro-level Planning : A Case Study of Karnal Area, Haryána (India), K.G. Publications, New Delhi.

Bhatt, M.P. (1977) : Some Aspects of Urbanization in Developing countries, Presidential Address to Economics, Commerce and Management Section, 2nd All India Academy of Social Sciences, Varanasi (unpublished).

Bhole, H.G. (1983) : Role and Potentiality of Traditional Market Systems in the Third World Urbanization, International Asian Forum, 14 pp. 345-362.

Bourne, L.S. (1973) : Comments on Behavioural Approaches in Geography, in John Rees and Peter Newby (eds.), Behavioural Perspectives in Geography, Middlesex Polytechnic, Monographs in Geography, No. 1, London.

Brinkmann, To (1935) : The Economics of the Farm Business, Berkeley, (Translation with Introduction and Notes by E.T. Benedict, Stippler, H.H. and M.R. Benedict).

Buchanan Francis (1811-12) : An Account of the District of Bihar and Patna, Book III.

Bromley, R.J. (1973) : The Spatial Pattern and Temporal Synchronization of Periodic Markets, Swansea Geographer, II, pp. 15-25.

————. (1975) : Periodic Markets and Rural Development Policy, Cambria, pp. 155-64.

————. (1976) : Contemporary Market Periodicity in Highland Ecuador, Regional Analysis, l, pp. 91-122.

————. (1975) : Periodic Markets and Rural Development Policy, Cambria, pp. 155-64.

Bromley, R. and Bromley, R.J. (1975) : The Debate on Sunday Markets in Nineteenth Century Ecuador, Journal of Latin, American Studies, 7.

Bronger, Dirk (1977) : The Dilemma of Developing Country Research, Intereconomics, Nos. 9/10, pp. 245-50.

Brush, J.E. (1953) : The Hierarchy of Central Places in South-western Wisconsin, Geographical Review, Vol. 43, pp. 380-402.

Bromley, R.G. (1971) : Markets in Developing Countries : A Review, Geography, 56, pp. 124-32.

Bhattacharya, Dr. V.R. (1982) : New Face of Rural India, Metropolitan, New Delhi, p. vii.

Carruthers, Ian (1958) : A Classification of Service Centres in England and Wales, "Geographical Journal, Vol. CXXIX.

(1981) : Census of India.

Christaller, W. (1966) : Central Places in Southern Germany, Translated by C.W. Baskin, Prentice Hall.

Clark, P.J. and F.C. Evans, (1954) : Distance to Nearest Neighbour as a Measure of Spatial Relationship in Populations, Ecology, 35, pp. 445-53.

Converse, P.D. (1949) : New Laws of Retail Gravitation, Journal of Marketing, 14, pp. 379-84.

Cox Kevin (1972) : Man, Location and Behaviour, John Wiley and Sons, Inc., New York.

Cordey-Hayes, M. (1968) : Retail Location Models, Centre for Environmental Studies, Working Paper 16.

Davis, Kingsley, (1966), "Urban Research and Significance", in Gibbs, J.P. (Ed.), Urban Research Method, New Delhi.

Davies, R.L. (1970) : Variable Relationships in Central Place and Research Potential Model, Regional Studies, 4, pp. 49-61.

————. (1976) : Marketing Geography with Special Reference to Retailing Methuen and Co., London.

Dixit, R.S. (1984) : Market Centres and their Spatial Development in the Umland of Kanput, Kitab Mahal, Allahabad.

Dickenson, R.E. (1932) : "The Distribution and Functions of the Smaller Urban Settlements of East Anglia", Geography, Vol. XVII.

————. (1981) : District Census Hand Book, Gaya, Bihar.

Eighmy, T.M. (1972) : Rural Periodic Markets and Extension of an Urban System : A Western Nigeria Example, Economic Geogrpahy, 48, pp. 299-315.

Funnel, D.C. (1973) : Rural Business Centres in a Low Income Economy : Some Theoretical Problems, Tidjdschrift Voor Econ. en. Geogrpahic, 64, pp. 86-92.

Good, C.M. (1975) : Periodic Markets and Travelling Traders in Uganda The Geographical Review, pp. 50-72.

Gormsen, E. (1972) : Considerations on the Formation of Central Place Systems in Developing Countries in Adams, W.P. and Helleiner F.W. (eds.), International Geogrpahy, 2, pp. 1293-95.

Galpin, C.J. (1915) : The Social Anatomy of Agricultural Community, University of Wisconsin, Agricultural Experiment Station, Research Bulletin, No. 34.

Gloward, A. and Stafford, Jr : "The Functional Basis of Small Town", Economic Geogrpahy.

Haggett, P. (1971) : Locational Analysis in Human Geogrphay, E. Arnold.

Haggett, P. et al., (1979) : Locational Models, Arnold Heinemann, I.

Harriss, Barbara (1974) : The Role of Punjab Wheat Markets as Growth Centres, Geographical Journal, 140, pp. 52-71.

Haggett, P. and Gunawardena, K.A. (1964) : Determination of Population Thresholds for Settlement Functions by the Reed - Muench Method, The Professional Geographer, XVI, pp. 6-9.

Harriss, Barbara (1976a) : Social Specificity in Rural Markets: The case of Tamilnadu, India, in Gormsen, e. (ed.), Mainzer Geographisches Studien, 10,pp. 39-48.

————. (1976b) : The Indian Idology of Growth Centres, Area, Institute of British Geographers, 4, pp. 263-69.

Hodder, B.W. (1965) : The Distribution of Markets in Yorubaland, The Scottish Geographical Magazine, 81, pp. 48-58.

————. (1969) : Markets in Yoruba Land, in Hodder, B.W. and Ukwu, U.I. (eds.). Markets in West Africa, Ibadan.

————. (1971) : Periodic and Daily Markets in West Africa, in C. Meillassum (ed.), Devlopment of Indigenous Trade and Markets in West Africa, London, Oxford University Press, pp. 347-58.

Huff, D.L. (1960) : A Topographical Model of Consumer Space Preferences, Paper and Proceedings of the Regional Science Association, 6, pp. 159-73.

Huff, D.L. (1963) : A probability Analysis of Shopping Centre Trade Areas, Land Economics, pp. 5381-89.

Isard, W. (1956) : Location and Space Economy, New York.

Jain, N.G. (1964) : The Emergence of Urban Centres in Eastern Districts of Vidarbha (Maharashtra), National Geographical Journal of India, X, pp. 148-49.

Jha, P.P. (1969) : Soils of Bihar 'Fertiliser News' Vol. 14, No. 10, October 1969.

Johnson, E.A.J. (1970) : The Organization of Space in Developing Countries, Cambridge.

Jones, Ronald (1967) : Central Place Theory and the Hierarchy and Location of Shopping Centres in a City, Edinburgh Institute of British Geographers Study Gorup in Urban Geogrpahy, Durban Conference.

Kansky, K.J. (1963) : Structure of Transportation Net Works: Relationship Between Geometry and Regional Characteristics, University of Chicago, Deptt. of Geogrpahy Reserach Paper.

Kar, N.R. (1960) : Urban Hierarchy and Central Functionss Around Calcutta, Lund Studies in Geography Series B. 1960, pp. 146-53.

Kumar, N. (1970) : Bihar District Gazatteers, Patna.

Kumar, B. (1983) : Regional Planning Approach to an Efficient Agricultural Market System, Dissertation for M.R.P., I.I.T. Kharagpur.

King, J.L. (1962) : The Functional Role of Small Towns in Centerbury, in Proceedings of 3rd New-Zealand Geographical Conference Palmerrston North.

Lakshmannan, T.R. and Hansen, W.G. (1956) : A Retail Marketing Potential Model, Journal of American Institute of Planners, 31, pp. 134-43.

Losch, A. (1954) : The Economics of Location, Translated by W.H. Woglom and W.F. Stopler, Yale University Press.

Malley, O. (1906) : District Gazetteer of Gaya.

Majumdar, R.C. (1968) : History and Culture of Indian People, Bombay.

Majumdar, S.N. (1924) : Cunningham's Ancient Geography of India, Calcutta.

Monkhoues, F.J. (1972) : A Dictionary of Geogrpahy, London, Edward Arnold.

Mandal, R.B. (1970) : Law of Village Anatomy and Rurban Centres Location on Loschian Landscape. Proceedings of Small Towns, Varanasi.

Marriot Mckim (1955) : Village India, The American Anthropological Association Memoir No. 83, p. 57.

Mayfield, R.C. (1960) : Conformations of Service and Retail Activities : An Example in Lower Orders of an Urban Hierarchy in a Lesser Developed Area, Lund Studies in Geography, Service B, pp. 77-86.

————. (1962) : A Central Place Hierarchy in Northern India, in Garrison, W.L.(ed.), Quantitative Geography, New York, Atherton Press, pp. 120-66.

————. (1963) : The Range of a Central Good in the Indian Punjab, Annals of the Association of American Geographers, 53, pp. 38-49.

Mukherji, A.B. (1975) : Urbanization in the Avadh Region, Uttar Pradesh, Avadh Geographer, I, pp. 13-29.

Mukherji, S.P. (1968) : Commercial Activity and Market Hierarchy in a part of Eastern Himalaya, Darjeeling, The National Geographical Journal of India, XIV, pp. 186-99.

Mumford, L. (1945) : The Culture of Cities, Secker and Warburg.

Murdie, R.A. (1965) : Cultural Differences in Consumer Travel, Economic Geography, 41, pp. 211-33.

Mandal, R.B. (1973) : Rurban Centres in Bihar Plain, Indian Geographical Studies, Research Bulletin, No. 1.

———— (1979) : Introduction to Rural Settlements, Concept Publishing Company, New Delhi.

Nanel, S.F. (1942) : A Black Byzentium : The Kingdom of Nupe in Nigeria. (For the International African Institute), Oxford University Press, London.

Nath, V. (1983) : Marketing and Social Structure in Awadh Plain, Ph. D. Thesis accepted by the University of Gorakhpur, Gorakhpur, (unpublished).

National Council of Applied Economic Research 1972 : Market Towns and Spatial Devlopment, New Delhi.

NCAER (National Council of Applied Economic Research), 1972 : Market Towns and Spatial Development, New Delhi.

Neale, W.C., et al., (1965) : Kurali Market : A Report on the Economic Geography of Marketing in Northern Pubjab, Economic Development and Cultural Chage, XIII, pp. 129-68.

Palomaki, N. (1967) : A Method for Grouping of Central Functions, Proceedings, Scandinavia - Polish Regional Science Association.

Pred, A. (1978) : Behaviour and Location, Lund Studies in Geography, Series B, Human Geography, No. 27.

Raju, V.T. and M. Von Oppen (1980) : Rural Marketing and Inter-regional Trade in India, National Seminar on Settlement Systems of India, Hyderabad (unpublished).

Ram, Udhaw (1982) : Periodic Markets and Rural Development in Lower Ganga-Ghagra Doab, Ph. D. Thesis accepted by the University of Gorakhpur (unpublished).

Roy, Choudhary, P.C. (1957) : Bihar District Gazetteers, Gaya.

Reddy, G.Y. (1982) : Role of Communications in Rural Development for Eradication of Rural Poverty, Indian Journal of Regional Science, XIV, pp. 104-109.

Reed, L.J. and Muench, H. (1964) : A Simple Method of Estimating Fifty Per cent End-points, American Journal of Hygiene, 27, pp. 493-97.

Reilly, W.J. (1931) : The Law of Retail Gravitation, Knicker Bocker Press.

————. (1969) : Methods of the Study of Retail Relationship, Bureau of Business Research, The University of Taxas, Austin, (Reprint of Research Monograph No. 4).

Richard, Fox (1969) : From Zamindar to Ballot Box, Cornell University Press, Itaha.

Sarma, P.K., J.K. Routray, and D.K. Singh (1984) : Spatial Analysis of Hierarchy of Market Centres and Domestic Market Potential Surface of Central Assam (India), The Indian Journal of Marketing Geography, II, I and 2, I.G.U. Special Number, pp. 45-64.

Sexena, H.M. (1975) : Geography of Transport and Market Centres : A Case Study of Hadoti Plateau, New Delhi.

Sen, L.K. and Wanmali, S. (1971) : Planning Rural Growth Centres for Integrated Area Development : A Study in Miryalguda Taluka, Hyderabad.

Shrivastava, K.R. (1983) : Periodic Markets and Central Places in Baghelkhand Region of Madhya Pradesh, Ph. D. Thesis accepted by Rani Durgavati Vishwa Vidyalaya, Jabalpur (Unpublished).

Shrivastava, V.K. (1974) : The Square Configuration of Central Places : An Indian Case, Oriental Geographer, 18, pp. 105-24.

————. (1976a) : Market Periodicity and Centrality : A Methodological Approach, Mainzer Geographisches Studien, 10, pp. 33-38.

————. (1976b) : Geography of Market Centres in the Tarai Region of Uttar Pradesh, I.C.S.S.R. Research Abstracts Quarterly, V, pp. 67-75.

————. (1977) : Periodic Markets and Rural Development Bahraich District : A Case Study, National Geographer, XII, pp. 47-55.

————. (1978) : Theoretical Norms and Interpretations of Market Place Participants' Spatial Behaviour, National Geographer, XIII, pp. 117-24.

————. (1979) : Agricultural Marketing in Uttar Pradesh in Noor Mohd. (ed.), Perspectives in Agricultural Geography, Vol. III, New Delhi.

————. (1980) : Central Place Theory in an Indian Context, Indian Journal of Regional Science, XII, pp. 195-206.

————. (1985) : Marketing and Rural Development in K. N. Singh, and D.N. Singh (eds.), Rural Development in India, Problerms, Strategies and Approaches, National Geographical Society of India, Varanasi, pp. 183-88.

————. (1987) : Storage of Foodgrains in Eastern Uttar Pradesh: Present Status and Future Planning, The Geographer, XXXIV, pp. 78-87.

Shrivastava, V.K. and K.R. Shrivastava (1984) : Geographical Personality of a Rural Market of the Indian Tarai, The Indian Journal of Marketing Geography, II, I.G.U. Special Number, 82-87.

Shrivastava, V.K. and H.P. Nayak (1980) : Origin and Development of Markets, Uttar Bharat Bhoogal Patrika, XVI, pp. 115-26.

Shrivastava, V.K. and J.P. Rai (1978) : Hierarchy of Market Centres : A Methodological Approach (A Case Study of Kopaganj Tahsil of Azamgarh District of U.P.), Uttar Bharat Bhoogal Patrika, XVI, pp. 97-104.

Shrivastava, V.K. J.P. Rai (1984) : Spatial Pattern of Social Services in the lower Son Basin, in Pandey, P. (ed.), Prof. Enayat Ahmad Felicitation Volume, New Delhi, pp. 251-57.

Shrivastava, V.K. and I. Richards (1975) : Spatial Distribution of Rural Settlements : A Methodological Approach, Uttar Bharat Bhoogal Patrika, XI, pp. 54-65.

Shrivastava, V.K. and Udhaw Ram (1982) : Nature and Demarcation of Market Area Regious of the Lower Ganga-Ghagra Doab, Uttar Bharat Bhoogol Patirka, 18, pp. 97-107.

Shrivastava, V.K. and V. Nath (1981) : Rural Marketing and Social Structure in North India : A Case Study, Proceedings International Conference on Urbanization and Regional Change in Developing Countries, Kharagpur.

Shrivastava, H.O. (1980) : Market Centres in the Saryupar Plain of Uttar Pradesh, Ph. D. Thesis accepted by the University of Gorakhpur, (unpublished).

Singh, J. (1979) : Central Places and Spatial Organization in a Backward Economy : Gorakhput Region, Uttar Bharat Bhoogol Parished, Gorakhpur.

Singh, Dr. J.N. (1981) : Population Geography of Magadh Plain. Unpublished Ph. D. thesis, M.U., Both-Gaya.

Singh, Dr. R.P. and Kumar Anil, (1970) : Monograph of Bihar, Bharati Bhawan, Patna-4.

Singh, O.P. (1968) : Functions and Functional Classes of Central Places in Uttar Pradesh, National Geographical Journal of India, XIV, pp. 83-127.

Singh, R.L. (1955) : Evolution of Settlements in the Middle Ganga Valley, National Geographical Journal of India I, pp. 69-114.

Sinha, Ashok Kumar (1988) : Planning Strategies for Drought Prone Areas of Bihar : A Case Study of Palamu District. Indian Journal of Landscape Systems and Ecological Studies, Calcutta, June, 1988, Vol. II, No. 1.

Singh, K.N. : Small Towns as Rural Development Centres in Uttar Pradesh, in Abstracts of Proceedings of Fifty Fourth Session, Indian Science Congress Association.

Singh, R.L. and Singh, S.M. (1960) : Mugra Badshahpur : A Rurban Settlement in the Ganga-Ghaghra Doab, West, National Geographical Journal of India, Vol. VI.

Skinner, G.W. : Marketing and Social Structure in Rural China, Journal of Asian Studies, 24, pp. 3-43; 195-228; 363-399.

Smailes, A.E. (1944) : The Urban Hierarchy in England and Wales, Geography, Vol. XXIV.

Srivastava, V.K. (1987) : Geography of Marketing and Rural Development, Inter-India Publications, New Delhi.

Sinha, Ashok Kumar (1989) : Some Aspects of Agricultural Productivity in South West Alluvial Plains Zone of Bihar, p. 2. A Paper Presented in National Seminar on Rural Development in India at Deptt. of Geography M.U., Bodh-Gaya in December, 1989.

Smith, C.A. (1971) : Examining Stratification Systems Through Peasant Marketing Arrangements, Economics Geography, 10, pp. 95-122.

Smith, R.H.T. (1971) : West African Market Places : Temporal Periodicity and Locational Spacing, in Claude Mei Massoux (ed.), The Development of Indigenous Trade and Markets in West Africa, Oxford University Press, London, pp. 319-46.

————. (1972) : The Synchronizaiton of Periodic Markets, in Adams, W.P. and F.M. Helleiner(eds.), International Geography, University of Toronto Press.

Stewart. J.Q. and Warntz, W. (1958) : Physics of Population Distribution, Journal of Regional Science, I, pp. 99-123.

Stine, J.H. (1962) : Temporal Aspects of Tertiary Production Elements in Korea in F.R. Pitts (eds.), Urban Systems and Economic Development, University of Oregon, School of Business Administration, Engene, Oregon, pp. 68-88.

Symansky, R. and R.J. Bromley (1974) : Market Development and the Ecological Complex, The Professional Geographer, 26, 382-88.

Tamasker, B.G. (1983) : Trader Travel Behaviour and Periodic Market Cycles in the Arvi Upland, The Indian Journal of Marketing Geography, I, pp. 22-27.

Taylor, D.R.F. (1974) : The Role of Small Urban Place in Development : The Case of Kenya, in E.E.I. Shakhs and R. Obudho, (ed.), Urbanization, National Development and Regional Planning, New York.

Thomas, E.N. (1960) : Some Comments on the Functional Bases for Small Towns, Iowa Business Digest.

Tinkler, K.J. (1973) : The Topology of Rural Periodic Market Systems, Geografiska Annaler, 55, pp. 121-33.

Ullman, E.L. (1956) : The Role of Transportation and the Bases for Interaction, in W.L. Thomas (ed.), Man's Role in Changing the Face of the Earth, pp. 862-80.

Vance, J.E. Jr. (1970) : The Merchants World : The Geography of Wholesaling, Prentice Hall, Inc. Englewood Cliffs, N.J.

Wanmali, S. (1972) : Ranking of Settlemetns : A Suggestion, Journal of Behavioural Sciences and Community Development, 5, 97-111.

Zemanian, A.H. (1986) : Multi Level Marketing Networks in Less Developed Countries, Applied Mathematics and Computation, 18, pp. 185-210.

Urban-Rural Difference in Southern Asia (1964), Report on Regional Seminar, Delhi, 1962, London.